POWER
THOUGHTS

POWER
THOUGHTS

12 STRATEGIES TO
WIN THE BATTLE OF THE MIND

JOYCE MEYER

New York Boston Nashville

Unless otherwise indicated, Scriptures are taken from the *Amplified Bible*®. Copyright © 1954, 1962, 1965, 1987 by The Lockman Foundation. Used by permission.

Scriptures noted NASB are taken from the *New American Standard Bible*®, copyright © 1960, 1962, 1963, 1972, 1975, 1977, 1995 by The Lockman Foundation. Used by permission.

Scriptures noted The Message are taken from *The Message*. Copyright © 1993, 1994, 1995, 1996, 2000, 2001, 2002. Used by permission of NavPress Publishing Group.

Scriptures noted NKJV are taken from the *New King James Version*. Copyright © 1979, 1980, 1982 by Thomas Nelson, Inc., Publishers.

FaithWords
Hachette Book Group
237 Park Avenue
New York, NY 10017

www.faithwords.com

Printed in the United States of America

First Edition: September 2010
20 19 18 17 16 15 14 13

FaithWords is a division of Hachette Book Group, Inc.
The FaithWords name and logo are trademarks of Hachette Book Group, Inc.

The publisher is not responsible for websites (or their content) that are not owned by the publisher.

Library of Congress Cataloging-in-Publication Data
Meyer, Joyce.
    Power thoughts : 12 strategies to win the battle of the mind / Joyce Meyer.—1st ed.
        p. cm.
    ISBN 978-0-446-58036-6 (regular edition)—ISBN 978-0-446-57414-3 (large print edition)   1. Thought and thinking—Religious aspects—Christianity.
2. Success—Religious aspects—Christianity.   3. Spirituality.   I. Title.
    BV4598.4.M49 2010
    248.4—dc22   2010008535

CONTENTS

POWER
THOUGHTS

PART I

It's All in Your Mind

Whatever you hold in your mind will tend to
occur in your life. If you continue to believe
as you have always believed, you will continue to act
as you have always acted. If you continue to act as you
have always acted, you will continue to get what
you have always gotten. If you want different
results in your life or your work, all you
have to do is change your mind.
—*Anonymous*

INTRODUCTION

One of my favorite sayings is, "Where the mind goes, the man follows." I wholeheartedly believe our thoughts lead us, charting the course for our lives and pointing us in certain directions that ultimately determine our destinations in life. Our thoughts cause us to have certain attitudes and perspectives; they affect our relationships; they determine how productive we will be personally and professionally; and they greatly influence the overall quality of our lives. We absolutely must understand the power of thoughts!

For instance, if you begin to think about starting your own business, getting a college degree, improving your health, or eliminating your debt, and you are really serious about it—which means that you firmly set your mind in that direction—you will eventually do it. Your goals may change as time goes by. Or perhaps life, as it so often does, will twist and turn along the way, putting you in a place you never expected to be and creating new options that you hadn't even considered. A good example of this can be seen in the life of a friend of mine. Several years ago, she decided to move across the country even though that would mean leaving a career of many years and starting over. She gave notice at her job, and in a thriving real estate market she put her house up for sale and started making plans for the move. Who would have expected that a sudden major real estate slump would leave her with a house that wasn't worth the balance of her mortgage? With too little savings to sell at a large loss and make up the difference, she stayed in her home and found another job that was below the level of her old one. As a result of working for her new employer, two years later she met the man who would become her husband. Although her initial goal wasn't realized, she would tell you with great assurance that deciding to move was the best decision she ever made—even though she still lives where she did all those years ago. Had she not taken the steps she did, she is sure she never would have met her husband.

I firmly believe that each thing we do in life gives us experience for the next thing we will do and that our thoughtful planning is perfected by God as we place our trust in Him.

Success in every aspect of life begins with a thought; so does failure. If you think you cannot do or attain something, chances are you will not be able to. Your mind has *that* much influence over your life.

Just think about it. Take a moment now to consider the successes and failures of your life. What kinds of thoughts were you thinking before and during your greatest achievements? And what kinds of thoughts filled your mind before and during your most significant failures or missteps? Can you see how your mind has worked either for you or against you over the course of your life?

Many times, we succeed in life because other people encourage us and we think about their affirming comments to the point that we believe them. Anyone who has ever been told "You can do it!" knows how easy it is to turn those inspiring, confidence-building words into a thought. When "You can do it" becomes "I can do it," then "it" happens—whether it's scoring a point in an athletic competition, making a good grade on a test, getting a job, losing weight, or buying a house. When we believe or think we can do something, then somehow, someway—even if we face challenges—we still manage to get it done. The same is true when we think negatively and come to believe we cannot do something. Discouraging words from others and thoughts such as "I'm not smart enough, attractive enough, talented enough, or diligent enough" often become self-fulfilling prophecies. Why? Because they become ingrained in our thinking to the point that they exert influence over our decision-making processes—and where the mind goes, the man follows.

James Allen, a British philosopher around the turn of the twentieth century, said, "All that a man achieves and all that he fails to achieve is the direct result of his own thoughts." The way we think is far more powerful than we often realize and our thoughts impact every aspect of our existence, either positively or negatively. Whatever we think and believe *feels* real to us, even if it is not true at all. If we think something is true, we respond and act as though it is. Our thoughts affect our relationships, our self-image, our finances, our health (physical, emotional, and spiritual), our productivity at work and at home, the way we manage our time, our priorities, and our ability to enjoy life.

The connection between our thoughts and the rest of our lives is clear in Scripture. Proverbs 23:7 says, "For as he thinks in his heart, so is he." In other words, we become what we think. If we think positive thoughts, we will be positive people enjoying fruitful lives. Conversely, if we think negative thoughts, we will be negative people with no joy or success.

Let me be clear that I am not saying that we can think into existence anything that we want. That view of the power of thoughts is a form of humanism, which is an ungodly philosophy. But, simply recognizing the fact that thoughts are powerful is not humanistic at all. In fact, it's quite biblical, and you will see that throughout this book.

Our minds must go through a process of renewal in order to experience God's plan for us. His thoughts are above our thoughts (see Isaiah 55:8, 9), so in order to walk with Him and experience His good plans for our lives, we *must* learn to think as He thinks (see Romans 12:2). It is impossible to change our lives unless and until we change our thoughts. When people say they are miserable or frustrated, I say that a "stinking" life can be the result of "stinking thinking." Most of the time, these people don't realize they have the ability to make choices concerning their thoughts and that doing so will make a difference in their lives.

Indeed, very few people realize that we have the ability to choose our thoughts and decide what we want to think; most of us passively meditate on whatever comes into our minds without ever realizing our enemy, Satan, uses our minds extensively to control us and keep us from fulfilling God's destiny for our lives. Each person regenerated through receiving Jesus Christ as their Savior receives a new spirit and a new heart from God, but does not receive a new mind—the mind must be renewed. The intent of one's heart may be pure and yet the mind is still confused. The Bible declares emphatically that we must be transformed by the entire renewal of mind and attitude (see Romans 12:2). This is accomplished by a complete, diligent, and thorough study of God's Word.

I understand completely that choosing right thoughts is not always easy. One of the greatest breakthroughs I have ever had in my life took place when I finally realized I had the ability to control my thoughts, and one of the greatest challenges I have ever faced was the challenge to change my thinking once I realized it was possible to do so. I'll tell you more about my journey toward right thinking and encourage you in yours as this book unfolds.

Sometimes thinking correctly seems to be a battle—and I'm here to tell you that it is a battle. That's because the mind is the battlefield; it is where we win or lose—where we become victims or victors—in life. In 1995, I wrote *Battlefield of the Mind*, which is based on the fact that the biggest problems we face in life often result from wrong thinking. Since that book was released, many people have come to understand that guarding our minds is critically important and have learned to develop healthy thought patterns. In the years since that book was released, I've had more experience observing how my own thoughts affect my life, as well as how powerful thoughts are in the lives of people I minister to, and I am more convinced than ever that the mind is the battlefield. It is the battlefield on which we wage war not only with our enemy and God's enemy, the devil, over our personal lives and destinies, but also with worldviews and concepts or ideas that threaten to deceive us. It is the battlefield on which we make the decisions that lead to frustration and defeat or to strength, health, joy, peace, and abundance.

The battle in our minds will continue until our earthly lives are complete. We will never become so spiritual that the enemy decides to stop harassing us, but we can become stronger and stronger against him as we grow in our relationship with God and in understanding His Word. We can learn to live in greater measures of power and authority over the enemy, which will result in greater abilities to enjoy our lives, receive God's blessings, and fulfill the good plans He has for us.

In *Power Thoughts*, I want to take the next step beyond *Battlefield of the Mind* and give you specific insights and strategies to help you build powerful mind-sets to empower you to live in a place of strength, success, and victory every day.

In Part 1 of this book, I will share with you some potentially life-changing truths and insights on the power of our thoughts and on the importance of the way we think. You'll see how important your thoughts are to your physical health, your mental and emotional well-being, and your spiritual growth. You'll discover how vital a godly positive attitude is and you'll learn how to develop and maintain the kind of optimistic outlook that will help you change your life for the better.

In Part 2 of this book, I'll offer you twelve "power thoughts" that can revolutionize your life if you will believe them, allow them to take root in your mind, and act on them in your everyday life. In these pages, I am giving you tools that can make you strong where you have been weak, triumphant where you have been defeated, positive where you have been negative, courageous where you have been afraid, and successful where you have failed in the past.

The goal of this book is not simply to provide you with good information you can read and store away in the bottom drawer of your mind. My aim is to help you change your life. The only way to change your life is to change your thinking, and I want to give you a head start on that by sharing with you twelve of the most important thoughts you can ever think. These thoughts may not agree with the way you currently think; you may have to retrain your brain by using these power thoughts to build new mind-sets. You may need new mental habits, which won't happen immediately, but it *can* happen if you commit to renewing your mind. You can start with the twelve thoughts introduced in this book and then continue on throughout your life developing and perfecting new thought patterns and habits.

Some experts say forming a new habit takes thirty days; others say it takes three weeks. Perhaps you can break old habits and develop new ones more quickly than that, or it may take you longer. All I ask is that you prayerfully approach this book and use it as a pattern in your life. You may want to focus on one power thought per week for twelve weeks and put yourself on a three-month "program" of teaching your brain to think differently. You may choose to focus on one power thought each month for twelve months, using this book over the course of one year to help you establish new mind-sets and ways of thinking that can change your life. I suggest that you use the three-month program and repeat it four times in a year. This book is laid out in a way that will allow you to record your progress at the end of each week and make notes about the changes you are beginning to see in your life as a result of your new thoughts. Whatever you decide is a good pace for you to go through this book, make a commitment to it. More than that, make a commitment to God and a commitment to yourself. Commit that you are going to change the things about your life that need changing—and see this book as a tool that can help you do so.

Simply reading this book will not be enough to accomplish the transformation I know can happen in your life. You will have to apply the principles you learn and discipline your mind to think in new ways. These new ways of thinking have the ability to improve your everyday existence and make your life much better. If you are tired of the way you have been living, you can change it by learning to think differently. You must be determined and even if you have to repeat the twelve-week program many, many times just remember that each time through you are making progress. The choice is yours; no one else can do it for you. You alone are in charge of your mind, and your mind affects every area of your life. I believe with God's help you can change your mind, and as you do, you can change your life. God does not control us. He guides us in what is right. He gives us the spirit and fruit of self-control and the freedom to do our own thinking. Satan, who is the enemy of your soul, will try to control your life by controlling your thoughts. Sadly, a great deal of our thinking is instigated by the way we have been raised, the world around us, and evil forces at work in the world today, but the truth makes us free. You can learn brand-new ways to think that will change you and your life forever. I believe by studying this book you are embarking on a "truth journey" that will produce amazing results in your life.

Your mind can be a junkyard or a treasure chest, and you alone have the ability to choose what it will be. You can make it one or the other by deciding whether you will think thoughts that are negative, cheap, common, and low or thoughts that are positive, pure, honorable, and valuable in God's eyes. You can think "power-enhancing" thoughts or "power-draining" thoughts. Let me encourage you to think about this book as a map that will lead you to the valuable things you need to make your mind a source of power and a treasure chest.

I believe with all my heart that you, as an individual, are a treasure, and there are incredible treasures within you. Some of these treasures you have never unearthed, because your thinking has not enabled you to realize they exist. This book can change that.

If you sincerely want to be different from how you are now, or you want some aspect of your life to be different, you must begin to think differently. If your current thinking would qualify more as "trash" than "treasure," you can change it. Don't poison your life with wrong thinking patterns. I challenge you to invest the time you need—whether it's twelve weeks, a year, or some other amount of time—to renew your mind and see if you don't reap an unbelievably wonderful dividend. Use this book to help you get started, and keep it handy for an entire year or perhaps a lifetime as you learn to change your life by changing your thinking. If you take no action, things might remain the same or they could even get worse. If you invest now, you can look forward to great improvement in every area of your life.

How to Use This Book

Power Thoughts is meant to be *used,* not simply read. As you go through this book, mark passages that apply to your life, make notes on points that cause you to think in new ways, or take time to journal. Read mindfully—you may need to stop and reflect on a particular thought or passage. Do that! This is not a book to be raced through. Stop and pray along the way, and ask God to help you change your thinking so you can change your life. Trust me—it will be time well spent.

Throughout this book, you'll see the words *Think about It*, sometimes followed by a question or two. Please take time to answer the questions, preferably in writing, because they are designed to help you make even more progress than reading alone will provide on your journey toward a powerful life—a life in which circumstances do not determine whether you are happy or not and stress does not overwhelm you, a life of confidence in God and in who He made you to be, a life in which you feel you can do and be everything He intends for you.

When you reach Part 2, the section devoted to twelve specific power thoughts, you'll continue to see questions throughout the chapters, and at the end of every chapter, you'll see a "Power Pack." Each Power Pack is a group of Scriptures that reinforce the principles in each power thought. If you will read them, memorize them, meditate on them, obey them, and allow them to become rooted in your mind, you will see remarkable improvements in your life.

I know that the Word of God can turn a weak or mediocre existence into a powerful, exciting, fulfilling life. In various places throughout this book, I will suggest that you find Scriptures that apply to a particular mind-set or circumstance in your life. You can accomplish this several ways:

- Use the concordance in your Bible. For example, if you want to find a verse about peace, simply look up the word *peace* in the concordance and you will see listings for Scriptures about peace. Some Bibles do not have concordances; comprehensive concordances are available separately.
- Use a topical index, which you use the same way you use a concordance. Where a concordance lists Scriptures with the exact word you are looking for, a topical index lists those Scriptures and others related to the topic.

- Use an online Bible or Bible software program that has concordance and topical index capabilities.
- Use my book *The Secret Power of Speaking God's Word*, which is arranged topically.
- Use the section titled "The Word for Your Everyday Life" in *The Everyday Life Bible,* available through Joyce Meyer Ministries or everywhere books are sold.

You are about to step onto the battlefield to remove the land mines of self-doubt, fear, and anxiety that the enemy has planted. So in the words of Paul, I remind you to "put on God's whole armor... that you may be able successfully to stand up against [all] the strategies and the deceits of the devil" (Ephesians 6:11). I encourage you to be determined from the beginning of your journey that you will not give up. It is those who finish the race who receive the prize.

It is my prayer that the Holy Spirit will guide you as you read and contemplate the power thoughts found in this book; that He will instill in you the patience to reflect on the truths and meditate on the Word as you examine the role that each thought can—and will—play in your life.

CHAPTER

1

The Power of a Positive You

Olympic gold medalist Scott Hamilton has said, "The only dis-ability in life is a bad attitude." It's true. Nothing will hinder or handicap you in life as severely as a bad attitude. When I use the word *attitude,* I am referring to the system of thoughts, the mental posture, the mind-set, or the way of thinking with which a person approaches life. For example, if a person has a bad attitude toward work, he will think thoughts such as these:

- *I have the most boring job on Earth.*
- *My boss is too demanding.*
- *This company needs to pay me more and treat me better.*
- *I should get more vacation time.*
- *I always have to do the "grunt work."*
- *No one here appreciates me.*
- *I may have to work with these people around me, but I don't have to be nice to them.*

All those thoughts combine to make one big bad attitude. How could a person with those thoughts running through his mind all day ever enjoy his work, become a positive employee, or make valu-able contributions to his company? He can't—unless he changes his thoughts and develops a better attitude. Even if your employer definitely needs to make changes and improve in several areas you must realize that being negative about your job does not change your employer, but it does change your attitude into one that is "power-draining."

Do you think the person I just described would be a good candidate for a raise or a promotion? Certainly not. But, what about a man whose attitude is built on thoughts like these?

- *I am so thankful to have a job.*
- *I am going to do my very best every day.*
- *I believe that God gives me favor every day with my boss.*
- *I am glad to be part of a team with my coworkers even though none of us are perfect.*
- *The work environment may not be ideal, but I will do my part to make it pleasant for myself and those around me.*
- *I am committed to be focused and diligent while I'm on company time.*
- *I would like a raise, so I will work hard to earn it.*

No doubt, this person's positive attitude will position him for promotion in his company, and if he has the same type of attitude in other areas, he will enjoy a happy and fulfilling life. Even if his employer never recognizes his attributes, God does and will either change the employer's heart or provide better employment. God always rewards openly what we do in secret for His honor and glory.

It's Up to You

All of us have the privilege and responsibility of choosing our attitudes, no matter what circumstances or situations we find ourselves in. The key word here is *choosing*. Attitudes don't just happen; they are the products of our choices. Over time, the thought patterns established in our minds can put us on "autopilot," which means that when certain types of situations occur, we are preprogrammed to think about them in certain ways. We have to interrupt this autopilot function and learn to stop our minds from going in the directions they have gone for years if that direction is not producing good things in our lives. For example:

- You may have spent years dreading being with your family for holiday celebrations, but this year, you can choose to think, *Being with family may not be my favorite activity, but I am going to purposefully look for something good in each of my relatives.*
- You may have a habit of complaining of feeling overwhelmed when bills arrive in your mailbox every month, but you can begin to think, *I am going to pay as much as possible on this bill, and little by little I am getting out of debt.*

It is vital for you to understand that you can choose your own thinking. You may be in a habit of merely thinking whatever falls into your mind, but you are now in the process of retraining your mind one thought at a time. As you learn to think as God thinks it enables Him to partner with you in accomplishing whatever you need to accomplish.

Think about It

What do you believe is the most important thought or attitude you need to change in your life?

An Attitude Adjustment

Winston Churchill noted that "Attitude is a little thing that makes a big difference." I couldn't agree more. All of us need "attitude adjustments" at times, and an attitude adjustment is the result of changing the way we think.

If we keep our attitudes up and positive, we will continue to climb higher and higher in life and be able to soar. But if our attitudes are down and negative, we will fall and stay on the ground of life, never able to make the journeys God intends for us or reach the destinations He has planned for us.

You may have heard the saying: "Your attitude determines your altitude." In other words, a positive attitude will cause you to "fly high" in life, while a negative attitude will keep you down. Just as pilots have certain rules to follow to keep planes oriented, with the right attitudes and altitudes, I want to share a few rules you can follow in life to help keep your attitude positive so you can keep your "altitude" where it should be.

Rule #1: Maintain the right attitude when the going gets rough.

No matter what happens to you, determine to go through it with the right attitude. In fact, determine *beforehand* that you will keep a positive attitude in the midst of every negative situation that presents itself to you. If you make this decision and meditate on it during a good time in your life, then when difficulty arises you will already be prepared to maintain a good attitude. For example, if an unexpected bill or major repair presents itself to you, make up your mind that you will not complain because you have to tighten your belt financially for a few months to make up for it. Instead, look at the challenge as an adventure and decide you will find creative ways to cut costs for a while and look for ways to enjoy life without spending money. I have witnessed over and over how God helps people who keep a good attitude in challenging times. I recently heard of a couple who were struggling financially but were also determined to keep a good, positive, and thankful attitude. The man, who we will call John, worked in a restaurant and one day a customer had a heart attack while eating lunch there. John had some medical training from being in the armed forces and was able to administer CPR to keep the man breathing and his heart beating until the paramedics arrived. As it turned out, the man whose life was saved happened to be very wealthy and in appreciation he gave John a check for five thousand dollars as a way of saying, "Thank you for saving my life." The good attitude the couple maintained in their financial struggle opened the door for God to work miraculously in their lives.

Throughout history, we have examples of people who have maintained good attitudes in the face of difficult times and thereby turned their problems into opportunities. Specifically, I think of various individuals who were imprisoned and composed some of the most influential writing the world has ever known, such as: "Letter from Birmingham Jail" by Martin Luther King Jr., *Pilgrim's Progress* by John Bunyan, and Sir Walter Raleigh's *The History of the World*. While the famous composer Ludwig van Beethoven was not literally imprisoned, he was almost totally deaf and suffered great sorrow during a period of his life—and that was when he wrote his greatest symphonies. No doubt, these people could have had terrible attitudes as they faced trouble, but they made a decision and maintained the best of attitudes through the worst of times and made contributions that are still read and heard in the world today.

I don't think they were simply born as positive people—I believe they had to make a choice and decided to make one that would benefit themselves as well as the world. One of the worst mistakes we can make in our thinking is to believe we are just not like *those positive people* and we can't help it. If you think you can't do anything about your thinking and attitude then you're defeated before you even begin to try.

No matter what difficulty you encounter, *maintaining* the right attitude will be much easier than *regaining* the right attitude, so as soon as you sense your attitude losing altitude, make an adjustment. Remember to resist the devil at his onset (see 1 Peter 5:8, 9). In other words, as soon as the enemy sends negative thoughts into your mind, stop them. Determine that you will not agree with them and decide that you will not listen to his voice anymore. Discipline yourself to stand strong with your positive attitude in every circumstance. Misery will always be an option; you can always choose to be unhappy and pessimistic, but you can also choose to be optimistic and happy.

Think about It

How can you begin to make attitude adjustments now to help you maintain a good attitude the next time you find yourself up against a challenge? It may be as easy as saying, "I realize that life is not perfect but with God's help I am going to be stable even during the storms of life."

Rule #2: Realize the rough times won't last forever.

I have heard many people who live in parts of the world where there are four distinct seasons talk about how much they enjoy winter, spring, summer, and fall. They like the variety and the unique beauty, qualities, and opportunities of each season. The Bible tells us God Himself changes times and seasons (see Daniel 2:21). Seasons change; this is true in the natural world and it is true in regard to the seasons of our lives. It means that difficult times do not last forever. We may have "off" days, tough weeks, bad months, or even a year that seems to have more than its share of troubles, but every negative experience does come to an end.

Some of the trying situations we find ourselves in seem to go on far too long. When this happens, we are usually tempted to complain or become discouraged. Instead, we need to promptly adjust our attitudes and ask God to teach us something valuable as we press through the situation at hand. According to James 1:2–3, God uses trials and pressure to produce good results in our lives. He always wants to bless us. Sometimes His blessings come through unexpected circumstances we may view as negative, but if we will keep positive attitudes in the midst of those situations, we will experience the positive results God desires to give us.

If you are going through a difficult time right now, let me remind you that this probably isn't the first challenge you've ever faced.

You survived the last one (and probably learned some valuable lessons through it) and you will survive this one too. Your trials are temporary; they won't last forever. Better days are on their way. Just keep your attitude "up" instead of "down," and remember that this is just a season and it *will* pass.

Think about It

Look back over the course of your life and remember some of the trials you have faced. How has God used them to bring something good into your life?

_____

_____

Now, remind yourself He will also bring good out of the current situation and the next one too!

When David faced the giant Goliath, he remembered the lion and the bear he had already defeated and it gave him courage in his current situation.

Rule #3: Don't make major decisions during a storm.

No one's entire life is like one big, long sunny day. At some point, we all face storms—whether they come in the form of unexpected illness, job loss, financial crisis, marital difficulties, problems with children, or any number of other scenarios that are stressful, intense, and important. I have faced many storms in my life—some like the quick afternoon storms that are common in summertime and some that seemed like category four hurricanes. If I have learned anything about weathering the storms of life, I have learned that they don't last forever, as I mentioned in Rule #2, and that if at all possible, I do not need to make major decisions in the midst of them.

When the storms of life arise, it's best to keep your mind and emotions as still as possible. Thoughts and feelings often run wild in the midst of crises, but those are exactly the times we need to be careful about making decisions. We must remain calm and discipline ourselves to focus on doing what we can do and trusting God to do what we cannot do.

Just as a pilot's bad decision can cause a plane to be diverted from its intended destination or even to make a dangerous emergency landing, a bad decision can divert or delay you from reaching your destiny. Next time you face a storm or crisis in your life, I hope you'll remember these words, which I often say: "Let emotions subside before you decide." Do your best to let things settle down before you make major decisions. You may not always have that choice, but as much as possible, put significant decisions on hold until your storm passes. Just as the wind blows about wildly during a storm, our thoughts can become quite wild and frantic, and that is not the best time to make major decisions.

Think about It

What do you consider your biggest mental or emotional challenge when storms arise in your life? Is it fear, anxiety, impatience, overreacting, or something else?

_____

_____

Determine today to wait on wisdom and not respond emotionally or out of panic and fear.

Rule #4: Stay in touch with the "control tower."

Air traffic controllers are the only people on Earth who can see the "big picture" of what's going on in the sky and who have the knowledge and authority to tell planes to slow down or speed up, fly higher or fly lower, avoid or navigate through storms, or take alternate routes to their destinations. According to the National Air Traffic Controllers Association, air traffic controllers in the United States handle about eighty-seven thousand flights every day, and sixty-four million takeoffs and landings per year. Interestingly, air traffic controllers manage not only commercial flights, but also private aviation, military, and cargo air traffic, as well as air taxis. If all the flights air traffic controllers handle at any given time were to be posted on monitors in airports, more than 460 monitors would be needed. With so many flights taking off and landing each day, pilots have to stay in touch with the control towers if they want to make safe, on-time flights.

Just as airplane pilots must maintain contact with air traffic control towers, you and I must stay in touch with God—the one who sees the big picture of our lives and who orchestrates everything that involves us. He makes sure everything that needs to happen in our lives happens at the right time, moves at the appropriate speed, and causes us to arrive safely at the "destinations" He has planned for us.

If we want to stay on track with God and do so with good attitudes, we have to make communication with Him a priority in our daily schedules. He will help you navigate the ups and downs of life, and find your way through the "cloudy" days when you can't seem to see the next step you need to take. I can't urge you strongly enough to communicate with Him frequently through prayer, reading His Word, worship, and simple acknowledgment of His presence and guidance throughout every day. If you want to learn more about how to stay in touch with God moment by moment and develop a close relationship of communication with Him, I recommend my books *The Power of Simple Prayer* and *Knowing God Intimately.*

Think about It

How is your personal relationship with God? If it's less satisfying than you would like, what adjustments can you make to improve it?

Rule #5: Try to keep things in perspective.

One of the definitions for *perspective* in *Webster's Dictionary* is "the interrelation in which a subject or its parts are mentally viewed." Interesting, isn't it? This definition makes a clear distinction. It implies that our mental capacities can cause us to see things in ways that may not be accurate.

When we lack proper perspective, we may consider minor situations to be major crises, or we may do the opposite and view significant situations as "no big deal." Either tendency—exaggerating things or minimizing them—can lead to problems, so we need to do our best to see things as they really are and not allow them to be out of proportion.

I know a young man who spent many years of his life frequently trying to prove he was right in every disagreement. He habitually argued and became angry, and in fact that happened so often that he lost a lot of friends. He simply was not enjoyable to be with. After this continued for a period of years I finally began to notice a big change in him. He wasn't argumentative if someone had a different opinion from his or did not want to do something his way. I asked him what had made him change and he said, "I have discovered that being right is highly overrated." When he looked at being right in proper perspective and compared it to the turmoil he experienced, he finally realized it just was not worth it.

Try to form a habit of looking at the whole of life instead of centering on one thing that may be upsetting you. Thinking excessively about the problems we encounter in life only makes them appear to be larger than they really are. When you are experiencing any issue that is upsetting to you take time to purposely recall the good things that you enjoy also. King David did this during times of depression and it helped him keep things in perspective (see Psalm 42).

Think about It

Are you good at keeping things in perspective or is this an area in which you need to improve?

_____

_____

A Positive You Is a Powerful You

An organization once offered a bounty of five thousand dollars apiece for wolves that were captured alive. Enticed by the idea of such money, Sam and Jed eagerly set out through the forests and into the mountains in search of the animals that could secure their fortune.

They fell asleep under the stars one night, exhausted after days of enthusiastic hunting. Sam awoke in the middle of the night and saw about fifty wolves surrounding him and Jed—hungry wolves, baring their teeth, with their eyes glistening at the thought of easy human prey.

Realizing what was going on, Sam nudged his friend and said eagerly, "Jed, wake up! We're rich!"

A positive attitude enables you to make the best of every situation, and that gives you power over your circumstances instead of allowing your circumstances to have power over you. This was certainly true for Sam. While most people would be terrified when surrounded by a wolf pack, Sam saw the opportunity he'd been waiting for.

Make a commitment today to be a positive person. The more positive you are, the more powerful you'll be.

CHAPTER

2

Teach Your Mind to Work for You

Do you know that your mind can either work for you or against you, depending on how you train it? When it works for you, it helps you stay positive, reach your goals in life, and think the kinds of thoughts that enable you to enjoy each day. When it works against you, it can make you negative and discouraged, hold you back from accomplishing what you want or need to do, and cause you to think the kinds of thoughts that result in self-sabotage.

As a physical structure and an organ of the human body, your brain engages in many functions that take place without your knowledge, without your help, and outside of your control. It has all sorts of jobs in your body. Your heart rate, breathing, blood pressure, movement and coordination, balance, body temperature, hunger and thirst, sensory processing, sight and hearing, emotions, learning, and memory are all areas with which the brain is involved.

But your brain is also the "home" of your thoughts, your mind. Dr. Caroline Leaf, a leading Neuro-Metacognitive learning specialist and committed Christian, notes in her teaching on the brain that "The Word and science believe that the mind and the brain are one." The way you think is voluntary, and you can control your thoughts. I want you to give your brain a new job and begin to teach your mind to work for you instead of against you. One important way to do this is to make the intentional decision that you will begin to think positively. I realize your brain won't be able to fulfill the new role completely overnight. You may be asking it to undergo a radical transformation, and that will take time. So give it a little grace, but determine that with your diligence and God's help, your brain will go to work *for* you instead of against you and become a powerful, positive force in your life.

I like what Dr. Leaf says—that the human brain takes "eighteen years to grow and a lifetime to mature." Don't miss this point. While every other organ in the body is fully formed when a person is born, and simply gets bigger as the body gets bigger, the brain actually takes a full eighteen years to grow. Once it's fully formed, it continues to mature until the day a person dies. This means, no matter how old you are, your brain is still maturing. This is great news because it means you do not have to be stuck in any old or wrong thought patterns. Your brain is still maturing, so you can still mature in your thinking.

Think about It

What comes to mind immediately when I ask: In what way(s) is your mind working against you?

It'll Help Your Health

Your thinking can have a positive effect on your physical health. People have suspected an interrelationship between the mind and the body for generations, but in recent years, a variety of scientists and researchers from all over the world have studied and proven it.

In a 2004 article in *USA Today*, Carol Ryff of the University of Wisconsin-Madison said, "There is a science that is emerging that says a positive attitude isn't just a state of mind. It also has linkages to what's going on in the brain and in the body." Ryff's research has proven that people who have higher than normal levels of well-being show "lower cardiovascular risk, lower levels of stress hormones, and lower levels of inflammation, which serves as a marker of the immune system."[1]

In addition, a study conducted in the Netherlands in 2004 found that people who are optimistic have healthier hearts than those considered "grouchy." Fewer self-described "optimists" died of cardiovascular disease and they had lower death rates overall than those of pessimists.[2]

Dr. Becca Levy of Yale University led a study that concluded that "a positive attitude towards aging was greater than physiological measures such as low blood pressure and cholesterol, each of which is thought to add a maximum of four years to life." This study also found that optimistic people live longer than people who worry constantly and that positive attitudes can add more years to a person's life than exercising or not smoking.[3] In some ways, I find this research astounding, but in other ways, I have no trouble embracing these findings because I have learned that the mind is extremely powerful and I am not surprised by the extent of its influence in our physical lives.

According to the world-renowned Mayo Clinic, thinking positively may also result in the following health benefits:[4]

- Decreased negative stress.
- Greater resistance to catching the common cold.
- A sense of well-being and improved health.
- Reduced risk of coronary artery disease.
- Easier breathing if you have certain lung diseases, such as emphysema.
- Improved coping ability for women with high-risk pregnancies.
- Better coping skills during hardships.

Further affirming the mind-body connection in an interesting way, I was fascinated to see that in 2005, the Associated Press released an article that reported, "New research suggests that once Alzheimer's disease robs someone of the ability to expect that a proven painkiller will help them, it doesn't work nearly as well."[5] Isn't that amazing? As long as people are able to think painkillers work, these medicines seem to help us, but when we stop thinking they are effective, they actually stop being effective. Our minds are incredible!

We know positive thinking is good for our attitudes and emotions, but the research I have referenced in this section, plus an enormous amount of research available in various forms today, clearly indicates that positive thinking is also extremely beneficial to our physical well-being. If we want to live healthy lives, we have to have healthy minds—and that starts with thinking positively instead of negatively.

The Results of Positive Thinking

You have read about a number of studies and experiments that prove how our thinking influences us. One case I find especially interesting is an experiment conducted by an MIT professor named Dan Ariely and some of his colleagues. They established a bogus testing facility where they asked people to undergo a series of electric shocks before and after receiving a certain pain reliever. The participants first received shocks with no pain reliever and then took pills called "Veladone-Rx" before receiving the shocks again. The testers told some people the Veladone-Rx pills cost $2.50 each, while they told others the pills cost only ten cents each. Almost all the people who thought the pills cost $2.50 each reported pain relief when they got the second series of shocks, but only half of those who thought the pills were ten cents each reported any relief at all. The truth about Veladone-Rx: the pills were nothing more than vitamin C tablets.[6]

What was the key to Dr. Ariely's experiment? People *think* expensive products work better than inexpensive ones. The pills that supposedly cost $2.50 each didn't have any actual pain-relieving effect at all on those who took them, but the people *expected* the pills to be effective because they cost a lot. Their expectations set them up to think positively about the pills and report positive results, even when the pills provided nothing but a boost of vitamin C.

Clearly, positive thinking often yields positive results. In the next section of this book, I want to share and elaborate on four specific things positive thinking "does" to facilitate positive results in our lives:

- Positive thinking releases the power of potential.
- Positive thinking encourages positive responses.
- Positive thinking keeps things in perspective.
- Positive thinking helps you enjoy life.

Think about It

On a scale of 1 to 10, with 1 being "not good at all" and 10 being "outstanding," how would you rate yourself as a positive thinker?

_____

_____

Positive Thinking Releases the Power of Potential

People who think positively can see potential in even the most discouraging situations, while those who do not think positively are quick to point out the situations' problems and limitations. This goes beyond the proverbial idea of simply seeing a glass "half-full" or "half-empty" and extends to actually making decisions and taking actions based on either positive thinking or negative thinking.

One of the best stories I know about how positive thinking releases the power of potential took place centuries ago, when many parts of the ancient world were still unsettled. God promised the people of Israel they would possess a rich and fertile country, known as Canaan. He didn't promise them they could step across its borders without opposition, but He did promise them they would inhabit it—and when God makes a promise, He means it.

Taking God at His Word, the Israelites appointed twelve men to go into Canaan to "spy out the land" and bring back a report. Upon their return, ten spies admitted that the land flowed with milk and honey, and acknowledged that the fruit in Canaan was large and beautiful, but then remarked that the land was full of giants who would be impossible to overcome. They allowed the presence of the giants to detract from the promises of God.

In contrast, Joshua and Caleb brought back good reports, full of faith and confidence in God, and Caleb spoke up with confidence, saying, "Let us go up at once and possess it; we are well able to conquer it" (Numbers 13:30). The ten spies thought the giants in the land were too big to kill, but Joshua and Caleb thought they were too big to miss. Joshua and Caleb were the only two men who were positive in the face of opposition from the giants. They didn't ignore the challenges, but they did not over-emphasize them—and they were the only two who entered the Promised Land.

The spies who died in the wilderness only saw what was and failed to see what could be. Their negative thinking produced defeatist attitudes and caused them to try to persuade Moses that God's Word to Israel was not true, that possessing the Promised Land was not really possible.

Being positive does not mean we deny the existence of difficulty; it means we believe God is greater than our difficulties. Believing in God can cause us to win any battle we face. When we are closed to "positive possibilities" we only see what is right in front of us, not what we could see if we would simply be positive and creative.

Train your brain to trust and believe God and to think positive thoughts that are based on His Word. Determine that you will think as Joshua and Caleb did, not as the ten negative spies who never got to enjoy the Promised Land. Choose to see the power available to you through God if you trust Him more than your circumstances. Always remember that nothing is impossible with God!

Think about It

In what specific situation do you need to believe God is greater than your difficulties?

_____

_____

Positive Thinking Encourages Positive Responses

The way we think affects the way we speak, and the way we speak affects the way others respond to us. If you think and speak negatively, you are likely to hear a negative response. The opposite is also true. Positive thoughts and positive speech encourage positive responses.

For example, let's say you are an overnight guest in someone's home. Your host says to you just before bedtime, "It's supposed to be cold tonight, but there are probably enough covers on the bed. You don't think you'll need an extra blanket, do you?" Think about it. You would probably respond something like this, "No. Whatever is on the bed should be fine."

Now, consider this scenario. Your host says to you, "It's supposed to be cold tonight, so you'll probably want an extra blanket, won't you?" Most people in that situation would answer, "Yes."

I'm sure you can recall many situations in your life in which the way you communicated to someone influenced his or her response to you. I recently heard myself ask a clerk at a checkout counter, "You don't have a tissue behind the counter, do you?" Of course, she quickly said, "No." Maybe, if I had asked the question in a positive way, she would have been more diligent to look for one.

The most common type of negativism that draws negative responses from others is what I call the "flat-world attitude." This happens when a statement is not true, but people believe it based on hearsay, past experience, or what is considered "common knowledge." Let me explain.

Christopher Columbus believed the world was round. Therefore, he reasoned, if he set sail, he would eventually reach land—previously undiscovered territory—or end up back where he started. The people around Columbus *thought* the world was flat, so when "scholars" and "experts" examined his plans, they said his idea was impossible. Because they believed the world was flat, they assumed he would surely sail off the edge of it and disappear. But Columbus was right. He didn't fall off the edge of the world, but proved it was round and ended up discovering America in 1492.

During the early 1900s, an impressive array of scientific wizards scoffed at the idea of an airplane. They said, "It is an opium-induced fantasy—a crackpot idea." Really? Orville and Wilbur Wright didn't think so, and have gone down in history as the "first in flight." With similar skepticism toward airplanes, Marshal Ferdinand Foch said in 1911, "Airplanes are interesting toys, but they have no military value." Foch later became supreme commander of the Allied forces during World War I. Though airplanes were not widely used in the early days of the war, they became increasingly important and Foch and others discovered that they were valuable after all.

Thomas Edison tried to persuade Henry Ford to abandon his fledgling idea of a motor car because he was convinced that it would never work. He said, "Come and work for me and do something really worthwhile." Although Edison was a great inventor it sounds as if he was only positive about what he could do and rather pessimistic about other people's ideas. Next time you get in a car to go somewhere, be glad Ford didn't allow Edison's negative outlook on automobiles to influence him. Let this example remind you to never let a pessimistic person talk you out of your dreams.

All these people, and thousands of others throughout history, had a "flat-world mentality." They were convinced certain things could not be done—even though no one had ever tried. I am sure Christopher Columbus, the Wright brothers, and Henry Ford had to be determined to maintain their positive, can-do attitudes. Even though they were surrounded with negativity, they stayed positive and eventually found success. I wonder how much more they might have accomplished had they simply been surrounded with positive encouragement instead of ridicule? There is no telling!

Don't let someone else's limited thinking limit you. Negativity can be contagious; you have to pay attention if you don't want to catch it! Even if you are the only positive person in your family, your social circles, or your work group, be the one with an optimistic attitude and outlook in every situation.

Remember, negative attitudes produce negative responses while positive attitudes encourage positive responses. In the story about Joshua and Caleb, this was certainly true. After the ten spies gave their negative report, the Israelites wept all night and became terribly discouraged (see Numbers 14:1). Those ten men and their bad attitudes caused an entire nation to lose heart and doubt God's promises.

Then, the Israelites became so negative that they wanted to stone Joshua and Caleb, who were positive (see Numbers 14:10). Similarly, the enemy, often working through other people, likes to silence people with faith-filled, can-do attitudes. Don't let anyone silence you. Learn to get positive and stay positive in every way.

A soldier was assigned to stand at the end of the chow line and offer apricots to everyone who passed through the line. He decided to test the theory that the way people ask questions impacts the answers they receive. To the first hundred men who came by him, he said, "You don't want any apricots, do you?" Ninety percent of them said no. To the next hundred men, he said, "Would you like some apricots?" Fifty percent said yes; 50 percent said no. He changed his strategy slightly for the next hundred men, asking them, "Would you like one serving of apricots or two?" Forty percent took two servings and 50 percent took one. By simply changing the way he asked the soldiers about the apricots, he saw a complete turnaround in the percentage of men who took apricots!

Take a lesson from the soldier. Learn to be aware of the way you think and the way you talk to people. Train your mind to think positively toward every situation and train your tongue to speak positively to everyone you meet.

Think about It

Can you remember an occasion when your negative attitude pro-voked a negative response? How could you have been more positive in that situation?

_____

_____

Positive Thinking Keeps Things in Perspective

As I said in Chapter 1, thinking positively helps us keep things in perspective. When we think positively, we avoid "making moun-tains out of molehills." Negative thinking tends to blow things out of proportion, viewing them as larger and more difficult than they really are. People who think negatively magnify the unpleasant or undesirable aspects of a situation while failing to see anything good in it. I believe every person's life and even his circumstance includes more right than wrong and more good than bad if he simply deter-mines to think positively about it and look for the good elements in it. You see, I still believe that God is bigger than the devil!

Think about It

Have you made a mountain out of a molehill lately? Is there some-thing in your life that you are blowing out of proportion?

_____

_____

Positive Thinking Helps You Enjoy Life

Years ago, a man named Captain Edward A. Murphy was work-ing on a project for the United States Air Force. He became angry and cursed a technician who made a mistake, noting that, "If any-thing can be done wrong, this man will do it." Over time, such thinking became known as "Murphy's Law," which basically states, "Nothing is as easy as it looks; everything takes longer than you expect; and if anything can go wrong, it will—at the worst possible moment." How negative! Who could enjoy life if they lived accord-ing to Murphy's Law? They would always expect the worst, so they would probably get it!

I believe God has laws that completely disagree with Murphy's Law. The world may expect Murphy's Law to operate in their lives, but we need to resist that kind of negative thinking and embrace God's Law instead, which says something like this: "If anything can go right, it will; nothing is as difficult as it appears; everything is more rewarding than it appears; if anything good can happen to anybody, it will happen to me."

Negative thinking always produces a negative life. How much more could you enjoy your life if your thoughts agreed with God's Law, not Murphy's? God has a great life for you, one He wants you to enjoy thoroughly and live to the fullest. I challenge you to live by God's Law and consistently fill your mind with positive thoughts.

Think about It

In what specific circumstance do you need to start believing God's Law instead of Murphy's Law?

Don't Let the Positive Become Negative

See the Big Picture

When we focus excessively on the negative elements of a certain situation to the exclusion of its good aspects, we are "filtering out" the positive and exaggerating the negative. Very few situations are 100 percent negative; most of the time, we can find something good in every circumstance, even if we have to be really diligent about it.

Let's say you are a stay-at-home mom with young children and your husband leaves the house for work each day. Your four-year-old colors on the walls, cuts holes in his new pants, kicks his sister, and spills grape juice all over your freshly cleaned carpet. Let's also say he finally learned to apologize to his sister without being reminded, confessed to cutting his pants instead of saying "The dog did it," makes an attempt to clean his room, and says you are the best mom in the whole world. To say he was absolutely horrible all day long and forget about his good moments would be filtering out the good, and it would leave your mind with nothing but negative thoughts. Though there certainly would have been some negatives about that day, it had its positive experiences too.

I can't emphasize too strongly how important it is that you resist the temptation to characterize something as totally negative or to focus excessively on negative aspects of a situation. Look at the situation as a whole and find something positive about it. That will help you become a positive person.

Think about It

What is the most negative situation in your life? Now, list three positive things about it. If you are not used to doing this it may stretch you but try anyway.

Don't Make It Personal

Automatically blaming ourselves when something goes wrong or thinking everything that goes wrong is intended against us as individuals is called "personalizing" and it makes positive thinking very difficult. This happens often with young people on sports teams, when they miss the last shot, goal, or run of the game and feel they are solely responsible for a loss. They need to realize that both winning and losing are team efforts. It takes a whole team to win; it takes a whole team to lose. Even if one individual missed the last opportunity to win the game, there were many others missed along the way that added to the end result.

Similarly, let's say a group of women decide to gather for lunch and at the last minute, Julie cancels. If Suzie is one who takes everything personally, she will automatically assume Julie didn't want to be with her, when in reality, Julie may have had a family crisis, an unexpected houseguest, or a dental emergency.

Think about It

When was the last time you blamed yourself for something that wasn't your fault? Was there another way you could have viewed the situation that didn't make you the villain?

Do you get your feelings hurt a lot? Could it be that you are personalizing some situations? How can you avoid that in the future?

Anticipate the Best

One of the world's largest shoe manufacturers sent two market research-ers, independent of one another, to an underdeveloped nation to find out whether or not that country was a viable market for them. The first researcher sent a telegram to the home office saying, "No market here. Nobody wears shoes." The second researcher sent a telegram back home saying, "Unlimited potential here—nobody has any shoes!"[7]

I am sure the second researcher went on his trip expecting to send good news back to his employer—and he did. He could have perceived the fact that everyone in the nation he visited was bare-footed as a challenge or an obstacle, as the other researcher did, and then his attitude would have been negative. But because he anticipated the best, he saw the situation in a positive light.

In any situation, a habit of thinking about what can go wrong or envisioning worst-case scenarios is a bad habit that needs to be broken. Let's say you and a friend are planning a hiking trip. Most hiking trips have their challenges, but the person who will be able to overcome the challenges is the one who expects the trip to turn out well and is determined to enjoy it. The one who thinks, *Well, maybe it is a beautiful trail, but it's full of mosquitoes and it'll be hot and my feet will hurt after a while. And what if we get lost and can't find our way back?* is doomed to have a long, miserable day! This person has already decided not to enjoy the journey before it ever begins. Many things in life come with challenges, but most of them can be overcome with a positive outlook that expects the best.

Think about It

Think about a challenge you are facing right now. How can you expect the best? What are two good things that could emerge from this challenge?

Accept a Few "Grays"

If we want to stay positive, we have to realize that everything is not black or white. Life has some gray areas, some "in-betweens." Everything can't be perfect all the time and everything isn't horrible all the time. Deciding to skip a meeting or social event simply because you are running five minutes late or have a blemish on your face, canceling an entire trip because a flight is delayed, or feeling like a terrible human being over one innocent mistake is a way of thinking known as "polarizing," and it leads to frustration and negativity.[8] To stay upbeat about life, accept that you won't be perfect all the time, and neither will the people or things around you.

If we expect perfection out of life in general we usually tend to expect the same thing from people. That type of "unrealistic expectation" not only meets with a great deal of disappointment when our expectations are not met, but it also places unbearable pressure on people we care about and can eventually destroy relationships. Why not give people a break and stop demanding something from them that they have no ability to produce? The apostle James said that we all often stumble, fall, and offend in many things (see James 3:2). So if we *all* make mistakes *often*, why not realize that it is part of the human experience and relax?

Think about It

In what specific ways do you need to be more accepting of the "imperfect areas" in your life or in the way someone else's imperfect areas affect you?

CHAPTER

3

More Power to You

A young woman was going to meet her boyfriend's parents for the first time. Of course, she wanted to look her best, but when she glanced at herself in the mirror, she saw that her leather pumps looked a bit dull. She grabbed a paper towel she had used to blot grease from the bacon she had for breakfast that morning, polished her shoes, and off she went. Upon arriving at the boyfriend's parents' home, they greeted her—and so did their spoiled, temperamental poodle. The dog followed her around happily all evening, because of the smell on her shoes. As her visit drew to a close and she prepared to leave, the parents remarked, "Our dog is an excellent judge of character, and she certainly likes you! Welcome to the family!"[1]

In this story, the boyfriend's parents made a decision based on something they *thought* was true—but wasn't true at all! Obviously, they couldn't smell the bacon grease on their son's girlfriend's shoes, but the poodle certainly could and he responded favorably to the girl because of it. They decided the young woman would be a welcome addition to their family because the dog was such a great judge of character. People allow what they think to influence them in many ways, both big and small!

Thoughts Are Powerful

In recent years, much has been made of the fact that thoughts and attitudes influence people in many ways. Many medical schools and hospitals have received funding to study the mind-body connection and implement programs to help patients heal physically by becoming healthier mentally. It's terrific that the medical community is paying attention to the mind-body connection, but the understanding of the power of thoughts is not a new development. In fact, it is addressed in both the Old and New Testaments, written thousands of years ago!

In Romans 14:14, the apostle Paul indicates his strong belief that thoughts are very powerful. Responding to a heated debate over whether or not Christians in the early Church should eat meat that had been offered to idols, he wrote, "I know and am convinced (persuaded) as one in the Lord Jesus, that nothing is [forbidden as] essentially unclean (defiled and unholy in itself). But [none the less] it is unclean (defiled and unholy) to anyone who *thinks* it is unclean" (emphasis mine).

Paul did not believe meat offered to idols could be tainted because he knew idols were nothing but wood or stone. However, many people did not see things as Paul did, and he understood that. So his advice to them was not to eat the meat if they *thought* it was unclean. He knew that eating meat they considered defiled would affect their conscience in the same way as it would have had the meat actually been unclean. In other words, in a sense, perception is reality.

The more I ponder Romans 14:14, the more amazed I am by the depth of Paul's insight. The principle he understood was true when applied to meat offered to idols in ancient times, and it is still true today in any area of life. For example, a person who thinks, *I will never get a good job* is not likely to get one. People whose thoughts have convinced them they can never do anything right tend to make more mistakes than normal and have a high rate of failure. People who consider themselves accident prone seem to have one accident after another. In its extreme form, allowing thoughts to become realities can result in conditions such as anorexia, in which patients whose weight and body fat are far below normal are convinced in their minds that they are grossly overweight. They are so deeply convinced that even when they look in the mirror, the image they see appears a great deal larger that it actually is.

We can never move beyond what we think and believe. Many people today don't even bother to think rationally about what they believe and sometimes end up building their entire lives on beliefs that simply are not true. For them, whatever "they" say becomes truth—and "they" may be the news media, a celebrity, a group of friends, or others who enjoy sharing opinions, but may or may not really have any idea what is true. When we believe lies, our minds can actually limit us and even keep us from doing what God created us to do. But, if we will contend for the truth, embrace the truth, and build our lives upon the truth, we will succeed in every endeavor.

Think about It

What one thought do you believe limits you more than anything else? Do you believe you can change it?

_____

_____

The Battle for Truth

In Paul's day, many people believed the lie that meat offered to idols was unclean. That situation may still be relevant in some cultures today, but not universally. However, the world you and I live in is also riddled with lies. Many people do not believe there is such a thing as "absolute truth," and think whatever truth does exist applies only to certain individuals or in situation-specific settings. Satan has constructed this entire mentality in order to push aside

God's eternal truths. It enables people to believe what is convenient and easy for them, rather than believing and living by God's principles, which are designed to give life, peace, and victory to us and to give glory to Him.

One of the problems in the world today is that people want to "do their own thing" even if it makes them miserable. They don't want to take direction from anyone or be told what to do. And they don't want to read words of truth in a book called the Bible. This kind of arrogant independence and rebellion is responsible for many unpleasant results and even tragedies. I am sure, if you stop and consider it, you know of situations in which people have been determined to go their own way and ended up with terrible problems. This does not have to happen! God has given us instructions for life. They are true—and they work.

To be able to enjoy life and avoid unnecessary problems, we must live according to the truth which is found in God's Word and not according to the lies we hear from other people, the world, or the enemy. The enemy is always out to deceive us by tempting us to believe things that are not really true, but can become personal realities for us if we buy into the lies surrounding them. When we are deceived, we don't know, enjoy, or live by the truth. But when we live according to the truth, there are great benefits. If we don't know the truth because we are deceived, there is no way we can enjoy the benefits. We must know how to separate what is true from what is not. We can do this, but the battle for truth takes place in our minds, and we won't win it without a fight. We must examine *what* we believe and *why* we believe it. It is wise to be firmly convinced so when the devil challenges us concerning God's Word, we are prepared to stand firm.

We often find the children of Christian parents reaching an age where they begin to wonder if they really believe what their parents have taught them or not. Sometimes they go through a "crisis" period concerning their faith in God. They need to find their own faith because they can no longer live on the faith of their parents as they have done in the past. This can be a very healthy process. Most of them usually realize they do believe that Jesus is their Savior, but it was a decision they needed to make for themselves. We cannot stand through the storms of life based on someone else's faith. We must be fully assured in our own hearts and minds.

Once we make the decision to change our thinking to align with God's truth, we enter into an all-out war with the enemy, and our minds are the battlefield on which this war is waged. Satan knows that if he can dominate our thinking, he can dominate our lives. But God has given us the ability to overcome Satan, and we can start by understanding his nature and his strategies against us.

Understanding the Enemy and His Strategies

Think again about Romans 14:14 and the fact that what we believe becomes "truth" in our minds. This is why we must be diligent to know and understand the "true truth," the truth of God, and know how to recognize and refuse lies. If we are not careful, we will believe lies and they will influence us in negative ways. This is *exactly* what the enemy wants.

John 8:44 clearly identifies the enemy as "a liar [himself] and the father of lies and of all that is false." Everything about him and everything he tries to get us to believe is a lie. He is the great deceiver and he gains entrance into the life of various individuals by deceiving them.

In the natural world, there is a creature that also practices deception and, like the enemy, it knows no other way to live. You've probably never heard of the Portia spider, but this little insect clearly illustrates how the enemy works.

The Portia spider is a master predator whose chief weapon is deception. To begin with, says Robert R. Jackson in *National Geographic*, the spider looks like a piece of dried leaf or foliage blown into the web. When it attacks other species of spiders, it uses a variety of methods to lure the host spider into striking range.

Sometimes it crawls onto the web and taps the silken threads in a manner that mimics the vibrations of a mosquito caught in the web. The host spider marches up for dinner and instead becomes a meal itself.

The Portia spider can actually tailor its deception for its prey. With a type of spider that maintains its home inside a rolled up leaf, the Portia dances on the outside of the leaf, imitating a mating ritual.

Jackson writes, "Portia can find a signal for just about any spider by trial and error. It makes different signals until the victim spider finally responds appropriately—then keeps making the signal that works."[2]

Don't Be Ignorant

The Bible says we should not be ignorant of the enemy's devices (see 2 Corinthians 2:11, NKJV). Interestingly, the word *device* is defined as "a scheme to deceive." Clearly, one way he uses his devices against us is to plant in our minds thoughts that have evil purpose. Dr. Caroline Leaf teaches that the moment our thoughts become toxic (in other words, filled with anxiety, burdened by depression, influenced by lies, or harmful in other ways—poisonous!), our brains cannot function as God designed. She believes, and so do I, that the enemy knows this and takes advantage of it by waging war on the battlefield of the mind.

I have found that worry and reasoning are two of Satan's greatest devices in life. It's important to know your "weak spots," and pray that when you are tempted in those areas you will be able to recognize and resist the temptation. Worry and reasoning are temptations just like lying, stealing, or any other sin. We normally don't see things like worry as being sin, but whatever is not of faith is sin according to Romans 14:23. We certainly do not worry by faith so we must face the fact that it is sin and very dishonoring to God.

I used to worry about and try to figure out many things. I couldn't seem to relax and be at peace unless I thought I had everything all figured out. I realize now that it was my desperate but foolish attempt to feel in control of life and therefore safe. When I allowed myself to worry and reason, I gave place to Satan in my thinking (see Ephesians 4:27). Over the years, this and other areas of weakness allowed him to develop a variety of strongholds in my mind. Let me explain.

The enemy does not simply try to plant individual lies in our minds; he has a larger and more subtle strategy than that. Second Corinthians 10:4–6 is an important passage for us to remember now.

> For the weapons of our warfare are not physical [weapons of flesh and blood], but they are mighty before God for the overflow and destruction of *strongholds,* [inasmuch as we] refute arguments and theories and reasonings and every proud and lofty thing that sets itself up against the [true] knowledge of God; and we lead every thought and purpose away captive into the obedience of Christ (the Messiah, the Anointed One), being in readiness to punish every [insubordinate for his] disobedience, when your own submission and obedience [as a church] are fully secured and complete (emphasis mine).

Tucked away in this passage is a key word: *strongholds.* What the enemy wants to do in our minds is to build strongholds. The American Heritage Dictionary defines a *stronghold* as "a fortress; an area dominated or occupied by a special group." So, strongholds are wrong mind-sets and thought patterns that are based on lies and enable the enemy to dominate certain areas of our lives.

As a child, I always felt the need to take care of myself because nobody else was doing it. Through fear, which was manifested in worry and reasoning, Satan gained entrance into and built a mental stronghold in those areas. I also felt ashamed because my father sexually abused me when I was a child and Satan used that circumstance to build a stronghold in my mind of insecurity and low self-worth. This wrong thinking affected every area of my life for many years.

The enemy knows strongholds are effective. If he can trap us in them, he can work all kinds of destruction. God doesn't want us held captive in fortresses of the enemy's lies, so He teaches us through His Word how to destroy them. This process is called "renewing the mind," which is simply learning how to think properly. We need to examine what we believe and begin to ask why we believe that particular way. Millions of people are trapped in miserable lives because they believe lies. They may believe like I once did that they have no value and wonder why they were even born. They might have a root of rejection in their lives, which is a deep sensing that nobody wants them or feels they have any value. Should a person have such a root of rejection they will imagine all kinds of things that are not true at all. They have such an expectation of being rejected that they actually end up behaving in ways that cause people to be uncomfortable and unable to enjoy them. They frequently do get passed over in life, but it was their own thinking that created the problem.

Think about It

Worry, reasoning, and insecurity were some of the enemy's most effective devices against me. What are his greatest devices against you?

Tearing Down Strongholds

The way to get rid of darkness is to turn on the light, and the only way to destroy a stronghold of lies is to dispel them in the light of truth. The greatest weapon you and I have is the truth of God's Word. Second Corinthians 10:5 says we must lead every thought away "captive into the obedience of Christ." I can assure you, if we don't lead wrong thoughts away captive, the wrong thoughts will lead *us* away captive.

During the days when Jesus lived on earth, Pilate asked Him a question that has been raised down through the centuries and is still being asked today: "What is Truth?" (John 18:38). Jesus had already answered this question plainly and simply: "I am the Way and the Truth and the Life" (John 14:6). When praying to God in John 17:17, Jesus also said, "Your Word is Truth." He not only knew the truth but when His own mind was being attacked by Satan, He spoke the truth of God's Word out loud (see Luke 4:1–13). This is one of the most effective ways to "cast down" wrong thoughts, reasons, theories, and imaginations. I look at it as interrupting the devil in the midst of his temptation.

That is what God taught me to do when the thoughts of worry and reasoning arose. And that is what He wants you to do with the wrong thoughts the enemy uses against you. When your mind is being bombarded with wrong thoughts, simply speak out loud the portion of God's Word that opposes the lie in your mind. For example: if you find yourself thinking that you are useless and always fail at what you try to do, then say out loud, "God has a purpose for my life and He causes me to triumph and succeed."

We are partners with God. Our part is to trust Him, to know His Word and believe it, and His part is to do whatever needs to be done in every situation. We cannot know the Word of God unless we dedicate ourselves to diligent reading and study. Nobody would expect to be a successful doctor without studying and I don't know why people expect to be strong in their faith without doing the same thing.

Jesus clearly stated in Matthew 6:25–34 that we are not to worry about anything because God is faithful to provide all we need, when we need it. Proverbs 3:5, 6 says, "Lean on, trust in, and be confident in the Lord with all your heart and mind and do not rely on your own insight or understanding. In all your ways know, recognize, and acknowledge Him, and He will direct and make straight and plain your paths."

As God opened my eyes to the truth of His Word, I began to trust what the Scripture said over what the enemy said. The more I meditated on Scriptures like the ones just mentioned and others, the more my thinking changed and my freedom and joy increased. Little by little, as the truth of God's Word became rooted in my mind, the enemy lost ground in my thinking.

Having my mind renewed didn't happen overnight. Satan had very patiently and diligently built wrong thought patterns in my mind. He had been working since I was born and intended to continue until I died. We must have the same tenacity as he does and be willing to spend the rest of our lives working with God to undo the damage the devil did. God wants to restore everything the devil has stolen from us, and cultivate the character of Christ in us (see Isaiah 61:7 and 1 Thessalonians 5:23, 24). Make a decision now that you won't ever give up until you experience victory in all areas of your life. I also encourage you to be patient and determined even if you don't get instant results. God is working in you and in your life and you will see results in due time.

God's Word, the Bible, is truth. It teaches the truth; it teaches us a way to live that produces life. God's Word has stood the test of time and been proven in millions of people's lives over thousands of years. It works, if followed; I know this from years of personal experience and from countless times I have seen other people's lives change in amazing ways simply because they believed and obeyed God's truth.

Break Free and Stay Free

Once we learn how to break free from the enemy's influence in our minds by believing and applying God's truth to our lives, then we need to learn how to stay free. It's not enough to just lead wrong thoughts away captive; we also have to choose to think the right thoughts in the future. I found this to be true in my battle against worry and reasoning. As soon as I learned that God didn't want me to worry or try to figure everything out, I made every effort not to do so. When wrong thoughts came into my head, I did my best to take them captive. I would say, "No, I am not going to think that!" For a moment, my mind would find freedom. But before long, the old thoughts came back. Again, I would say, "No, I'm not going to think that!" But sooner or later, the same thought, or one just like it, would return. This cycle went on and on, and sometimes, by the end of the day I was completely exhausted.

One day I remember praying, "God, I can't go on like this day after day. As soon as I capture these wrong thoughts, they come back. What am I supposed to do?" As you fight the battle in your mind, you may find yourself praying the same prayer, so I want to share with you the simple answer God gave me. He said that all I needed to do was to think about something else! When you think about something good, there is no room for wrong thoughts to get into your mind. Concentrating on not trying to think wrong thoughts can actually increase them, but simply filling your mind with good things leaves no room for bad things to get in. The Bible says that if we walk in the Spirit we will not fulfill the lusts of the flesh (see Galatians 5:16), and this simply means that if we concentrate on the thing God desires, then we will not have room in our lives for what the devil desires.

This was a life-changing revelation for me. I realized I couldn't wait for something good to just fall into my mind. I had to *choose* my thoughts *on purpose.* I needed to fix my mind on "whatever is true, whatever is worthy of reverence and is honorable and seemly, whatever is just, whatever is pure, whatever is lovely and lovable, whatever is kind and winsome and gracious" (Philippians 4:8). The Bible says in Deuteronomy 30:19 that God sets before us life and death, blessings and curses. If you and I do not choose thoughts that lead to life, the enemy will make the choice for us—and he will choose thoughts for us that lead to death. But when we choose thoughts that lead to life, our lives will be blessed. Once again I want to remind you that "You can choose your own thoughts" and should do so very carefully. I encourage you to have what I call "Think Sessions." Take time to roll good thoughts over and over in your mind and this will help you form the habit of thinking good things. You must believe you can do a thing or you won't even try. So I repeat: "You can choose your own thoughts!" You can "overcome (master) evil with good" (Romans 12:21).

Write It Down

Writing things down seems to really help me learn. For example, I have found that writing a list of all the positive points about a situation or a person, along with writing down related Scriptures, helps me remain joyful and avoid seeing things out of proportion. After I make such a list, I sometimes carry it with me so I can refer to it, or I go over it each morning. This helps me when I'm tempted to give place to wrong thinking. I call it "fighting the good fight of faith." God has used this method to renew my mind in many areas. I have learned that the more I magnify and meditate on what's good, the smaller my problems become. The same can happen for you. Just give it a try. Doing these exercises will help you form new thinking habits that eventually become very natural for you rather than something you have to work at.

Think about It

Think about a person or situation that is difficult for you and make a list of positive elements about it. Keep it with you and read it (aloud, if possible) when you are tempted to give in to wrong thinking.

Agree with God

We need to *constantly* renew our minds with the truth of God's Word. I am not only writing a book about thoughts right now but I am also reading one for my own study and edification. We need to be "lifetime learners."

I used to be a very negative person, so it took daily determination for me to reprogram my thinking. It took time, but gradually, as I applied new knowledge to this challenge, I developed a new way of thinking. Even though approaching things from a positive perspective has now become my normal response I still make it a point to read and study in this area periodically to give myself "refresher courses." I know it was a major weakness for me and I never want to assume I have learned all there is to learn and know all there is to know. The dumbest person in the world is the one who thinks they know it all and have no more need to learn.

If we can learn to agree with God in our thoughts—to think the way He wants us to think—then we can have what He wants us to have, be who He wants us to be, and do what He wants us to do.

I have said many times, "We have to think about what we're thinking about," and I believe it now more than ever. If you're in a bad mood, ask yourself what you have been thinking about, and you'll probably find the root of your mood. If you're feeling sorry for yourself, just think about what you're thinking about; your attitude may need adjustment. Remember, "Where the mind goes, the man follows." Our moods are directly linked to our thoughts, so good thoughts will produce good moods.

Think Responsibly!

We need to take responsibility for our thoughts. We must stop acting as if there is nothing we can do about them. God has given us the power to resist the devil by choosing to think on things that are godly and good. It gives me tremendous hope when I realize that I can be assured of a better life by thinking good thoughts. That is exciting!

God will show us what to do to "clean up" our thinking, but He will not do it for us. He gives us His Word to teach us, and His Spirit to help us, but only we can make the decision to do what we should do.

You can learn to think properly and powerfully if you want to; it will take time but it is an investment that pays great dividends.

The Bible is a record of God's thoughts, ways, and deeds. As we agree with it, we are agreeing with God!

Think about It

Have you taken personal responsibility for your thoughts and attitudes? If not, write down that today is the day that you begin to take responsibility for how you think, jot down the date, and sign it as if you are making a contract with God.

_____

_____

CHAPTER

4

On-Purpose Thinking

It's amazing how quickly and completely our thoughts can change our moods. Negative thinking of any kind quickly steals my joy and causes a variety of bad moods. When we are negative and gloomy, other people don't enjoy being with us, and when our thoughts are down, everything else goes down with them. Our moods, countenance, conversation, and even our body can begin to droop in a downward position. Hands hang down, shoulders slump, and we tend to look down instead of up. People who tend to be negative in their thoughts and conversation are usually unhappy and rarely content with anything for very long. Even if something exciting does happen, they soon find something wrong with it. As soon as they see one thing wrong, they tend to fix their minds on it; any enjoyment they might have is blocked by concentrating on the negative. They may occasionally experience momentary enthusiasm but it quickly evaporates and gloom once again fills their entire demeanor. They probably do not realize they could be happy if they would simply change the way they think. We must stop merely *waiting* for something good to happen and take action to ensure that something good will happen.

I am truly amazed when I consider the fact that we have the ability to make ourselves happy or sad by what we choose to think. The Bible says we must be satisfied with the consequences of our words, whether they are good or evil (see Proverbs 18:20). It also tells us "Death and life are in the power of the tongue, and they who indulge in it shall eat the fruit of it" (Proverbs 18:21). Our words begin with our thoughts, so the same principle that applies to our mouths also applies to our minds. We need to be satisfied with the consequences of our thoughts because they hold the power of life and death. I would add that they hold the power of contentment and discontent, of joy and sadness.

The longer I live, the more I'm amazed by the fact that my mind so profoundly affects my moods. I still need to fight the battle in my mind and I doubt anyone reaches the point of being entirely "battle-free." Of course, I have learned to discipline my mind more quickly than I once did, but there are still times when my mind comes under attack.

God has given us the fruit of self-control (see Galatians 5:22, 23), which means we do not have to allow our thoughts to be out of control, but we can be intentional in our thinking. We can control what we think, and we can choose our thoughts. God has given us the ability to make choices about so many things in life, including our thoughts, and we must be responsible to make those choices carefully. In the realm of the mind, exercising self-control and making wise choices is called "on-purpose thinking."

Think about It

What are the most obvious ways your thoughts affect your moods? Can you think of a person or situation you tend to be negative about?

_____

_____

Great Thinking, Great Life

One of the most life-changing revelations we can have is to find out that we can do something about our thoughts. We can practice "on-purpose thinking." We do not have to meditate on everything that pops into our minds; we can choose what we want to think about. We can choose power-enhancing thoughts—not power-draining thoughts. We can be deliberate about what goes on in our minds. We can break up with bad habits and form good habits. In fact, learning to think great thoughts on purpose is the key to a great life.

We often allow ourselves to buy into the world's idea of a "great life." We may equate greatness with fame, fortune, athletic success, celebrity status, remarkable business or scientific achievements, or physical attractiveness. But none of these things constitutes a truly great life. In fact some of the most famous and wealthy people in the world are some of the most miserable ones. To really have a great life, I believe a person has to have love, peace, joy, right standing with God, good relationships, and other qualities the world does not necessarily consider "great." Without these things, how could anyone's life be great? Just think about it: what do we really have without peace and joy; life is full of strife and misery; and no one considers that a great way to live.

Think about It

What is your own personal definition of a great life?

_____

_____

Three Keys to On-Purpose Thinking

God makes it clear in His Word that thinking is directly connected to quality of life. Through many years of studying, teaching, and writing about the mind, I can honestly say that your thinking *will* be transformed and your life *will* be changed *if* you will follow God's instructions concerning your thoughts. In this section, I want to share with you three keys to great thinking. They all work, but none of them happens accidentally or without effort. If you want them to be effective in your life, you will have to incorporate them into your thinking on purpose.

1. Set your mind and keep it set.

The apostle Paul gives us valuable instruction about our thinking in Colossians 3:2: "And set your minds and keep them set on what is above (the higher things), not on the things that are on the earth." He clearly tells us to think about things that are important to God ("the higher things"), and doing so will always fill our minds with good thoughts.

"Setting" your mind is probably one of the greatest and most beneficial things you can learn to do. To "set" your mind means to make up your mind firmly. Wet concrete can be moved with ease and is very impressionable before it dries or "sets." But once it does set, it is in place for good. It cannot be easily molded or changed. The same principle applies to setting your mind. To set your mind is to determine decisively what you will think, what you believe, and what you will or will not do—and to set it in such a way that you cannot be easily swayed or persuaded otherwise. Once you set your mind according to the truth of God's principles for a good life, you need to keep it set and not allow outside forces to reshape your thinking. To set your mind does not mean to be narrow-minded and stubborn. We should always be open to learning, growing, and changing, but we must consistently resist the temptation to conform our thoughts to the world and its ideas. To set your mind on things above means to be firm in your decision to agree with God's ways of living no matter who may try to convince you that you are wrong.

When I began to conform my way of thinking and living to God's Word I met with a great deal of opposition and had to be firm in my decision. For example, I discovered that when I tried to be positive it was not received well by those who had a habit of being negative. They told me that I was trying to live a fairy tale and that real life just wasn't that positive. They told me that I could not "think" my way into success. I was actually accused of trying to operate in "mind control" as if it were something evil and even demonic. But, the truth is that God does tell us to control our minds and not to do so is inviting every form of misery into our lives.

Although it is sad, I had to realize that Satan would even use my family and closest friends to try to prevent me from making progress. They loved me but just did not understand and, sadly, we usually find fault with what we don't understand. I had to know for sure that God was leading me, and I had to be firm in my resolve to think right thoughts so I could see right results in my life. My friends were accustomed to doing the same thing I had always done, which was to think according to what we saw and felt. It seemed strange to them that we could believe and think according to what could be instead of what was.

The reason setting your mind and keeping it set is so important is that there's really not much hope of being able to resist temptation if you don't make up your mind ahead of time concerning what you will do when you are tempted. The Bible states that because Abraham was "fully assured" concerning the promise of God, he did not waver or doubtingly question (see Romans 4:20, 21). In other words, he had set his mind and was able to keep it set during temptation. You will be tempted; that's just a fact of life. So, you need to think ahead of time about the situations that can pose problems for you. If you wait until you are in the midst of a situation to decide whether or not you will stand firm, then you are sure to give up.

When we go on a diet, we must apply this principle of "setting your mind and keeping it set," in order to be successful. You can easily commit to a diet after dinner on Sunday evening, but the real test comes on Monday afternoon when you start to feel really hungry. People who have set their minds will stick with their decisions, realizing that they have to make it through the hungry times in order to eventually get the result they desire. This same principle must be applied to every area in which we need to make a change. It can be applied to exercise, getting out of debt, cleaning out the garage, or any number of other things.

Make up your mind ahead of time that you are going to go all the way through with God. Some people spend their entire life starting and quitting. They never follow through. They may set their mind but when temptation comes, when things get difficult, they don't keep it set. I strongly encourage you to be one of the ones who finishes what you start by keeping your mind set in the right direction all the way through to victory.

> But we do [strongly and earnestly] desire for each
> of you to show the same diligence and sincerity
> [all the way through] in realizing and enjoying
> the full assurance and development of
> [your] hope until the end.
> (Hebrews 6:11)

Whatever challenges you the most, *decide now* that you are going to set your mind for total victory. Talking to yourself ahead of time is one of the ways to set your mind. Some examples of what you might say to yourself as you set your mind in areas that commonly cause temptation include:

- "I am not going to think bad thoughts about other people and I am not going to gossip. I will not gossip. When someone around me begins to talk to me about someone else critically, I will not let myself get involved in it. I am not going to participate in ruining someone's reputation. I will not offend the Holy Spirit."
- "I am not going to overeat when I sit down for meals today. I will stop when I begin to feel full. I will make good food choices and I will not eat emotionally."
- "I am not going to be excessive in any area of life. I am a balanced person. I am not going to complain about anything. I have a lot to be thankful for and I will think on those things."
- "I am going to live to please God, not people. I want to be accepted but I will not compromise my faith and moral integrity."
- "I am going to eliminate unnecessary stress from my life. I will slow down, not overcommit, and try to keep life as simple as possible."
- "I am going to think positive thoughts and speak positive words."

If you think thoughts such as these, then when you are tempted to gossip, overeat, or face whatever your particular temptation may be, you already have a foundation in place. The message you have recorded inside yourself will begin to play back to you, and making the right decision will not be nearly as difficult as it would have been had you not yet made up your mind about what you would do when that situation presented itself.

If you prepare your mind ahead of time, then when temptation comes, you'll be in good shape to say "no" to it. Don't just wait to see what you feel like when temptation arises. Jesus told His disciples to pray that they would not come into temptation (see Luke 22:46). This is another way of setting your mind and heart in the right direction. Recognizing your weak areas and knowing what kinds of situations are challenging to you in life is wise. Firmly setting your mind to overcome them is the pathway to victory.

Think about It

In what specific situations can you apply these principles of preparedness?

_____

_____

2. Renew your mind.

No teaching on the mind is complete without Romans 12:2: "Do not be conformed to this world (this age), [fashioned after and adapted to its external, superficial customs], but *be transformed (changed) by the [entire] renewal of your mind* [by its new ideals and its new attitude], so that you may prove [for yourselves] what is the good and acceptable and perfect will of God, even the thing which is good and acceptable and perfect [in His sight for you]" (emphasis mine).

An unrenewed mind is one that is never changed after receiving Jesus Christ as Savior. The spirit is regenerated but the mind remains the same. This condition furnishes fertile ground for the devil to operate. It is for this reason that Christians often have a reputation as being hypocritical. They say they believe something but their behavior does not match their so-called beliefs. They may go to church each week, but at home or at work they do not differ from the rest of the world. Not only are they miserable, but the example they set for others is terrible.

Many people who need Christ in their life are hindered from accepting Him due to the poor witness of others they know who say they are Christians.

An Improper Mind

If a child of God harbors sin in his heart, he is lending his mind to wicked spirits for their use. For example, the Bible states clearly that if a man lusts after a woman in his heart, he has already committed adultery with her as far as his heart is concerned. He may be a Christian but he is fleshly and carnal. He has an improper mind. He does not control his thoughts. He has not renewed his mind or learned the power of his thoughts.

A woman may have improper thoughts toward another man if, when she sees him, she admires him excessively and tends to compare him to her own husband. Perhaps she would like her husband to have some of the qualities that she sees in this other man and her thoughts become improper as she even imagines herself married to him rather than the husband she has.

The woman may find herself feeling guilty about having such thoughts but fails to realize that she can refuse these thoughts that are "uninvited guests" instead of offering them a comfortable home.

The longer one allows improper thoughts, the more difficult they are to get rid of. Satan has built a stronghold in the man's mind that can only be torn down by strong determination and megadoses of God's Word.

Satan introduces many improper thoughts into the believer's

head. He knows he can hinder fruitfulness by doing so. He can keep the believer weak and powerless through controlling his thoughts. Satan might fill one's mind with criticism or prejudices. He might use jealous thoughts to hold him in bondage. Proud thoughts are among his favorites. If he can get us to think more highly of ourselves than we ought to and less of others than we should, he can be successful in hindering us from loving other people, which is the one new command that Jesus gave (see John 13:34).

Renewing your mind is not like renewing your driver's license or library card, which can be done quickly and doesn't have to be repeated for months or years. Renewing your mind is more like undertaking the job of renewing and refurbishing an old house. It doesn't happen quickly; it takes time, energy, and effort, and there is always something that needs attention.

Don't fall into the trap of believing you can renew your mind by thinking right thoughts one time. To get the mind renewed, you will have to think right thoughts over and over again, until they become rooted in your thinking—until right thoughts come to you more easily and naturally than wrong thoughts. You will have to discipline yourself to think properly, and you will have to guard against falling into old thought patterns—and this can happen very easily. When it does, don't feel badly, just start thinking rightly again. You will eventually come to the place where wrong thoughts actually make you uncomfortable and they just don't fit right into your thinking processes any longer.

The continual, ongoing process of renewing the mind extends to every aspect of your thinking. If you are like most people, many areas of your mind need to be renewed. These may include the way you think about yourself, your finances, your health, your family, time management, vacations and recreation, your job, your future, or any of a multitude of other topics. Don't assume you have renewed your mind just because you feel confident your thinking has changed in one area. You should celebrate concerning the mental junk you have eliminated, but don't be complacent and fail to keep pressing on.

Many times, the areas of thinking you find most challenging to renew are the ones that hurt you most and keep you from receiving the best God has for you. I was a workaholic and although I made progress against it little by little, it was a real battle for me. I was insecure and felt devalued due to being abused in my childhood and I fell into the trap of getting my worth out of what I accomplished. I was not able to really enjoy the new life God had provided through Jesus Christ because I worked constantly trying to deserve what He had already given by His grace and mercy as a free gift. Through persisting in renewing my mind, I have been able to better balance my life in ways that amaze me! But I want to emphasize over and over again that you will have to be willing to invest time and effort if you want to change your way of thinking.

Let me be quick to say that you should not feel condemned if you are struggling with your thought life right now or if you face struggles in the days to come. Condemnation only weakens you, and it never helps you make progress. Anytime we recognize that we are allowing wrong thoughts in our mind, we should ask God to forgive us and continue pressing on toward our goal. Celebrate every victory because it helps you not to feel overwhelmed by what still remains to be conquered, and remember that God is very patient and long-suffering. He is understanding and will never give up on you.

Think about It

In what areas of your life does your mind need to be renewed?

_____

_____

3. "Gird up" your mind.

First Peter 1:13 instructs us to "gird up the loins of your mind, be sober, and rest *your* hope fully upon the grace that is to be brought to you at the revelation of Jesus Christ" (NKJV).

You and I aren't accustomed to hearing the phrase "gird up" today. But in biblical times both men and women wore long skirt-like outfits. If they tried to run in those clothes, there was a good chance they could get tangled up in the long fabrics and stumble. When they needed to move quickly, they gathered the material of their garments and pulled it up so they could walk or run freely. They would gird up their clothing.

When the Bible tells us to "gird up the loins" of our minds, I believe it means to get our minds off of everything that would cause us to stumble as we run the race God has set before us. I think it may also refer to concentrating on the thing at hand rather than allowing our thoughts to wander all over the place. God has a good plan for each of us, but we must walk the path that leads us to it. Focus and concentration are both real challenges in our world today. We have a great deal of information coming at us all the time and to keep our minds on what our purpose is requires great determination and even training.

You might get up on Monday and fully intend to start your day by spending time with God in prayer and Bible study. Then you intend to get three specific projects finished that day. You need to go to the grocery store, get some maintenance done on your car, and finish cleaning out a closet that you started working on last week. Your intention is good, but if you don't focus on those projects you will surely be pulled away by other things or people. Girding up your mind is another way of saying "stay focused on what you need to do."

Uninvited Guests

Do you experience thoughts flashing through your mind that seem to come from nowhere? They do come from somewhere and they are often designed to hinder you from reaching your goals. These thoughts are actually uninvited guests looking for a home and it is our job to tell them that we have no room for them.

How would you respond if people that you barely knew showed

up at your front door with their baggage telling you that they wanted to move in? Well, of course you would tell them they were not welcome and no matter how persistent they were, you would hold firm to your decision that you could not provide a home for them. We should take this same attitude with flashing thoughts that are in reality uninvited troublesome guests who come knocking at the door of our mind.

For example, if you decide to take some college courses to improve your education and when you go to register thoughts begin to flash through your mind like: *You are too old to go to college. It will be too hard for you and take too much time. You didn't do that good in high school and college is much more difficult.* Stop right away and ask yourself if these thoughts are yours or if they are coming from somewhere outside of you. Are you choosing them or are they uninvited guests that the devil has sent to you. Instead of offering them a home, "gird up" your mind and think the way you want to think. Stay focused on your goal, not the fear the devil is trying to instill in you. Think like this: *There will be a lot of people younger than I am in my classes, but I have a good mind and a destiny to fulfill, so I'm going to get myself enrolled and I'm going to do my very best. Even if I'm the oldest person in the entire college, I'm not too old to improve myself.*

You may want to get out of debt, live a healthier lifestyle, improve your marriage, or a variety of other things. Whatever your specific situation is, be diligent to gird up the loins of your mind and get rid of any thoughts that are standing in the way as you seek to move forward.

Think about It

Have you developed an ability to concentrate and focus or do you allow uninvited guests to get you off course?

Have Some "Think Sessions"

I believe in having a "think session" every day. If we were to sit down regularly and say to ourselves, "I am going to think about a few things for a few minutes," and then deliberately think about some of the things the Bible tells us to think about, our lives would improve dramatically. Disciplining ourselves to think properly by having "on-purpose think sessions" will train us to begin thinking properly in our everyday lives.

There are thoughts you need to think every day in order to set your mind and keep it set, renew your mind, and gird up the loins of your mind. In the next section of this book, I am going to share some of those thoughts with you and help you understand how incredibly powerful they are. For example, one of the things all believers need to think every day is this biblical truth: *I am in right standing with God.* Let me ask you, can you see anything at all wrong with thinking such a thought several times a day? I certainly can't! Why not think something on purpose that will benefit you rather than merely meditating on whatever happens to fall into your mind?

We use our thinking abilities every day, but most of us need to change the content of our thoughts. Instead of thinking, *I'm no good; I mess up everything; I never do anything right,* we can use our mental energy to think about how much God loves us and how we are in a right relationship with Him through Jesus Christ.

Or, think about how much more effectively you could overcome fear in your life if you took time to think, *I will not be afraid; I will not let fear control me; I know it will come from time to time, but even if I have to do something of which I'm afraid, I am going to do it.* This would be a way of setting your mind and keeping it set against fear. Then, when faced with the temptation to be afraid, you would be better able to resist.

As you spend more time thinking correctly, great transformation will take place in your life. You might have to put notes around your house saying "What have you been thinking today?" You might have to put a note in your car to remind you to think right thoughts today—or even write out what those thoughts are and post them on a mirror or on your computer screen. This type of exercise would not be uncommon for a college student facing final exams. They do everything they can do to keep the right answers in front of them prior to the test to assure that they graduate. If you will discipline yourself to remind yourself to spend time thinking right thoughts on purpose for several minutes each day, you will find things improving so radically you will be absolutely amazed. Before you know it, you'll be enjoying the good life God has predestined for you.

> For we are God's [own] handiwork (His workmanship),
> recreated in Christ Jesus, [born anew] that we may
> do those good works which God predestined (planned
> ⁻ beforehand) for us [taking paths which He prepared
> ahead of time], that we should walk in them [living
> the good life which He prearranged
> and made ready for us to live].
> (Ephesians 2:10)

Think about It

How can you work a ten-minute "think session" into your daily routine?

Breaking Up with Bad Habits

God offers each of us a great life, but we must renew our minds and learn to think on purpose if we want to experience all He has planned for us. Perhaps one of the areas we need to be most deliberate and purposeful about is the area of habits. Habits are actions we do repeatedly, sometimes without even thinking about them, or things we have done so often that they become our natural responses to certain situations.

For example, I have a habit of putting on lipstick after I eat when I am out in public. My friends tease me because I do it so often. I get out my pocket mirror and my lipstick, and I apply it. When I am home I use a lip moisturizer instead. I don't believe I ever consciously think about it; I have just done it for so long that it is a habit. The moment I sense my lips feeling dry, I apply something to moisturize. I also wiggle my toes a lot. I don't even know why I do it; it is just a habit. At least it keeps blood circulating in my feet, which is a good thing.

Some people make a habit of putting their car keys in the same place every time they enter their homes or offices. Some make sure absolutely nothing is left in their in-box (whether it's physical or electronic) at the end of each work day. Some have a habit of daily exercise or eating healthfully. Some fill their gas tanks when they are halfway empty instead of almost all the way empty. These are good habits. Of course, people have bad habits too—biting their nails, interrupting others when they are speaking, not turning lights off when they leave certain rooms, leaving messes for others to clean up, or being chronically late.

We all have habits such as the ones I mentioned; many of them are unique to us as individuals and we may not know anyone else who does what we do exactly the way we do it. Some habits that are harmless are not necessarily the ones we must be concerned with, but our harmful habits need to be broken and replaced with good ones. Bad habits are not broken simply because we want to break them; we must break them on purpose and that will require determination and diligence.

I found thirty-four references in the *Amplified Bible* for the word *habitually*. That tells me that God expects us to form good habits. The psalmist David said that the man who wants to prosper and succeed needs to *habitually* ponder and meditate on God's Word by day and by night (see Psalm 1:2, 3, emphasis mine). This tells me that establishing the habits necessary for success takes discipline and consistency, especially in our thought life. With enough discipline and consistency, we can break bad habits and new ones can be formed.

Think about breaking a bad habit like you would breaking up with a bad boyfriend. Interestingly enough, we could miss the boyfriend even though we knew we did the right thing in breaking up with him. We might feel lonely for a while and be tempted to go back to him, but if we remain firm in our resolve we will eventually no longer miss him and find someone else that provides a healthy relationship for us. In like manner, we may break a bad habit and yet miss it for a while, even being tempted to go back to old ways. This is the time to set your mind and keep it set in the new direction because you don't want to remain in bondage to the old and miss the good new thing God has for you.

In the New Testament, Paul writes that we must habitually put to death the evil deeds prompted by the body if we want to truly and genuinely live (see Romans 8:13). He is simply saying that we must learn to discern what is not God's will, and therefore not good for us, and we must habitually say no to those things. Doing the right thing once or even a few times does not equal success, but *habitually* doing right will produce a life worth living. It may not be easy, but it will be worth the effort.

Don't get discouraged if at first you feel you are making little or no progress in forming new habits. Remember that habits take time. As I mentioned in the Introduction to Part 1, some experts say a habit can be developed in twenty-one days, while others say it takes a month. I don't know if these figures are accurate or not, but I do know from experience that anything I stick with thirty days does begin to get ingrained in my thinking, my character, and my routine. Thirty days gives me a good beginning and I would rather spend my time going forward rather than backward. So, if you need to form a new habit, give it a try for thirty days. At the end of that time period, see where you are. If it seems established, congratulations; you have a new habit. If not, stay diligent, disciplined, and focused and you will eventually succeed. The person who never gives up always sees victory.

Think about It

What good habits do you need to develop in your life? How will you start? When will you start?

_____

_____

The Importance of Meditating on God's Word

All of the successful people we read about in the Bible had a habit of meditating on God's Word. They knew that it was the way to keep their minds renewed to God's ways. To meditate simply means to roll over and over in your mind, to mutter softly or speak out loud. We all do know how to meditate but we often apply the principle in harmful areas. I can easily meditate all day long on my problems or something someone did that hurt me. I can actually do it without even trying, but I can also choose to meditate on something else that will benefit me and be pleasing to God.

Meditation is actually very powerful. I like to look at meditating on God's Word as chewing my food. If I swallow my food whole, then I don't get the nutrition that is in it and it does me virtually no good with the exception that I might get a stomachache. If I skim over God's Word or just hear a weekly sermon in church, it is like swallowing it whole, but never getting the good things out of it that God wants me to have. The Word of God actually has inherent power in it and I believe that power is best released as we think on it over and over.

A friend of mine that I will call Pete shared an experience from his own life that I believe makes this point very clearly. He shared that he had had a lifelong problem with lusting after other women in his thoughts. This was especially painful to him because he is a minister and knew that the principles he taught and believed in should be working in his own life. He had shared this with his wife for accountability and although they prayed about it diligently he found no relief. This of course greatly grieved Pete because he did not want to think these wrong thoughts, but no matter how hard he tried he could not seem to stop. If he saw a pretty woman, his mind would imagine all sorts of things that were unclean and inappropriate. After many years of absolute agony over this problem, his health began to fail and through the difficult circumstances he encountered he sought God in a deeper way than ever before in his life. God showed him several things that were helpful, but the one that was the most important concerned forming a habit of meditating on God's Word. My friend had no idea that this would solve his lifelong problem with lustful thoughts, but in obedience to God he began with a Scripture about loving others. We are called to freedom; our freedom should not be an excuse for selfishness, but we should serve one another out of love (see Galatians 5:13).

He meditated on this portion of Scripture diligently, thinking about it often throughout the day. This continued for several days and then he had an occasion to be at the swimming pool at the hotel where he was staying. He wanted to go to the pool with his family but actually dreaded it because he knew that he was likely to see women in bathing suits and feared that his mind would more than likely be filled with the same lustful thoughts he had fought for years. He did indeed see a very beautiful woman and she was dressed in a very scanty and extremely revealing bikini, but Pete surprisingly discovered that his first thoughts were, "I wonder if this woman dresses like this because she has never had anyone to genuinely love her, and I wonder if she has ever known the unconditional love of God?" He began praying for her much to his surprise and was delighted to realize that he was not even tempted to think lustful thoughts. I might add that this amazing victory has continued from that time until the present. Pete has continued his journey of meditating daily on portions of Scripture and has found it to be totally life-changing for him. Although he is a minister and was educated in God's Word, he was not getting the power out of it that was available to him because he had not developed a habit of meditating on it.

I pray that Pete's story will be fuel for the journey you have ahead of you.

In the next part of this book, I will offer and explain twelve specific power thoughts—ammunition for you to use as you wage war against the enemy on the battlefield of your mind. As I stated previously, this book is not meant to be merely read, but to be studied, and the twelve power thoughts need to be meditated on until they become habits. These simple, yet powerful, thoughts are keys to victory in the mental battle that we fight in life, and they will bring an amazing dimension of power to you. They have absolutely transformed my life, and I believe they will do the same for you. But remember, you have to meditate on them, which means to think them on purpose!

PART II

Power Thoughts

Watch your thoughts, for they become words.
Watch your words, for they become actions.
Watch your actions, for they become habits.
Watch your habits, for they become character.
Watch your character, for it becomes your destiny.
—Anonymous

The Power Thoughts Program

The twelve power thoughts you are about to study can completely transform your life. Each one is solidly based on God's Word, and though I have personally experienced the power of these thoughts, they are not merely my own ideas or opinions, nor are they some kind of "humanistic mind science." They are all scriptural, and their purpose is to encourage you to bring your thinking into agreement with God so you can enjoy Him and His good plan for you.

As you go through the power thoughts, you will see that I often suggest that you meditate on them or on a passage of Scripture that affirms them. Dr. Caroline Leaf teaches that the most important thing we can do is meditate because meditation, which she also calls being "interactive with information," is a process that causes the brain to function as it's designed to, using both the left and right hemispheres in the proper ways. Simply put, meditation is good for your mind! In addition to rolling these power thoughts over and over in your mind, I would also like to suggest that you repeat them out loud and verbalize the Scriptures relating to them. I find that writing things down and saying them out loud is part of my meditation process that really helps me form new mind-sets.

Even though meditation is an excellent way to use our brains, I find that some people today are uncomfortable with or afraid of the word *meditation* because it is frequently used in eastern religious practices that are false and in New Age practices, which leave God out of everything or present Him as whatever a person wants Him to be. Actually, meditation was a biblical principle before anyone else decided to use it for other purposes. Those who adopted it for ungodly use simply found a God-ordained principle that worked and began using it in a humanistic way. Don't be afraid of meditation and the principle of positive thought and confession; just be sure what you say and meditate on agrees with God's Word.

The Twelve-Week Plan

1. First, read through the rest of the book so you have an idea of what the twelve power thoughts are. You will probably feel right away that some of them are what you need right now more than others, but all of them are important and necessary to maintain the good life God desires for us.

2. After reading the book, go back to the first power thought and meditate on it for one week. Make that thought part of your everyday life. Speak it out loud several times a day. More is better than less!

3. Write down the power thought that you are studying in large letters and put it in several places where you will see it every day—the more places the better!

4. Get a journal and write down your own thoughts about the power thought for the week. Use this time to get to know "you" in a deeper and more honest way. Talking to a friend or family member about what you are learning is another good way to get it rooted in your heart. Just make sure you choose someone who will be encouraging to you.

As the days go by you will find the power thought of the week becoming a part of you that affects all your actions. As you move to the next power thought, the previous one will still be part of your meditation but you won't have to work at it as much. You will find each of them becoming part of who you are.

5. Repeat steps 2, 3, and 4 for each of the twelve power thoughts.

At the end of your twelve weeks of focusing on each of the twelve power thoughts, I recommend that you start all over and repeat the process, especially with the ones that you feel you need most. I believe that repeating this process for an entire year would be the most beneficial plan, and that at the completion of the program you will be amazed with the results you are enjoying.

Norman Vincent Peale, a pastor who wrote the best-selling book *The Power of Positive Thinking,* said, "Change your thoughts and you change your world." I have certainly experienced the truth of these words over the course of my lifetime and I want you to experience it too. Are you ready to begin the process of changing your life and changing your world? The rest of this book is dedicated to helping you accomplish that purpose, so let's get started.

1

I can do whatever I need to do in life through Christ.

"I have strength for all things in Christ Who empowers
me [I am ready for anything and equal to anything
through Him Who infuses inner strength into me;
I am self-sufficient in Christ's sufficiency]."
Philippians 4:13

The first thought I want to focus on that has the power to transform
your life is simple: *I can do whatever I need to do in life through Christ.*
In other words, I can handle whatever life hands me. I wonder, do
you believe you can do whatever you need to do in life? Or are there
certain things that trigger dread, fear, or cause you to say, "I could
never do *that!*" when you think about them? Whether it's suddenly
losing a loved one, facing a serious unexpected illness, having your
adult child with two toddlers move into your meticulously clean
and quiet house after you've had an "empty nest" for years, going
on a strict diet because your life depends on it, putting yourself on
a budget to avoid foreclosure on your home, or suddenly having to
care for a disabled elderly parent—most people have some kind of
circumstance that truly seems impossible to them, something they
aren't sure they can handle.

The fact of the matter is, while some situations may be intensely
undesirable or difficult for you, you *can* do whatever you need to do

in life. I know this because God tells us in His Word that we have the strength to do all things because Christ empowers us to do so (see Philippians 4:13). He doesn't say everything will be easy for us; He doesn't promise we will enjoy every little thing we do, but we can enjoy life in the midst of doing them. He does guarantee us the strength for everything we need to do because He Himself empowers us and we are sufficient (which is another way of saying we have everything we need) in His sufficiency.

Think about It

What in your life do you need to begin to believe you can do?

_____

_____

Not Alone

We must understand that Philippians 4:13 does not say we can do anything we want to do because we are strong enough, smart enough, or hard-working enough. No, in fact, it leaves no room at all for human effort or striving of any kind. The secret to being able to do what we need to do is realizing that we cannot do it alone; we can only do it in Christ. For some reason, we often fail to use our faith to believe and act on that truth. Instead, we think *we* have to do it all and, forgetting that the power of Christ works through us, we are defeated before we even begin. As I have mentioned previously, we are partners with God. We cannot do His part and He will not do our part. He wants us to believe and take action on His direction and leading, but He insists that we trust (lean and rely on) Him every step of the way.

I hear so many people make comments such as, "This is too hard. I just can't do this. It's too much for me." But I need to tell you, as a believer in Jesus Christ, you are full of the Spirit of God, and nothing is too difficult for you if God is leading you to do it. God will not call you to do anything He will not enable and empower you to do. He will not allow you to go through anything that is impossible for you. Our attitude toward unpleasant things is a vital part of going through them successfully. Although God never authors bad things, He does use them for our spiritual growth. For example, He may use a grouchy person to help us become more patient. God did not cause the person to be grouchy, but neither does He remove them from our life when we asked Him to. Instead, He uses them to change us!

Most of our trials in life are the result of someone else's failure, carelessness, ignorance, or sin and understandably, we pray for God to change them. I have discovered that just because I am asking God to change someone, that does not mean they want God to change them and although my prayers open a door for God to work, He will not go against their free will to answer my prayer. While God is continuing to work in their life, they may be the tool He uses to form us into the vessel He wants us to be. I can pray for them to be pleasant, but I must joyfully accept each day as it comes, trusting God totally to enable me to do whatever I need to do that day.

God has given you the gifts, talents, abilities, and grace you need to do His will in life. God's grace is actually His power and He will not only give you grace, but promises grace and more grace (see James 4:6). He never runs out of power—and His power is available to you! Now, if you don't keep the right mind-set, the enemy can defeat you with thoughts of inadequacy, but if you make up your mind that you can do what you need to do, you'll find yourself able to do it—not in your own strength, but in the strength God gives you.

Don't speak out of your emotions because how we feel does not always agree with God's Word. That is why it is important to realize that even though you feel overwhelmed, you should still say, "I can do whatever I need to do in life through Christ."

Do you consider yourself a person who has faith in God? If so, has your faith reached your thoughts and words? We can easily deceive ourselves into thinking we have great faith but if we are easily defeated by challenges, then perhaps our faith is not as great as we thought it was.

The Bible says that out of the heart the mouth speaks. We can learn a lot about ourselves by listening to ourselves. Do your thoughts and words reflect your complete dependence on God, realizing that His abilities (not your own) empower you to do anything you need to do in life? I had to examine my own thoughts and words and ask myself if I portrayed a person who had great faith in God, and I encourage you to do the same. I didn't like all of my answers but the exercise in self-examination did open my eyes to understanding that I needed to make some changes. Realizing we are wrong in an area is never a problem. The problem comes when we refuse to face truth and continue making excuses.

Be willing to face anything God wants to show you and ask Him to change you. If you are trusting in your own strength, begin to trust God instead. If you are trying to do things out of your own human abilities and growing frustrated, tell God you want Him to work through you and let His sufficiency be your sufficiency.

When challenges arise I encourage you to develop a habit of saying immediately, "I can do whatever I need to do through Christ Who is my strength." Remember that words are containers for power, and when you say the right thing it will help you do the right thing. Don't fill your container (words) with things that disable you, for truly you are able to do all things through Christ.

As you meditate over and over on the power thought "I can do whatever I need to do in life through Christ," you will find that you are not as easily overwhelmed by situations that arise. Each time you roll that power thought over in your mind or speak it, you are developing a healthy mind-set that enables you to be victorious.

Think about It

How often do you say, "This is too hard for me" or "I just can't do this"?

Frequently_____

Occasionally_____
Almost never_____

What will you now begin to say to reflect your confidence in God's ability to help you do whatever you need to do?

_____

_____

Miracles Come in Cans

Perhaps you have heard the words "You can't" repeatedly throughout your life. Many people are good at telling others what they cannot do. Even people you wouldn't necessarily consider to be "against" you may have tried to discourage you from doing something you wanted to do by telling you that you couldn't do it. Parents, teachers, coaches, friends, family members, and leaders of church groups or social activities often fail to realize the power of their words over young lives. So many children and teenagers grow up thinking "I can't" when that isn't true at all! No matter how many times you have heard someone say to you, "You can't," I want to say to you, "Oh, yes, you can!" I believe that miracles come in cans—our belief that we can do whatever we need to do through Christ Who is our strength.

I believe in you; God believes in you; and it's time for you to believe in yourself. Today is a new day! Put the past and all its negative, discouraging comments behind you. Negative words and words that speak of failure come from the enemy, not from God, so decide right now not to allow the power of "you can't" to influence you anymore. In contrast, God's Spirit encourages you and will do everything to urge you forward toward success in every area of life. God tells you to have courage, so always remember if you feel "dis-couraged," that is from the enemy and if you feel "en-couraged," that is from God. Choose to agree with God and say to yourself, "I can!" And let the power of your positive thoughts and words outweigh the power of the negative words anyone else has ever spoken to you.

Think about It

Complete this sentence: Yes, I can

_____

_____

Rock Your Box

A long time ago, before some of the medical advances available to us today, a little boy was crippled, and doctors said there was nothing they could do to help him. So the boy's mother took an orange crate and made a box for him. She put him in the box, tied a rope to it, tied the rope around her waist, and pulled him around with her so she could keep a close watch over him. Everywhere she went, she pulled him along behind her.

After a while, the boy developed a habit the mother didn't like. He began to rock his box. This made taking him places more difficult because not only did she have to drag him, he was rocking his box. She pleaded with him to stop, but he kept rocking. Sometimes, he rocked his box to the point that it tipped over and he fell out of it. No matter how many times she put him back in the box, he kept rocking. Eventually, he rocked his box until he was finally able to get out of it. Then, to everyone's amazement he learned how to walk and ended up with a great life.

That little boy did something that the doctors and not even his loving mother believed could happen. He refused to settle for life inside a box someone had put him in. Has somebody or something put you in a box that you want to get out of? If so, keep rocking your box until you are free. The world and people in it are experts at telling us what we can and can't do. They don't always celebrate anything "out of the box," which is something out of the ordinary. Time after time I have seen ordinary people do extraordinary things when they believed they could and refused to give up.

Everyone faces challenges in life. Some people are completely overwhelmed by their challenges while others, like the little boy in the box, refuse to give up. My question to you is, "Do you want to be able to meet all challenges head-on and overcome them?" Then get mentally prepared for whatever comes. Remember, according to Colossians 3:2, the way to be prepared is to "set your mind and keep it set." Don't be caught off guard and unprepared. Repeatedly thinking and saying, "I can do whatever I need to do in life through Christ," will help you set your mind and keep it set in that direction, and it will set you up to win in life. Remember, where the mind goes, the man follows!

Do not allow yourself to think thoughts such as, *I just cannot take any more trouble!* Or, *If one more thing happens I am going to go over the edge!* Or, *If things don't change soon—I am giving up!* There are many varieties of this kind of thinking—and you may have a favorite thought or saying of this type that you use when you feel overwhelmed. But do you realize these thinking patterns actually prepare you to be defeated before you even encounter a problem? There is nothing strong, powerful, enabling, or victorious in thinking you will "go over the edge" or deciding to quit. Those are losing attitudes, not winning attitudes. Don't say things like "I feel like I am losing my mind," or "This is going to kill me." Instead you can say, "I have the mind of Christ," and "This trial is going to work out for my good."

Be a person who is mentally prepared for any challenge that crosses your path, and do not allow yourself to be easily discouraged and defeated. Always remember that apart from Jesus you can do nothing (see John 15:5), but in Him you can do whatever you need to do in life (see Philippians 4:13). Decide to rock your box until it falls apart.

Think about It

What box do you need to rock?

_____

_____

Exchange Things That Are Not Working

I'm sure you have walked into a store before with something to exchange. Maybe it was an article of clothing that you decided you didn't like, a pair of shoes that were uncomfortable, or a gadget that didn't do what you'd expected. You entered the store with something that didn't work for you, exchanged it, and left with something that did work for you—something that looked better, fit better, or was more functional. You had to trade what was not effective for something that was.

The same principle applies to your thinking. If you will exchange your "I can't" thoughts for "I can" thoughts and begin to say "I can do whatever I need to do in life because God strengthens me. I am strong in the Lord and in the power of His might, and whatever He asks me to do, I can do," you will see remarkable changes begin to happen. If you will build into your character the thought that, with God's help, you are able to do whatever you need to do in life, you will have more zeal and enthusiasm about facing every day. I have found that I even have more physical energy when I think "I can" thoughts. It helps me to not dread anything that is an energy drainer.

It's never too late to begin saying, "I can." Don't think or say things like: "My marriage is in too big of a mess. It will never work," "There's no point trying to clean this house. It's in such bad shape it just overwhelms me when I walk in and look at it," or "I can't get out of debt because I am in too deep." "I will never own a home or have a new car," or "I can't enjoy my life because I have too many personal problems." Some of the challenges you face may be very difficult ones, however God never allows more to come on us than we can bear, but with every temptation He always provides a way out! (see 1 Corinthians 10:13). That Scripture not only says He provides a way out, but it also says that He gives us strength to bear up under our challenge patiently. That means we can go through it with a good attitude!

Your attitude is actually more important than your challenges in life. If you will change your attitude to a more positive, faith-filled one, you will find that your trials are not as bad as you thought they were. I challenge and encourage you right now to consistently believe you are able to do anything that comes your way, with God's help. You must also believe He wants to help you and will help you if you ask Him to do so. The devil may provide one of those "flashing thoughts" I mentioned that says, "You don't deserve God's help so don't bother asking." You can remind him that God doesn't help you because you deserve it, but because He is good, and while you're at it, why not remind the devil that you know he is a liar!

Think about It

Which "I can't" belief in your life do you need to exchange for an "I can"?

_____

_____

Overcomers Everywhere

On July 2, 1932, in Atlantic City, New Jersey, a baby boy was born. Six weeks later, a couple adopted the infant, but when he was five years old, his mother died. His father moved from state to state, looking for work and taking his young son with him. At age twelve, the boy landed his first job at a restaurant counter—and loved it. When he was fifteen, his father wanted to move again, but by then the young man was working at the Hobby House Restaurant in Fort Wayne, Indiana, and didn't want to leave his job. So he dropped out of school, moved into the local YMCA, and went to work full-time.

Several years later, his Hobby House boss offered him an opportunity. The man owned four Kentucky Fried Chicken (KFC) outlets that were failing. In four years, with hard work and determination, the young man turned the restaurants around financially, sold them back to KFC, and received a portion of the profits from the sale—he was once a high school dropout, but now he was a millionaire at age thirty-five.

Who was this man? Dave Thomas, who started Wendy's Old Fashioned Hamburgers and became an innovative and respected leader in the fast-food business. And, by the way, he also earned his GED forty-five years after he dropped out of school.

The world is filled with people like Dave Thomas, people who have overcome seemingly insurmountable odds. They have faced tragedies, sickness and disease, accidents, poverty, and deprivation in every area and yet they have pressed through and become some of the world's most respected and admired individuals. I can assure you that they did not do so by thinking, *I can't*. They had to make a decision about what they wanted out of life and think accordingly. Then, they had to work hard to accomplish their goals. I don't believe any of them could have expended the effort they needed to or made the sacrifices they made had they not believed wholeheartedly that they could do what they wanted to do.

A lot of people start out in the right direction, with great "want to," but no ability to push through when challenges arise. We hear and read about the ones who start out and keep going to achieve amazing results, especially in the face of tremendous odds. But even in the everyday, ordinary aspects of life, we all have obstacles to overcome. It's easy to see how much working out at the gym has improved your friend's energy and body shape and then decide, "I'm going to do that." But when it is time to go, will you do it? When you get so sore that you have to fall in a chair to sit down and pray that you can get up will you keep going? When something that sounds like more fun comes along, will you keep going? There will be plenty of opportunity to think, *I just can't do this. It's too hard.* But, if the thought *I can do whatever I need to do in life* is ingrained in you, then it gives you the determination to press through the difficulties.

God does not want us to be afraid or discouraged in the face of difficulties. In 2 Timothy 1:7, Paul wrote to his young associate Timothy that God has not given us a spirit of fear, but that He has given us power, love, and a sound mind. Timothy faced many challenges in the huge tasks in front of him and, no doubt, had days like you and I do—days when he was overwhelmed, days he thought he could not take any more pressure. He had fearful thoughts, he worried, and in my opinion, his stomach problem that Paul mentioned may have been an ulcer due to stress. The young man was overwhelmed! In the midst of such pressure, Paul encouraged him, writing to him to keep his mind filled with peace, balance, discipline, and self-control (see 2 Timothy 1:7). Paul knew Timothy needed to think properly if he was to accomplish God's will.

It is impossible to think "power-draining" thoughts and then be powerful when situations arise that call for extra strength. I want to encourage you to think and say at the beginning of each day, "I can do whatever I need to do in life through Christ." Don't fear the day, but instead look forward to it with passion, zeal, and enthusiasm.

Think about It

How can you push through and overcome a particular obstacle in your life?

_____

_____

Throw Away Your Excuse Bag

One of the reasons many people do not enjoy life, miss out on some of the blessings God wants to give them, or feel badly about themselves is that they do not finish what they start. They never taste the joy of a goal accomplished or a desire fulfilled because they do not press past the challenges that arise. Most of us would not want to say, "I am a quitter," so we make excuses or we blame the failure on someone or something.

Every single one of us has an "excuse bag." It's a little invisible accessory we carry around with us all the time. Then, when something that seems difficult arises, challenging us or giving us more than we want to deal with, we pull out an excuse, such as:

- "That is just too hard."
- "I don't have enough time."
- "I hadn't planned on this today."
- "I can't see how that would ever work."
- "I just don't feel like it."
- "I have too many personal problems and too much going on in my life right now."
- "I don't know how to do that."
- "I have never done this. I don't even know anybody who's ever done this."
- "I don't have anyone to help me."
- "I'm afraid."

I urge you today to throw away your excuse bag! Go get a "can-do bag" and fill it with biblical, faith-filled reasons you *can* do what you need to do. Stop making excuses and start doing what God is telling you to do. Stop looking at all your weaknesses because His strength is made perfect in our weakness. It is through our weakness and inability that God shows His strength. God actually chooses people on purpose who absolutely cannot do what He is asking them to do unless they allow Him to do it through them. You don't need ability, you need availability and a "can-do" attitude.

Think about It

What excuse do you use most? Will you determine today that you will stop making excuses and start believing God gives you strength to do what you need to do?

I Did It!

Until I turned sixty-four, I'd never exercised in a serious way. I had walked and done a few things to stay in decent shape, but I was not dedicated to exercise. I had reached into my excuse bag many times over the years, and come up with all kinds of "reasons" I could not exercise. But, the Lord spoke to me and encouraged me to begin a serious workout program so I could be strong for the last third of my journey through life. I already had good eating habits, but when it came to going to the gym several times a week, I used the excuse that I simply could not do that because of my travel obligations. I truly couldn't figure out how I could manage to put serious workout time into my already busy schedule. I finally decided to do what I could do instead of focusing on what I couldn't do.

The thought of getting started with a serious workout routine was overwhelming to my mind, so I had to put Philippians 4:13 to work in a very practical way and discipline myself to say, "I can do this. I can do whatever I need to do in life, and God says I need to be on a serious workout program." I had to take the challenge one day at a time because if I looked at my calendar for the year, it looked as if I was attempting something that was truly impossible. I strongly urge you to face your challenges one day at a time. Looking too far down the road only tends to overwhelm us in our thinking. Trusting God requires that we believe He gives us our "daily bread." In other words, we receive what we need as we need it and usually not before.

As I started seeing the benefits of working out regularly I felt it was important enough to me that I needed to eliminate a few other things I was doing that cluttered my schedule to make room for the exercise. I quickly discovered that if we want to do something strongly enough, then we find a way to do it.

I still continue to this day to have challenging times with the workout program. I still get sore and some days I have to go to the gym by sheer determination, but I refuse to give up. At one point after I had been working out for three or four months, my coach put me on circuit training. I didn't even know what circuit training was, but I quickly found out that circuit training is doing five exercises in a row, as quickly as you can. It took me thirty-five minutes to do seventy-five lunges on each leg, one hundred bench presses,'' seventy-five dumbbell dead lifts, seventy-five abdominal crunches, and seventy-five exercises with a pulley. After that, I was so sore I thought I might not survive.

When my coach had originally told me what he wanted me to do that week I quickly said, "That is going to be too much for me." I reminded him of my age and that working out was fairly new to me. He said, "Don't let your mind get in your way; you can do whatever you decide to do. Our motto here is 'No excuses, only results.'" With that encouragement, I thought, *Okay, I'm going to get a good mind-set about this. I can do this.* I had to tell myself over and over again, "I can do this." I got started and did okay, but by the fourth set, I began to get dizzy. I told my coach, "I'm getting dizzy" and he responded, "Then you don't have to do all five sets. You can stop with four." Something rose up in me when he said that, and I said, "I am not quitting with four sets. I'm going to do the fifth one." And when I did, I was so proud of myself!

The same principle that applied to me as I began working out also applies to many other areas of life—getting out of debt, cleaning and organizing your house, solving marriage problems, disciplining your children, being on time for work, or completing a project. Whatever you need to do in life, you can do it. Remember, Philippians 4:13 says you are ready for anything and equal to anything because God gives you strength. Nothing is too much for you when He is on your side.

Think about It

What have you been wanting or needing to do that you haven't done yet because even the thought of it overwhelmed you?

You Can Handle It

As Christians we often hear people quote Romans 8:37 which says, "Yet amid all these things we are more than conquerors and gain a surpassing victory through Him Who loved us."

For years, I have pondered what being "more than a conqueror" means. I'm sure other people have other perspectives, but I have come to the conclusion that being more than a conqueror means you have such confidence that no matter what comes up in your life, you know that through Christ you can handle it. You know before you are ever faced with a problem that you're going to have victory over it. You believe you can do whatever you need to do in life. So therefore, you don't dread things, you don't fear the unknown, you don't live in anxiety about what's going to happen in situations. It doesn't really matter what the specifics of the situation are, you know you can handle it through Christ. For you, defeat isn't an option!

If you will begin to think every day, *I can handle whatever life hands me. I can do whatever I need to do in life. I am more than a conqueror. I am equal to anything through Him who infuses inner strength into me,* even before you get out of bed in the mornings, just let it roll over and over in your mind, your confidence will skyrocket and you will find that indeed, you can do whatever you need to do in life.

Right thinking is the first step toward a better life. Wishing won't work. Being jealous of someone who has what you desire does no good. Self-pity is a waste of time and energy. Discovering God's will through an accurate knowledge of His Word and beginning to think as He thinks is the beginning of a new life for anyone who desires one.

Think about It

In what specific situation do you need to believe you are more than a conqueror?

_____

_____

Make It Work for You

In the Old Testament, a prophet named Habakkuk was complaining to God about the conditions of the world during his time. God told him to write down his vision, or what he wanted, plainly, so everyone passing by could read it easily and quickly (see Habakkuk 2:1, 2). Habakkuk and the Israelites needed to have their minds renewed. They had looked at the way things were for too long and needed to be reminded of the way things could be if they trusted God and obeyed Him. They needed to have words of vision and hope in front of them to remind them not to be overly impressed with their circumstances.

As you renew your mind and become established in the fact that you can do whatever you need to do in life, you will also need to be deliberate about getting that truth ingrained in your mind. I encourage you to write Philippians 4:13 from the _Amplified Bible_ or one of the Scriptures from the Power Pack at the end of this chapter on a cardboard sign or sheet of paper and make it large enough to see even if you're just passing by. Each time you do, say, "I am able." Also, several times each day I encourage you to say aloud, "I am able to do whatever I need to do in life through Christ Who strengthens me." I believe that some of you who feel physically tired most of the time will find that this more positive approach to life actually energizes you. Remember, moods and physical body functions are connected at least in part to our thoughts and words.

If we think about negative circumstances too long, they can

easily overwhelm us. No wonder the Bible says we should look away from those things that distract us unto Jesus Who is the Author and Finisher of our faith (see Hebrews 12:2). Jesus said, "Come to Me, all you who labor and are heavy-laden and overburdened, and I will cause you to rest. [I will ease and relieve and refresh your souls.]" (Matthew 11:28). We must remember that He is the one Who empowers us to do all things, and look to Him regularly throughout each day. With His help, there's nothing you can't do!

Power Pack

"I have strength for all things in Christ Who empowers
me [I am ready for anything and equal to anything
through Him Who infuses inner strength into me;
I am self-sufficient in Christ's sufficiency]."
Philippians 4:13

"Yet amid all these things we are more than conquerors and
gain a surpassing victory through Him Who loved us."
Romans 8:37

"Looking away [from all that will distract] to Jesus,
Who is the Leader and the Source of our faith
[giving the first incentive for our belief] and is also
its Finisher [bringing it to maturity and perfection].
He, for the joy [of obtaining the prize] that was set
before Him, endured the cross, despising and
ignoring the shame, and is now seated at
the right hand of the throne of God.
Hebrews 12:2

POWER THOUGHT

2

God loves me unconditionally!

"Even as [in His love] He chose us [actually picked us
out for Himself as His own] in Christ before
the foundation of the world, that we should be holy
(consecrated and set apart for Him) and blameless in
His sight, even above reproach, before Him in love."
Ephesians 1:4

What is wrong with me?" If you are like most people, you have asked
yourself that question many times throughout your life. I know I
asked myself that for many years and it's a common question the
enemy plants in people's minds. It is designed to make you feel like
you are not what you need to be and to prevent you from enjoying yourself. It encourages insecurity and all kinds of fear. We frequently compare ourselves with other people and if we are not what
they are, we assume something is wrong with us. There is, however, an antidote for this type of thinking that poisons our life. It
is thinking frequently *God loves me unconditionally!* Not only does
God love us but He chooses to view us as being right with Him,
accepted and blameless. This all comes through our faith in Jesus
Christ as our Savior and Lord. So we can accurately say, "I am the
righteousness of God in Christ. I am chosen in Christ, and in Him I
am blameless before God." This is our inherited position with God

through our faith in Jesus and it is not based on our own works of right or wrong, but entirely on faith. God wants us to learn proper behavior, but He accepts and loves us first and once we are rooted and grounded in the knowledge of His unconditional love then He can begin the work of transforming our character into the image of His Son. The truth is that if you want your behavior to improve, then your knowledge of the unconditional love of God must be the foundation for the "new you." The more we experience God's love, the more we desire to do what pleases Him.

Knowing God loves us unconditionally is an absolute necessity in order to make progress in our walk with Him. Jesus didn't die so we could be religious; Jesus died so we could have deep, intimate, personal relationships with God through Him. Religion offers us rules and regulations to follow in order to be close to God. But relationship lets us know we can be close to Him because He has chosen us. We will not draw near to God if we are afraid He is displeased with us. It is vital that you learn how to separate how important "you" are to God from what you do right or wrong. How can we hope to have an intimate relationship with God, His Son Jesus, and the Holy Spirit if we are not confident that we are loved unconditionally?

Good relationships must be based on love and acceptance, not on fear. All too often we are deceived into thinking that our acceptance is based on our performance, and this is totally unscriptural. We are loved and accepted by God, and made right with Him because we place our faith in Jesus Christ and the work He accomplished for us on the cross. He paid for our sins and misdeeds. He absolved us from guilt and reconciled us to God. Now, when we stand before God, we have "rightness," not "wrongness." And we have it because He gave it as a gift, not because we have earned it. Blessed is the man who knows he has right standing with God apart from the works he does.

Think about It

In your own words, how do you believe God feels about you?

_____

_____

Now say, "God loves me unconditionally!"

The World Is Wrong

Something about the culture in which we live often makes us feel that we are always the ones who are "wrong." Modern societies are full of messages that say to us, "Something is wrong with you because you are not like I am. Something is wrong with you because you like that and I don't. Something is wrong with you because you can't do this as well as I can." So we repeatedly hear the message, "What's wrong with me?" "What's wrong with me?" "What's wrong with me?" After hearing it long enough, we get convinced something is desperately wrong with us and we become disabled emotionally. This wrong thinking negatively affects all relationships and everything we try to do.

People can find all kinds of reasons to say, "Something is wrong with you." The world tells us how we need to look, how we need to behave, and what we should find entertaining. People seem to have an opinion on everything we think, say, and do. When we don't agree with the world or accept its standards and values, we begin to wonder what's wrong with us and questions begin to run through our minds about our abilities. These thoughts nag and haunt us, and even though we may not verbalize them, they often play like broken records in our minds. Same song, different verses:

- *My spouse hardly speaks to me anymore. What's wrong with me?*
- *I don't like the same things my friends like. What's wrong with me?*

- *My parents didn't want me. What's wrong with me?*
- *My parents abused me. What's wrong with me?*
- *People in my class don't like me. What's wrong with me?*
- *I wasn't chosen to serve on the committee. What's wrong with me?*
- *I haven't had a date in five years. What's wrong with me?*
- *My teenage children treat me terribly. What's wrong with me?*
- *I have never received a promotion at work. What's wrong with me?*
- *My business failed. What's wrong with me?*
- *My grades in school are not as good as my brother's. What's wrong with me?*

The enemy wants us to become self-focused by making us try to figure out what's wrong with ourselves. When we ask ourselves questions such as these, we are playing along with his plan. God, on the other hand, does not want us to be tormented by questions such as these and the feelings that accompany them. He wants us to know how much He loves us and to understand in the depths of our hearts that we are in right relationship with Him through faith in Jesus Christ. When we really believe we are right with God and accepted by Him, the enemy will no longer be successful in his attempts to make us feel bad about ourselves.

Think about It

List five things that are right or good about you. You may find this difficult if you have never done it, but be bold.

You're Expensive!

Obviously, Satan works hard to give us what I call "wrong-ness." He wants us to continually feel and believe that we just don't measure up to what we should be and that something is inherently wrong with us. God gives us "right-ness" through Jesus Christ, or as the Bible says, "we are now justified, (acquitted, made righteous, and brought into right relationship with God) by Christ's blood" (Romans 5:9).

The fact that God sent His only beloved Son to die a painful death in our place assigns value to us and lets us know God loves us immensely. The Bible says we are bought with a price, a price that is precious—the blood of Jesus (see 1 Peter 1:19). He paid for our misdeeds, secured our justification, made our account with God balance and absolved us from all guilt (see Romans 4:25). Jesus is our substitute. He stood in our place taking what we deserved (punishment as sinners), and freely giving us what He deserves (every kind of blessing).

This is huge! We immediately are transferred from a state of being wrong to a state of being viewed by God as right through faith in Jesus and the work He did on the cross. We are transferred out of the kingdom of darkness into the kingdom of light (see 1 Peter 2:9 and Colossians 1:1). We might also say we go from death to life as far as our *quality* of life is concerned. The grace of God purchased our freedom and faith is the hand that reaches out and receives it.

Though nothing ever done on Earth could match or even come close to the awesome gift Jesus gave us on the cross, I once heard a story that provides a good illustration to help us begin to understand what He did for us.

One winter's night in 1935, it is told, Fiorello LaGuardia, the irrepressible mayor of New York City, showed up at a night court in the poorest ward of the city. He dismissed the judge for the evening and took over the bench. That night a tattered old woman, charged with stealing a loaf of bread, was brought before him. She defended herself by saying, "My daughter's husband has deserted her. She is sick, and her children are starving."

The shopkeeper refused to drop the charges, saying, "It's a bad neighborhood, your honor, and she's got to be punished to teach other people a lesson."

LaGuardia sighed. He turned to the old woman and said, "I've got to punish you; the law makes no exceptions. Ten dollars or ten days in jail." However, while pronouncing the sentence, LaGuardia reached into his pocket, took out a ten dollar bill, and threw it into his hat with these famous words: "Here's the ten dollar fine, which I now remit, and furthermore, I'm going to fine everyone in the courtroom fifty cents for living in a town where a person has to steal bread so that her grandchildren can eat. Mr. Bailiff, collect the fines and give them to the defendant."

The following day, a New York newspaper reported: "Forty-seven dollars and fifty cents was turned over to a bewildered old grandmother who had stolen a loaf of bread to feed her starving grandchildren. Making forced donations were a red-faced storekeeper, seventy petty criminals, and a few New York policemen."[1]

Mayor LaGuardia made an important point when he said she must be punished and then paid her fine. His example reminds us that God's justice required that our sins be paid for and Jesus paid for them.

When the mayor took up money from everyone in the courtroom to help the grandmother buy food, his point was: Something is wrong with a world in which a grandmother has to steal! Something is wrong with a place where children don't have anything to eat. He refused to allow the "wrongness" of the world to affect that grandmother. I think his message was that we all need to help those who are less fortunate than we are. He stepped in and made the situation right for her—he did not ask if she deserved it; he simply helped her.

Think about It

Do you regularly receive God's grace and freely give it to others?

Performance Canceled

We must get comfortable with the thought that we are loved unconditionally and in right standing with God—not because of what we have or haven't done, but because of what Jesus did for us. Our experiences in the world and with people have told us we cannot be accepted apart from "performing" well in life and that our performances determine how much acceptance we receive. We have been deceived into believing that what we *do* is more important than *who* we are. This leaves us constantly working to prove to ourselves and others that we have value by what we do.

As long as we think God's love is conditional, we will keep trying to earn it by attempting to prove that we are worth loving. When we make mistakes, then we feel we are no longer valuable and therefore do not deserve love. We suffer the guilt, shame, and condemnation of believing we are not lovable and should be rejected. We keep trying harder and harder until sometimes we are exhausted mentally, emotionally, spiritually, and even physically. We try to keep up a good front, but inside we are weary and often very afraid.

Once we believe God's love is based on Who He is and what Jesus has done, and not on what we do, the struggle is over. Now we can cancel our "performance" and serve God because we know that He does love us and we do not need to "get" Him to love us. We already know we have His love and that under no condition will He ever stop loving us. We no longer have to live in fear of being rejected by Him because of our mistakes. When we do something wrong, all we need to do is repent and receive God's forgiveness and refuse the guilt that comes with sin, but is no longer applicable when sin is forgiven and removed.

I used to think almost constantly, *What is wrong with me?* I don't think that way now. I still do things that are wrong, but I have learned the difference between my "who" and my "do." I urge you today to understand that you are not your performance; your "who" and your "do" are separate. God loves you because of your "who"! He loves you because you are His child.

Is God ever displeased with us? Yes, He is displeased when we sin (this is our "do," not our "who") and He loves us enough to correct us and continue working with us to bring us into better and more godly behavior (see Hebrews 12:10). We are destined by God to be molded into the image of Jesus Christ (see Romans 8:29), and I am grateful that He has sent His Holy Spirit to convict us of sin and to work God's holiness in and through us. This is a work of God's grace and it takes place little by little as we study God's Word (see 2 Corinthians 3:18).

There are certainly times when God is displeased with our behavior, but He always loves us. Don't let anything separate you from the love of God because the knowledge that He loves you enables you to be more than a conqueror in life.

An important verse to understand as we learn to believe we are loved and in right standing with God is 2 Corinthians 5:21: "For our sake He made Christ [virtually] to be sin Who knew no sin, so that in and through Him we might become [endued with, viewed as being in, and examples of] the righteousness of God [what we ought to be, approved and acceptable and in right relationship with Him, by His goodness]."

Knowing we are loved and accepted even in our imperfection is such a relief! Serving God from desire rather than obligation is incredibly liberating and brings great peace and joy to our lives. The Bible says that we love Him because He first loved us (see 1 John 4:19). Being assured of God's unconditional love gives us confidence and boldness.

Our confidence should not be in anything or anyone but Jesus— not in education, outward privilege, positions we hold, people we know, how we look, or our gifts and talents. Everything in this world is shaky at best and we should not place our confidence in it. He is the same yesterday, today, and forever (see Hebrews 13:8). We can count on Him to always be faithful and do what He says He will do—and He says He will *always* love us. He says we are righteous in His sight and we need to make a decision to simply believe it.

We become what we believe we are; therefore, as we become convinced that we are right with God, our behavior will improve.

We will do more things right and with less effort. As we focus on our relationship with God rather than our performance, we relax and what God has done in our spirit when we were born again is gradually worked out in our souls and finally seen through our daily life.

No matter what other people may have told you that you are not, God delights in telling you in His Word who you are in Him— loved, valuable, precious, talented, gifted, capable, powerful, wise, and redeemed. I encourage you to take a moment and repeat those nine things out loud. Say, "I am loved, valuable, precious, talented, gifted, capable, powerful, wise, and redeemed." He has a good plan for you! Get excited about your life. You are created in God's image and you are amazing! You may still be working on your "do," (that's part of being human) but your "who" is awesome!

Think about It

Do you believe God loves you unconditionally?

_____

_____

Take a piece of paper and draw a line down the center of it. On one side of the line, write "Who" and on the other side, write "Do." Begin to list different aspects of who you are according to God's Word under "Who," and under "Do" you can list things you do right and things you do wrong. This will help you separate your "who" and your "do." Now cross out the "do" section because it has nothing to do with God's love for you anyway. No matter how many right things you have listed, you can never do enough to deserve God's love, and no matter how many wrong things you have listed on your sheet of paper, they cannot prevent God from loving you forever.

God Is Not Angry with You

You may not feel like you're amazing or awesome, but God says that you are. Psalm 139 says that we are fearfully and wonderfully made. Studying how the human body functions reveals that we are truly an amazing creation. When you receive Jesus Christ as your Lord and Savior, something happens to you on the inside. Paul writes of it this way: "Therefore if any person is [ingrafted] in Christ (the Messiah) he is a new creation (a new creature altogether); the old [previous moral and spiritual condition] has passed away. Behold, the fresh and new has come!" (2 Corinthians 5:17). You may not notice any difference when you look in the mirror; your behavior may not change overnight; and your struggles may not suddenly disappear, but when you are "in Christ" a gradual and patient work of transformation is under way in your life. God sees the end of things from beginning, and He sees you complete in Him. He sees you, through Jesus Christ, as new and completely righteous.

Also, when you receive Jesus Christ as your Lord and Savior, you become part of the family of God. You are a child of God.

I think again about my children. They always have right standing with me, even though they don't always do everything right. I still go through times when I am displeased with their behavior in various areas, just as I am displeased with my own. But, my children are always in the family; they never cease being my children. I don't like all their choices; I don't like everything they do, but I love them and I don't withhold my love because they make mistakes. I still help them if they need help.

God loves us even more than we love our children. He does not reject us when we make mistakes. He knows our hearts. He knows we are on a journey and that we need time to renew our minds. We have a High Priest (Jesus) Who understands our weaknesses and infirmities because He was tempted just as we are and yet He never sinned (see Hebrews 4:15). I love the fact that Jesus understands me! He also understands you, so why not relax and be yourself, know that you are loved unconditionally, and do your best each day? Feeling guilty about every mistake that you make and comparing yourself with others only impedes your progress; it doesn't help it. Admit your faults, mistakes, and sins; ask God to forgive you and to help you change. Don't compare yourself with anyone else. God has created you unique and wants you to be all you can be. God will never help you be someone else so give yourself a big hug right now and rejoice in who you are!

Think about It

Do you have a good relationship with yourself?

_____

_____

Stop right now and meditate on Power Thought #2: "God loves me unconditionally!" Roll that thought over and over in your mind and speak it, placing an emphasis on the word *unconditionally*!

Your Account Is in Balance

Second Corinthians 5:18 gives us important insight into the way God sees us: "But all things are from God, *Who through Jesus Christ reconciled us to Himself [received us into favor, brought us into harmony with Himself]* and gave to us the ministry of reconciliation [that by word and deed we might aim to bring others into harmony with Him]" (emphasis mine). What does it mean to be reconciled to God? It means "your account is in balance." You don't owe anything! I once saw a bumper sticker that said, "I owe, I owe, so off to work I go." I immediately realized that was the mentality I lived with for years. I felt that I owed God something for all the wrong I had done and I tried every day to do good works to make up for my mistakes. I wanted to be blessed by Him, but felt I needed to earn His blessings. I finally learned that we cannot pay for His gifts, otherwise they are not gifts at all. God has received us into favor, which means He does good things for us even when we don't deserve them. He is merciful and kind to the just and the unjust. He loves us, looks favorably on us, and wants to bless us. He is not angry and frustrated with us, nor does He seek to punish us for every mistake we make.

God sees the heart of man and His dealings with us are based on the kind of heart we have. I don't do everything right but I do love God very much. I am very sorry for my sins and it grieves me when I know that I have disappointed Him. I want His will in my life. I am sure that if you are reading this book your heart attitude is the same as mine. Perhaps like me, you have been tormented for years by feelings of guilt and fear, but knowing that God loves you unconditionally releases you from those negative emotions and allows you to enjoy yourself while you are changing. In 2 Corinthians 5:20, Paul emphasizes again the reconciliation and favor God extends to us and encourages us to believe these things: "So we are Christ's ambassadors, God making His appeal as it were through us. We [as Christ's personal representatives] beg you for His sake to lay hold of the divine favor [now offered you] and be reconciled to God." Paul is actually begging the believers of his day to take hold of what God is offering and I also urge you to do the same. Don't wait another moment to believe that God accepts you, views you as being in right standing with Him, and loves you unconditionally.

Think about It

Do you really believe you are reconciled to God, that He is not angry with you, and that He is completely satisfied and pleased with who you are?

_____

_____

Take It Personally

The truth that God loves us unconditionally and gives us right standing with Himself is so amazing that I find it difficult to find the proper words to express the depth of the beauty of being made right with God. To release the power of this truth into your life, begin to meditate (think) on this truth and speak it aloud. Say, "I am the righteousness of God in Christ. I am a new creature in Christ, old things have passed away and all things are made new. I am precious in God's sight and I have value. I am God's child, the apple of His eye and He watches over me constantly." Say, "God loves me unconditionally" many times each day. This will help renew your mind to the truth of God's Word.

Go to bed at night and lie there thinking over and over, *God loves me unconditionally and I am made right with Him through faith in Jesus.* When you awake in the morning, lie in bed a few minutes and thank God because He loves you and will be with you all day, in everything you do.

Meditating on God's Word and confessing it is a central theme in God's economy (His way of doing things). Add some power to your life by believing what the Bible says about you. You are made right with God; you're precious, valuable, and loved unconditionally.

Think about It

How do you feel when you think about the fact that you are special and precious to God?

_____

_____

Power Pack

"For our sake He made Christ [virtually] to be sin Who knew no sin, so that in and through Him we might become [endued with, viewed as being in, and examples of] the righteousness of God [what we ought to be, approved and acceptable and in right relationship with Him, by His goodness]."
2 Corinthians 5:21

"Therefore if any person is [ingrafted] in Christ (the Messiah) he is a new creation (a new creature altogether); the old [previous moral and spiritual condition] has passed away. Behold, the fresh and new has come!"
2 Corinthians 5:17

"Because you are precious in My sight and honored, and because I love you, I will give men in return for you and peoples in exchange for your life."
Isaiah 43:4

"Even as [in His love] He chose us [actually picked us out for Himself as His own] in Christ before the foundation of the world, that we should be holy (consecrated and set apart for Him) and blameless in His sight, even above reproach, before Him in love."
Ephesians 1:4

POWER THOUGHT

3

I will not live in fear.

"For God did not give us a spirit of timidity
(of cowardice, of craven and cringing and fawning fear),
but [He has given us a spirit] of power and of love and
of calm and well-balanced mind and
discipline and self-control."
2 Timothy 1:7

The well-known advice columnist Ann Landers reportedly received some ten thousand letters per month. When asked to name the most prevalent problem in her audience's lives, she responded, "The one problem above all others seems to be fear. People are afraid of losing their health, their wealth, and their loved ones. People are afraid of life itself."[1]

Landers's assessment is not hard to believe. I see so many people who are ruled by fear. It can absolutely take over a person's life, which is why I believe this power thought—"I will not live in fear"—is so important. Until the power of fear is broken in our lives, we are held captive to it, which means we are not free to follow our hearts or to follow God. To fulfill His good plan for our lives and to enjoy all the blessings He wants to give us, we simply must refuse to live in fear.

If fear rules in our lives we cannot enjoy anything we do. Let's say Sarah is invited to a party. She is excited that she got invited but when she arrives she's afraid she doesn't look right. She becomes uncomfortable and starts comparing herself with the other guests. She begins watching to see who is talking to whom. Then she over-analyzes who is talking to her and how friendly they seem to be. She is so afraid of being rejected that she can't relax and simply enjoy the party.

Sarah is so focused on herself that she really can't reach out to anybody else, and that makes her appear aloof and unfriendly. As you might expect, she doesn't get invited to the next party. The result of all this is that in her mind all of her fears that she is unwanted and unacceptable are confirmed. The sad thing is that the entire scenario was created by her fear. The war on the battle-field of Sarah's mind was raging so fiercely during the party, that she felt confused and could not enjoy anyone or anything. She was too busy trying to sort out her negative emotions and engaging the enemy of fear. Fear brings torment and we must refuse to entertain it or our lives will be miserable.

Think about It

Take a moment to think about how your life would be if you were free from all fear. How would a fear-free life differ from the life you have today?

How Fear Operates

There are more types of fear than we could name or count, but they all have the same source and the same purpose. They are all from the enemy and they are intended to steal the life Jesus died to give us. We often think fear is simply an emotion or feeling, but it also affects us physically. In *Who Switched Off My Brain?* Dr. Caroline

Leaf notes that fear "triggers more than 1,400 known physical and chemical responses, and activates more than 30 different hormones and neurotransmitters" and that fear is at the root of all stress.[2] When fear causes a stress reaction through our bodies, it actually "marinates" the body in toxic chemicals. This, of course, is terribly unhealthy and threatening to our physical well-being.

There are many ways Satan uses fear to steal from us. For example, the fear that we will not be accepted as we are causes us to develop phony personalities that stifle our true selves and hide who God has made us to be. The fear of failure prevents us from ever trying new things or stretching ourselves to do more than we feel comfortable doing. The fear of the future can cause us not to enjoy today. Even something like the fear of flying can prohibit our being able to discover and enjoy the beauty and excitement of places we would like to visit. It can absolutely paralyze us and in its more advanced stages can drive us to do things that are completely irrational. It can even cause mental and emotional problems.

In an August 1989 issue, *Time* magazine printed a story that shows how utterly destructive and controlling fear can be. The brief article reported that Charles Bodeck, a retiree who had received several tick bites during fur-trapping expeditions, grew fearful that he had contracted Lyme disease when the disease garnered considerable media attention in the late 1980s. Bodeck was not only afraid of having the disease himself, he was also concerned he had transmitted it to his wife. Despite many medical tests and repeated assurances from doctors that he was not infected and that passing the disease to his wife was impossible (because he didn't have it), Bodeck remained terrified. His totally unfounded fear so completely controlled him that he eventually killed his wife and himself with a shotgun. When police searched his mailbox after the incident, they found it crammed with information on Lyme disease—and a note confirming yet another doctor's appointment for a Lyme-disease test.[3] Bodeck's story and countless other less dramatic instances prove that fear can be powerful in our lives. I fully believe it is the devil's tool to keep us miserable and out of the will of God. It drains our courage, presents everything from a negative viewpoint, and prevents us from making progress. Destinies are destroyed because of fear—fear of pain, fear of discomfort, fear of lack, fear of sacrifice, fear that life is going to be too hard, fear of losing friends, fear of being alone, fear of losing your reputation, fear that no one will understand you, fear that you're missing God, and on and on. Fear is the enemy's perversion of faith. He says, "Believe what I'm telling you. This is not going to work. Your prayers aren't any good. You don't have right standing with God. You are a failure."

Fear always tells you what you're not, what you don't have, what you can't do, and what you never will be. But Romans 8:15 says, "For [the Spirit which] you have now received [is] not a spirit of slavery to put you once more in bondage to fear, but you have received the Spirit of adoption [the Spirit producing sonship] in [the bliss of] which we cry, Abba (Father)! Father!" You do not have to live in bondage to fear or allow fear to control your life. You can be bold, courageous, and adventurous.

The word "Abba" was a term used by little children in addressing their father. It would be similar to the word "Daddy." This term is less formal than "Father" and denotes a comfortable closeness between a child and their father. Jesus said that we could call God "Abba" because He had delivered us from all fear. He will always take care of His beloved children and we can approach Him without fear of rejection. When we run to Him with any problem or pain, He is waiting with open arms to comfort and encourage us.

Boredom

God created you for adventure, for the exhilaration of a life that requires you to take bold steps of faith and see Him come through for you. So many people are unsatisfied with their lives simply because they won't step out into the new things they desire to do. They want to stay in "the safe zone," which may feel secure, but is not always where the joy and adventure of life can be found. Don't let fear keep you from the vibrant life God has for you or destroy your destiny. Even when you *feel* afraid, don't let it stop you! As I like to say, "Feel the fear and do it anyway!" Boredom is often the result of sameness. I encourage you to include more variety in your life. Try new things; when you start feeling that life is getting stale and tasteless add a little spice by doing something different. Start thinking and saying, "I will not live in fear."

Think about It

Is fear causing you to live a safe but boring life?

_____

_____

Catch It Early

In the United States, there is an over-the-counter medication advertised as the medicine to take at the first indication of a cold, to keep it from getting worse and becoming full-blown. I take a lot of vitamin C if I have a scratchy throat or a runny nose because it often keeps me from getting worse. Catching something before it goes too far is wisdom. The Bible says we are to resist the devil at his onset (see 1 Peter 5:8, 9). For years, I have used this principle against fear, and I guarantee you, it makes a difference.

I recommend that anytime you even begin to feel fearful about anything that you immediately begin to pray and confess, "I will not live in fear." You will see amazing results. When we pray, God hears and answers. When we confess His Word, we renew our own minds and come into agreement with His plans for us. No matter what God wants to do for us, we must agree with Him in order to receive and enjoy it (see Amos 3:3). He has good plans for us, but in order for them to become a reality in our lives we must have our minds completely renewed (see Romans 12:2). Simply put, we must learn to think like God thinks and talk like He talks—and none of His thoughts or words are fearful.

This power thought—"I will not live in fear"—will help you become courageous rather than fearful. Call it to mind the instant you begin to feel fear and meditate on it even during the times when you are not afraid. By doing this you will be even more prepared to stand against it when it does come. Remember that it will take time and be committed to stick with it until you see change. I still say, "I will not live in fear." I woke up this morning and said, "This is the day that God has made. I will enjoy this day and I will not live in fear." God taught me to use what I call the "power twins" to help me defeat the spirit of fear. They are "I pray" and "I say." When I feel fear, I begin to pray and ask for God's help and I say, "I will not fear!" Use these power twins as soon as you feel fearful about anything and you will be able to keep fear from controlling you. You may still feel fear, but you can move beyond it by realizing that it is merely the devil's attempt to prevent you from enjoying life or making any kind of progress. Do what you believe you are supposed to do even if you have to "do it afraid."

Think about It

What can you do to not let fear control you?

_____

_____

It Won't Go Away

The reason we must learn how to deal with fear before it goes too far is that it will never completely go away. Feeling fear is part of being alive. We may feel fearful when we are doing something we have never done before, or when the obstacles seem insurmountable, or when we don't have the natural help we feel we need. None of this means we are cowards; it means we are human. We can only be cowardly when we allow our fears to dictate our actions or decisions, instead of following our hearts and doing what we know is right for us. Feeling fear is simply the temptation to run away from what we should face and confront; feeling fear is not equal to being afraid because being afraid means letting fearful feelings get the best of us. I might feel angry but I can still choose not to act on my anger but to respond with forgiveness and love. In the same way, we can feel fear but not let it make our decisions.

We must accept the fact that fear will never go away completely, but also know we can live boldly and courageously because God has told us that He is always with us, and because of that we can choose to ignore the fear we feel. It's okay to feel fear; it's not okay to act on those feelings. You see, the word *fear* means "to take flight" or "to run away from," and it causes us to want to flee what God wants us to confront. It does not mean to shake or quake or have a dry mouth or weak knees. Fear is not a feeling; fear is an evil spirit that produces a feeling. So when we say, "I will not bow down to fear," what we mean is "I will not shrink back in fear." Fear causes us to cower, shrink back, and withdraw. Instead of having big faith, it causes us to have little faith, and if we entertain it long enough, we'll end up with no faith at all.

The only acceptable attitude for a Christian to have toward fear is "I will not fear." Do not shrink back from anything in fear. You may be going forward with something you feel God has spoken to you to do. Then something happens to make it appear that it's not working out or that people are not in favor of it. You realize that if you do what God wants you to do, you may risk losing some friends, some resources, or your reputation. When you feel that fear, the first impulse is to begin to shrink back, isn't it? God knows that, and that is why He says, "Do not fear." When He tells us not to fear, what He means is, no matter how you feel, keep putting one foot in front of the other and doing what you believe He has told you to do because that's the only way to defeat fear and make progress.

I have decided that I *am* confident, whether I happen to feel confident or not. Sometimes I feel more confident than I do at other times, but I go out every day confident that God is with me and because of that I can do whatever I need to do and enjoy the process.

I choose to be confident instead of fearful, even when potentially fearful situations arise. Confidence is the way I present myself, not merely a feeling I have. The devil hates it when we are confident that God is with us, and enabling us to do whatever we need to do in life.

I urge you to meditate on this power thought: "I will not live in fear." Roll it over and over in your mind because setting your mind ahead of time that you will not bow down to fear will help you not do so when fears arise. You will have already made the decision that you will not be afraid. Renewing your mind with these power thoughts prepares you to face whatever comes in life with confidence.

Think about It

What is the only acceptable attitude for a Christian to have toward fear?

_____

_____

Do It Afraid

When the Bible says, "God has not given us a spirit of fear," it does not mean we will never feel fear. As a matter of fact, when God said to so many people in the Bible, "Fear not," He was basically telling them, "Fear is going to come after you. You are going to have to deal with it." When God gave Joshua the job of leading the Israelites into the Promised Land, He said, "Be strong, vigorous, and very courageous. Be not afraid" (Joshua 1:9). He was basically saying, "You will be attacked by many fears and you will be tempted to turn back, but you have to keep going forward." No matter what you feel like, just keep going forward and you will arrive at your desired destination. I am not suggesting that we do foolish things and refuse to take any counsel from anyone, but if we are fully assured that we have direction from God then we must press forward no matter what we feel like or what people say. I often say, "Courage is not the absence of fear, it is progress in its presence."

Suppose a man desperately wants to make a career change because he hates his job and is totally unfulfilled and miserable in it. Let's say he is in the accounting department at a large manufacturing firm, but the desire of his heart has always been to work in sales. He believes he is gifted in being able to sell things he really believes in, so why doesn't he just change jobs? He starts to, but then he stops and thinks about the fact that in the accounting department, he always gets his paycheck every two weeks and it is always for the same amount. He can depend on it and plan around it. In the sales area, he would work on commission and his income would depend on how much he sold. It might fluctuate, which would necessitate better financial planning or a stricter budget.

Then, more thoughts come to him: *You would have to build a reputation in sales and develop a customer base, and that will take time. Your income may be lower than it is now for a while. You will have to do without some things. Your family will have to sacrifice for a while. And what if it takes much longer than you think it will?*

Suddenly the man is afraid to make the change he desperately wants to make and he continues day after day going to a job he hates, being unfulfilled and miserable. Only the man can change his situation. He must take a step of faith, drive fear backward, and be unwilling to be trapped in a job he despises.

God is standing by to help him, but that can only happen if the man puts his faith in God. God cannot give us anything we are not willing to step out and take. The Bible says repeatedly that we are to "Fear not" because God is with us. We have two choices: Believe this truth and make decisions based on it, or live narrow, often miserable lives because we are afraid of change, risk, or new situations.

Although I did not appear to others to be a fearful person, I actually spent many years bowing down to internal feelings of fear. Then I finally learned to "do it afraid." What I mean by this is that

I learned to follow my heart as long as it agreed with God's Word and keep going forward even when fear was making me shake and telling me I was going to fail. Since the devil is a liar, we can be fairly sure that when he tells us something isn't going to work, it will. When God is trying to show us to back away from something, He does so by withdrawing our peace, not by trying to frighten us. I often back away from something because I lose my peace. We are to follow peace and let it be the umpire in our life, but we must not follow fear.

I started overcoming fear by praying and by thinking and saying, "I will not live in fear." I even learned to say, "Fear will always present itself to me, but I will ignore it and keep going forward." Remember, *fear* means "to take flight or run away from something." I learned that I had to stop running and stand still long enough to see what God would do for me if I let my faith in Him be larger than my fears. I finally realized that each time God was leading me into a new area that would eventually be better for me, the devil launched an attack of fear against me. Fear is the devil's favorite weapon and he uses it masterfully against people until they realize that through God they have the power to move beyond fear and keep making progress.

Think about It

Are you running from anything in your life? If so, will you keep moving forward—and see what God will do for you?

_____

_____

Be Filled with Faith

Fear is the opposite of faith. We receive from the enemy through fear, and we receive from God through faith. Fear is the enemy's brand of faith, his counterfeit of it. In other words, we can know and do God's will through placing our faith in Him, but we can cooperate with the devil's plan through fear. When we are afraid, we may fail to do what God wants us to do and, instead, end up doing what the devil wants us to do. The Old Testament man Job said that what he feared came upon him (see Job 3:25), which is exactly what the enemy wanted for him and what he wants for us. The enemy is the author of fear, not God. In fact, 2 Timothy 1:7 says God has not given us a spirit of fear, but of power, and we need to apply this truth to our lives and refuse to live any way other than powerfully.

I want to share something I have been practicing aggressively lately. I have found it very helpful, and I believe you will too. When fear knocks on the door of our lives, if it finds us full of faith, it cannot enter in. I strongly urge you to meditate on and confess that you are filled with faith. I say it like this, "I am a woman of faith. I think faith, talk faith, and walk in faith." I also choose portions of Scripture about faith and meditate on them. Hebrews 11:6 is a good example: "Without faith it is impossible to please and be satisfactory to Him. For whoever would come near to God must [necessarily] believe that God exists and that He is the rewarder of those who earnestly and diligently seek Him [out]." The more I meditate on faith and believe I am a woman filled with it, the stronger and more energetic I feel. Fear weakens us in every way, but faith adds courage, boldness, confidence, and actual energy to our lives.

In 1 Timothy 6:12, Paul encouraged Timothy to "fight the good fight of faith" (NKJV). We all need to fight this good fight and I believe meditating on and confessing God's Word is the way to do it. Remember, we are in a war and the battlefield is the mind.

If you are accustomed to allowing your mind to go wherever it pleases, meditating on the Word of God will require forming a new habit. Don't become discouraged if you find that you have good intentions but fail many times. I can assure you that everyone has the same experience in the beginning of this journey. Pray for God's grace to enable you and don't merely "try" to do it. Quite often, we try very hard without asking for God's assistance, but He always wants to help us obey Him, so all you have to do is ask. Ask Him to help you develop an ability to concentrate and focus on power thoughts that will enable you, rather than entertaining "Uninvited Guests" (thoughts) that will disable you.

When Satan comes to attack you with fear, make sure you are filled with faith so there will be no place of entrance for him. Fear and faith cannot coexist; where you have one, you will not have the other. God's Word builds faith in your heart, so use it—and you'll keep fear out of your life.

Think about It

How can you demonstrate faith instead of fear?

_____

_____

Freedom from a Great Fear

I actually believe it is possible to be so afraid people will disapprove of us—what we say, what we do, what we think, how we look, what we value, or the choices we make—that we become addicted to approval. "Approval addiction" happens when people need the approval of others so much that they are miserable anytime they feel they don't have it. They even make certain decisions to gain approval rather than to follow their hearts or to obey what they believe to be God's will for their lives. I am keeping this section rather brief, but because it is a huge problem, I have an entire book on the subject titled *Approval Addiction*. I highly recommend it if you feel you need help in this area.

I developed an out-of-balance need for approval because I did not have a healthy relationship with my father. I was not addicted to the approval of everyone around me, and in some cases I did not care what people thought at all. But when it came to authority figures in my life, especially male authority figures, I desperately craved approval. I know now that I was trying to get from men in positions of authority what I should have had from my father but never received.

Are you afraid of anyone in particular? Are you afraid of certain personality types? Locating a problem is the first step to defeating it so I strongly encourage you to isolate repetitive fears and make a decision to overcome them. Many people confess that they fear authority figures in their life and that is unfortunate because we all have to deal with others who have authority over us.

I once had an employee who was terribly afraid of me because of some unresolved issues from her childhood. Her fear not only made her miserable, but it made me very uncomfortable too. She was so fearful of not pleasing me that she often made mistakes that she would not have made had she been more confident. She could not relax and I felt that I had to be extremely careful about everything I said and did so she could hopefully remain confident, but it seemed that nothing worked for very long. It was difficult to tell her that she did anything wrong and needed to correct it. It was difficult to be direct and straightforward in communication, and I found myself trying so hard to keep her confident that it became an unbearable burden for me. Her fear was actually stealing my ability to be myself and eventually our working relationship just did not work and she had to move on to something else.

The sad thing is that she was a beautiful, kind, and caring individual who wanted to do her best and craved acceptance, but her fears continually stole the very thing that she desired.

It makes me sad when people are afraid of those who have authority over them, but unfortunately this is quite often the case. A great many people have been mistreated by an authority figure while growing up and they tend to transfer their fears onto other people who had absolutely nothing to do with their initial problem. I can always discern when someone is comfortable with me or uncomfortable and nervous. I lean toward those who are confident because I know they will not only be able to do the job, but I will also be able to enjoy my relationship with them.

It is important to realize that our fears not only affect us, but they can also affect the people around us. Nothing is more uncomfortable to me than having to tiptoe around a person because they have fears that make them touchy, fearful, and uptight. I feel sorry for them and I pray for them but, ultimately, fear cannot be conquered unless we recognize it and confront it by not letting it control us.

You may be like I was—afraid other people will not approve of you or afraid of an authority figure in your life. Whether you struggle with this fear or other fears, the path to freedom is the same: Study God's Word and apply it to your life; pray; and renew your mind.

Think about It

Do you have an out-of-balance need for approval? Is there anyone you are allowing to control you due to fear?

God Is with You

The truth we must believe to overcome fear is that God is with us. This makes all the difference in life and it is the key to being able to obey what God tells us to do so many times throughout the Bible, which is "Do not fear." If we are not confident that He is with us, we will fear. David was only able to face Goliath because he knew that God was with Him. He did not rely on his own ability, but he trusted God. We may not always know exactly what God is going to do, but we can relax by knowing that He will do what needs to be done at the right time. We can easily feel afraid if we think about the future and all the things that are unknown to us. We can look at it two ways. We can either be negative and fearful, or we can be excited about being part of God's mystery, knowing He knows exactly what's going to happen and is right there with us, helping us and directing us.

We may not know what to do in a tense situation, but God does. He is never surprised by anything. He knows everything before it happens and He has already planned our deliverance, so all we need to do is keep going forward. We simply need to take one step at a time and not worry about the next one because God will be there to guide us in the next step when the time comes.

God has said that He is with us at all times. This is a powerful truth that can absolutely demolish fear in our lives. We don't have to see or feel Him in order to believe that. Faith is a matter of the heart, not the natural senses. God is with you! Believe it and begin living courageously. Renew your mind to the truth that God is always with you by thinking about it and confessing it. The more aware you are of His Presence the more confident you will be.

Say "I will not fear. I will not be afraid of men because God is with me." As you take the next week and meditate on this power thought, I believe you will begin to feel more confident than ever before. You only have one life to live, so live it boldly and never let fear steal God's best for you!

Power Pack

"For [the Spirit which] you have now
received [is] not a spirit of slavery to put you
once more in bondage to fear, but you have received
the Spirit of adoption [the Spirit producing sonship] in
[the bliss of] which we cry, Abba (Father)! Father!"
Romans 8:15

"What then shall we say to [all] this?
If God is for us, who [can be] against us?
[Who can be our foe, if God is on our side?]"
Romans 8:31

"The Lord is on my side; I will not fear.
What can man do to me?"
Psalm 118:6

"For God did not give us a spirit of timidity
(of cowardice, of craven and cringing and fawning fear),
but [He has given us a spirit] of power and of love and
of calm and well-balanced mind and
discipline and self-control."
2 Timothy 1:7

POWER THOUGHT

4

I am difficult to offend.

"Great peace have they who love Your law; nothing
shall offend them or make them stumble."
Psalm 119:165

People who want to live powerful lives must become experts at forgiving those who offend and hurt them. When someone hurts my
feelings or is rude and insensitive to me, I find it helpful to quickly
say, "I will not be offended." I have to say those words quietly in
my heart if the person is still in my presence, but later when the
memory of what he or she did returns to haunt me, I repeat them
aloud. When I say, "I will not be offended," I always pray for God
to help me, realizing that I can do nothing without Him. So once
again, "I pray and I say!"

My husband, Dave, has always been difficult to offend. When
he is around people who could hurt him or in situations where he
could be offended, he says, "I am not going to let those negative
people control my mood. They have problems and they are not
going to give their problems to me."

On the other hand, I spent many years getting my feelings hurt
regularly and living in the agony of offense, but I am not willing
to live that way any longer. I am busy getting a new mind-set. Are
you willing to join me in becoming a person who is hard to offend?

If so, you will open the door to more peace and joy than you have ever known before.

Developing the mind-set that you are a person who is difficult to offend will make your life much more pleasant. People are everywhere and you never know what they might say or do. Why give the control of your day to other people? Being hurt and offended does not change the people, it only changes us. It makes us miserable and steals our peace and joy, so why not prepare ourselves mentally not to fall into Satan's trap?

Will You Take the Bait?

There is no doubt about it. As long as we are in the world and around people, we will have opportunities to be offended. The temptation to become hurt, angry, or offended comes just as surely as any other temptation comes, but Jesus said we should pray that we will not give in to temptation (see Matthew 26:41). Praying that temptation won't present itself to us does no good, but we can choose to take it or leave it. The same is true with offense. Author and speaker John Bevere calls offense "the bait of Satan," and I couldn't agree more. In his introduction to the book by this name, he writes:

> One of [Satan's] most deceptive and insidious kinds of bait is something every Christian has encountered—offense. Actually, offense itself is not deadly... But if we pick it up and consume it and feed on it in our hearts, then we have become offended. Offended people produce much fruit, such as hurt, anger, outrage, jealousy, resentment, strife, bitterness, hatred, and envy. Some of the consequences of picking up an offense are insults, attacks, wounding, division, separation, broken relationships, betrayal, and backsliding.[1]

As you can see, allowing ourselves to become offended is very serious and has devastating consequences. Satan will not stop tempting us to be offended, but we are the ones who choose whether or not to bite the bait.

One of the signs of the last days prior to Jesus' return is that offense will increase.

> And then many will be offended and repelled and will
> begin to distrust and desert [Him Whom they ought to
> trust and obey] and will stumble and fall away and betray
> one another and pursue one another with hatred.
> (Matthew 24:10)

Rudeness, quick tempers, and holding grudges seem to be very common today. People don't realize that they are playing right into the devil's hands when they allow these negative and poisonous emotions to rule them. Let us think of Becca, a young Christian who is making progress growing in Christ when suddenly something happens at her church that offends her. Becca had hopes of being chosen to sing in the choir but for some reason she got passed over. Satan takes advantage of the situation and fills her mind with all kinds of thoughts that are not even true. Becca begins to focus on what she imagines to be an attack of rejection, and she receives it as a personal attack instead of simply trusting God. The offense becomes a stumbling block to her and, as the Scripture above says, she begins to fall away from what should be important to her, which is growing in her relationship with God. Sadly, this scenario is repeated over and over in the world today. Sometimes I think we have more people in the world who are angry and offended than those who are not.

Satan is fishing all the time hoping to catch someone in his trap; don't take his bait! Start meditating on and saying, "I am difficult to offend."

Think about It

Why is "the bait of Satan" a good term for offense? What kinds of "bait" does Satan like to use with you?

_____

_____

Let God Do It

One of the reasons we find forgiving others difficult when we are offended is that we have told ourselves probably thousands of times that forgiving is hard to do. We have convinced ourselves and set our mind to fail at one of God's most important commands, which is to forgive and pray for our enemies and those who hurt and abuse us (see Luke 6:35, 36). We meditate too much on what the offensive person has done to us, and we fail to realize what we are doing to ourselves by taking the bait of Satan. Keep remembering that being offended will not change the person, but it does change you! It makes you bitter, withdrawn, and often revengeful. It keeps your thoughts on something that does not bear good fruit in your life.

While praying for our enemies and blessing those who curse us may seem extremely difficult or nearly impossible, we can do it if we set our minds to it. Having the proper mind-set is vital if we want to obey God. He never tells us to do anything that is not good for us, and never anything we cannot do. He is always available to give us the strength we need to do it (see Philippians 4:13). We don't even need to think about how hard it is, we just need to do it!

God is just! Justice is one of His most admirable character traits. He brings justice as we wait on Him and trust Him to be our vindicator when we have been hurt or offended. He simply asks us to pray and forgive—and He does the rest. He makes even our pain work out for our good (see Romans 8:28). He justifies, vindicates, and recompenses us. He pays us back for our pain if we follow His commands to forgive our enemies and even says that we will receive "double for our trouble" (see Isaiah 61:7).

As we renew our minds with thoughts such as, *I am difficult to offend,* or *I freely and quickly forgive,* we will find forgiving and releasing offenses easier than ever to do. The reason this is true is because "Where the mind goes, the man follows." As we mentally and verbally agree with God by obeying His Word, we become a team that is unbeatable.

The Bible teaches us about the power of agreement. Deuteronomy 32:30 speaks of the fact that one person can put one thousand to flight and two, ten thousand. In Matthew 18:19, Jesus says, "Again I tell you, if two of you on earth agree (harmonize together, make a symphony together) about whatever [anything and everything] they may ask, it will come to pass and be done for them by My Father in heaven." If people on Earth can get these kinds of powerful results simply by being in agreement, just imagine what will happen when we come into agreement with God.

I actually believe that forgiving those who hurt and offend us is one of the most spiritually powerful things we can do. The Bible says we "overcome (master) evil with good" (Romans 12:21). The best way to defeat the devil is to do what is right. I can't imagine how it frustrates him when we pray for those who hurt us instead of hating them. It makes me want to laugh out loud when I even think of it.

Think about It

In what areas do you frequently take the bait of Satan and fall into his trap of being offended? What is your new power thought that will prepare you ahead of time for victory?

Believe the Best

Believing the best of people is very helpful in the process of forgiving people who hurt or offend us. As human beings, we tend to be suspicious of others and we often get hurt due to our own imagination. It is possible to believe someone hurt you on purpose when the truth is they were not even aware they did anything at all and would be grieved to know that they hurt you. God calls us to love others, and love always believes the best. First Corinthians 13:7 makes this clear: "Love bears up under anything and everything that comes, *is ever ready to believe the best of every person*, its hopes are fadeless under all circumstances, and it endures everything [without weakening]" (emphasis mine).

In many ways, Dave and I are extremely different, yet we rarely ever argue or become angry with one another. That was not the case for many years, but we have learned to disagree agreeably. We each respect the other's right to have an opinion, even if our opinions differ.

I can remember, during the early years of our marriage, focusing on everything I considered negative about Dave and ignoring his positive traits. My thoughts went something like this: *We just don't agree about anything. Dave is so stubborn, and he has to be right all the time. He is insensitive, and he just doesn't care how I feel. He never thinks of anyone but himself.* In reality, none of these thoughts were true! They only existed within my own mind; and my wrong thinking caused a great deal of offense and disagreement that could have been easily avoided had my mind-set been more positive. I "thought" myself into being offended by believing lies—just exactly what the enemy wanted me to do.

Over time, as I grew in my relationship with God, I learned the power of believing the best of people and meditating on the things that were good. As that happened, my thinking sounded like this, *Dave is usually very easy to get along with; he has his areas of stubbornness but then so do I. Dave loves me and would never hurt my feelings on purpose. Dave is very protective of me and always makes sure I am taken care of.* At first, I had to think these things on purpose because I had a habit of always choosing the negative, but now I actually feel uncomfortable when I think negative thoughts and positive thoughts come more naturally because I have disciplined myself to think them.

There are still times when people hurt my feelings, but then I remember that I can choose whether to be hurt or to "get over it." I can believe the best or I can believe the worst, so why not believe the best and enjoy my day? I grew up in a home that was filled with turmoil and anger, and I refuse to live that way now. I help create a good atmosphere around me by thinking good thoughts about others and by choosing to not be easily offended or angered.

I encourage you to believe the best about others. Resist the temptation to question their motives or to think they hurt you intentionally. Believing the best about others will keep offense and bitterness out of your life and help you stay peaceful and joyful. So, always do your best to believe the best.

Think about It

About whom do you need to begin to believe the best?

_____

_____

Tired and Touchy

Sometimes we are more prone to be hurt or offended than at other times. Years of experience have taught me that when I am excessively tired, I am more touchy and apt to get my feelings hurt more than I am when I am rested. I have learned to avoid conversations that could be tense when I know I am tired. I have also learned to wait to bring up subjects that might be tense for Dave when he is tired. Times when we are tired are the worst times to confront something I think he is doing wrong or to mention something I would like him to change. I know I will end up hurt or angry if he does not respond the way I want him to, so I do not put myself in that position.

I encourage husbands and wives to learn to relate to each other in ways that minimize the potential for offense, just as Dave and I have learned to do. A woman should not greet her husband when he comes home from work with all the bad news she can think of, such as, "The children acted terribly all day and you need to correct them," and "The utility bills are higher than I have ever seen them," and, "You need to quit that golf league you are in because I am sick and tired of watching you have all the fun while I do all the work."

Similarly, when one of the children kept a mother awake all night with an illness, the others have misbehaved all day, the house looks like a cyclone hit it, and dinner is burned beyond recognition—that is not the time for a husband to announce, "I'm going fishing with the guys this weekend." Under the circumstances I mentioned, all his wife would want is encouragement, some assistance around the house, and someone to help with the children, not the news that she has to handle everything by herself all weekend long. Perhaps this couple does need to talk about the children, the utility bills, the golf league, and the fishing trip, but they need to do so at a good time, not when they are frustrated, frazzled, or exhausted.

I have also discovered I can be more easily offended than I typically am when I have been working too long without a break. I might not be physically tired, but I may be mentally fatigued and need some creativity or diversity. Learning to understand these things about myself has helped me avoid offense. I can say to myself, "I am tired and therefore touchy, so I need to shake this off and not get upset over something I wouldn't normally get upset about."

Talking to ourselves is a good thing! When I begin to get a bad attitude, I often say that I need to have a meeting with myself. Especially when we are tempted to sin (and being offended is sin), we may need to give ourselves verbal reminders or instructions such as, "I know I am tired and frustrated, but I am not going to sin. I am not going to open a door to the enemy in my life by being offended.

I am going to obey God and forgive this person, and not harbor hurt and offense in my heart."

Have as many meetings with yourself as you need to in order to figure out when you are most likely to be easily offended. As I mentioned, I am more sensitive to offense when I am tired or under stress and I believe most of us are that way. Get to know yourself in this way. Be aware when circumstances that make you touchy arise, and be diligent to refuse to be offended.

That Time of the Month

Many household arguments occur during a woman's monthly cycle. Men often say, "It's that time of the month again," and they say it with dread in their voice tone. I have two daughters and both of them have learned that they are more sensitive than normal at that time of the month and they try to keep that in mind when situations begin to frustrate them that normally would not bother them at all. They realize they are more prone to negative thoughts and have a greater tendency to feel overwhelmed. Reminding themselves of that fact helps them not to let their emotions have control.

Most women have moody days before they actually begin their cycle and for that reason they often don't connect the dots. They think, "My life is driving me crazy," and fail to realize that life is the same as always, they are the ones that are different. I urge women who have not yet gone through the change of life to mark this time on their calendars each month and pray ahead of time that they will not be easily offended due to hormone changes in their body. I urge men to mark it on their calendars also and use wisdom. This is a great time of the month to send flowers to your wife or give her extra encouragement and it is not a good time to correct her or be moody yourself.

Women should get more rest at that time of the month if possible and absolutely avoid trying to solve a crisis. The world has given this monthly event a name. It is called PMS, which means premenstrual syndrome. Whatever we decide to call it, the truth is that it is a time of the month when some women need to be cautious not to be offended, but to simply realize they are emotionally tender and need to be careful about the way they behave.

Women can experience varying degrees of the same thing during the change of life, so that is also a time to use caution and wisdom. Try to be patient because eventually that time of life will pass and things will return to normal.

Think about It

What increases your tendency to be offended? Is it being tired, being stressed at work, financial pressure, relational difficulties, or something else?

_____

_____

Life Is Precious—Don't Waste Your Time!

I have learned that any day I spend angry and offended is a wasted day. Life is too short and too precious to waste any of it. The older a person gets, the more they usually realize that, but I am sad to say that some people never learn it. The society we live in today is filled with angry, easily offended people who are stressed-out and tired most of the time. Jesus tells us we are not "of" this world (see John 8:23); we do live in the world, but we are not to be *of* the world in terms of behaving the way society does and reacting to situations the same way it does. Jesus teaches us a better way to live. I always like to say that Christianity begins with accepting Jesus as our Savior and then it is continued in a lifestyle based on His teachings. Jesus told the disciples that although the law said, "an eye for an eye," which meant whatever someone does to you, do it back to them, now He was saying to forgive your enemies, to love and pray for those who used and abused you. The people who heard Him were amazed, they had never heard of such a thing.

He taught them many other things that would be an entirely new way of living, but it was one that would produce a quality of life they previously had not known.

We can choose to live according to God's Word rather than to live the world's way or to give in to fleshly thoughts or emotions. The Bible tells us to walk in the Spirit (see Galatians 5:25) and in order to do that we must manage our emotions rather than allowing them to control us. We must take responsibility for our responses to daily events, especially the little offenses that tempt us to be angry.

Making the decision to not be offended does not always change how we feel about the way we were treated. One of our biggest problems is that we usually allow our feelings to direct our choices and thereby never get around to making the decisions we need to make. We must realize our feelings will eventually catch up with our decisions, so we need to be responsible to make the right decisions and let the feelings follow. Becoming established in the thought *I am difficult to offend* can prepare you ahead of time for any offense you may face. It will set you up to forgive and release the offender, which will keep you out of the snare of unforgiveness.

A wise person refuses to live with hurt feelings or offense in his heart! Life is too short to waste one day being angry, bitter, and resentful. The good news of the Gospel of Jesus Christ is that our sins are forgiven and I believe we have been given the ability to forgive those who sin against us. Anything God has given us, such as forgiveness and mercy, He expects us to extend to others. If it comes *to* us, it should flow *through* us—and that should be our goal. When we are offended, we need to quickly call to mind the fact that God has freely and fully forgiven us, so we should freely and fully forgive others.

Think about It

Is there an offense you have been holding onto? If so, write it down on a piece of paper. Then rip it into tiny pieces and throw it away.

Don't Drink the Poison

Many people ruin their health and their lives by responding to offenses by drinking the poison of bitterness, resentment, and unforgiveness. In Matthew 18:23–35, Jesus tells a story about one man who refused to forgive another. At the end, He makes the clear and strong point that those who do not forgive others get "turned over to the torturers" (see Matthew 18:34). If you have, or have ever had, a problem forgiving others, I'm sure you can attest to this truth. Harboring hateful thoughts and bitterness toward another person in your mind is indeed torturous.

You may have heard the saying, "Refusing to forgive is like drinking poison and hoping it kills the other person." We are not hurting the one who hurt us by being angry at them. The truth is that most of the time people who offend us don't even know how we feel. They go on with their lives while we drink the poison of bitterness. When you do forgive those who offend you, you are actually helping yourself more than you are helping them, so I say, "Do yourself a favor and forgive!"

We think, *But, it is so unfair for me to forgive them and then they just have no punishment for what they did. Why should I have the pain while they get the freedom?*

The truth is that by forgiving, we are releasing them so God can do what only He can do. If I'm in the way—trying to get revenge or take care of the situation myself instead of trusting and obeying God—He may sit back and allow me to try to handle things in my own strength. But, if I allow Him to deal with those who offend me by forgiving them, He can work good out of it for both parties concerned. The book of Hebrews tells us that God settles the cases of His people. When we forgive, we put God on the case (see Hebrews 10:30).

Think about It

How does forgiveness help you?

_____

_____

Forgive ... for YOUR Sake!

Mark 11:22–26 clearly teaches us that unforgiveness hinders our faith from working, so we can conclude in contrast that forgiveness enables faith to work for us. The Father can't forgive *our* sins if we don't forgive other people (see Matthew 6:14, 15). This is an illustration of the biblical law stating that we reap what we sow (see Galatians 6:7). Sow mercy, and reap mercy; sow judgment, and reap judgment. Sow forgiveness toward others, and reap forgiveness from God.

There are still more benefits of forgiveness. For one, I'm happier and I feel better physically when I'm not filled with the poison of unforgiveness. Serious diseases can develop as a result of the stress and pressure that result from bitterness, resentment, and unforgiveness. Our fellowship with God flows freely when we're willing to forgive, but unforgiveness serves as a major block to communion with God. I also believe it is difficult to love people while hating or harboring anger toward others. When we have bitterness in our hearts it seeps out in all of our attitudes and relationships. It is good to remember that even people we want to love may suffer when we hold bitterness, resentment, and unforgiveness. For example, I was very angry and bitter toward my father for abusing me and I ended up mistreating my husband who had nothing at all to do with the pain I had encountered. I felt that someone needed to repay me for the injustice in my life, but I was trying to collect from someone who could not pay and had no responsibility to do so. God promises to pay us back for our former trouble if we turn the situation over to Him, and if we don't, then we allow Satan to perpetuate our pain and take it from relationship to relationship. Forgiving our enemies sets us free to move on with our lives. Finally, forgiveness keeps Satan from getting an advantage over us (see 2 Corinthians 2:10, 11). Ephesians 4:26, 27 tells us not to let the sun go down on our anger or give the devil any such foothold or opportunity. Remember that the devil must have a *foothold* before he can get a *stronghold*. Do not help Satan torture you. Be quick to forgive when you are offended.

Think about It

List three benefits that you will receive by forgiving.

_____

_____

A Key Issue for Desperate Times

Some people say over and over, "I am just touchy and I get my feelings hurt easily. That is just the way I am and I cannot help it." This is what they believe about themselves, and this belief controls their words and actions, which is so unfortunate because it is so ungodly! It is also an excuse to continue the wrong behavior.

I cannot stress enough how important it is to become a person who is difficult to offend. Satan desperately tries to prevent us from making spiritual progress. If he can keep us focused on who we are angry with and what they did to offend us, then we cannot focus on God's Word and His plan for us, and we will not grow spiritually. Once again let me remind you that Satan is fishing, hoping to catch someone in his trap; don't take his bait!

Most of us sense that we are living in desperate times among desperate people and we should be more careful than ever before to not let our emotions take the lead role in our lives. Instead of being quick to become angry or being easily offended, we must take the Bible's advice and be wise as serpents and gentle as doves (see Matthew 10:16). In other words, we should be spiritually mature, patient, kind, and gentle with others and wise enough not to allow them to offend us. We cannot control what people do to us, but through God we can control the way we respond to them. The world seems to be getting darker and darker; everywhere we look, we hear and read about people whose anger leads them to do drastic, even tragic, things. We want to represent God and express His love in these difficult days, and to do so, we will have to guard our hearts diligently against offense and anger. Building a new mind-set that you are not easy to offend will be very helpful to you and all those you love.

This principle is also very important to teach our children. One of the reasons it was so difficult for me to forgive was because I never had it modeled in front of me. All the people I grew up around stayed angry most of the time and if anyone ever did anything to hurt or disappoint them, their natural response was to angrily shut that person out of their lives forever. What we do in front of our children affects them even more than what we say, so remember to set a good example for them. Take every opportunity to teach them the importance of prompt and complete forgiveness. If you train them early not to be easily offended, you can save them years of pain and frustration.

Think about It

In your own words, why is it important to become a person who is difficult to offend?

Power Pack

"Great peace have they who love Your law; nothing
shall offend them or make them stumble."
Psalm 119:165

"For if you forgive people their trespasses [their
reckless and willful sins, leaving them, letting them
go, and giving up resentment], your heavenly Father
will also forgive you. But if you do not forgive others
their trespasses [their reckless and willful sins, leaving
them, letting them go, and giving up resentment],
neither will your Father forgive you your trespasses."
Matthew 6:14, 15

"Love bears up under anything and everything that
comes, is ever ready to believe the best of every person,
its hopes are fadeless under all circumstances, and
it endures everything [without weakening]."
1 Corinthians 13:7

POWER THOUGHT

5

I love people and I enjoy helping them.

"I give you a new commandment: that you
should love one another. Just as I have loved
you, so you too should love one another."
John 13:34

The Roman philosopher Seneca made a statement we all need to remember: "Wherever there is a human being, there is an opportunity for kindness." I would add to that, "Wherever there is a human being, there is an opportunity to express love." Everyone on Earth needs love and kindness. Even when we have nothing to offer others in terms of money or possessions, we can give them love and show them kindness.

If I could only preach one message, it would probably be this: Get your mind off of yourself and spend your life trying to see how much you can do for others. From start to finish, in all kinds of ways, God's Word encourages and challenges us to love other people. To love others is the "new commandment" Jesus gave us in John 13:34, and it is the example He set for us throughout His life and ministry on Earth. If we want to be like Jesus, we need to love others with the same kind of gracious, forgiving, generous, unconditional love He extends to us.

Nothing has changed my life more dramatically than learning how to love people and treat them well. If you only incorporate one power thought from this book into your life, I urge you to make it this one: "I love people and I enjoy helping them."

Think about It

What are you doing to show love to others?

_____

_____

More than a Feeling

Some people think of love as a wonderful feeling—a sensation of excitement or gushy emotions that make us feel warm and fuzzy all over. While love certainly has its wonderful feelings and powerful emotions, it's so much more than that. Real love has little to do with gooey emotions and goose bumps; and it has everything to do with the choices we make about the way we treat people. Real love is not theory or talk; it is action. It is a decision concerning the way we behave in our relationships with other people. Real love meets needs even when sacrifice is required in order to do so. The Bible makes this point in 1 John 3:18: "Let us not love [merely] in theory or in speech but in deed and in truth (in practice and in sincerity)." Clearly, love moves us to take action—not just to theorize or talk.

I am amazed when I think about how often we know the right thing to do, but never get around to doing it. The apostle James said that if we hear the Word of God and don't do it, we deceive ourselves with reasoning that does not agree with the truth (see James 1:21, 22). In other words, we know what is right but we make an excuse for ourselves. We find reason to exempt ourselves from doing what we would tell others that they ought to do. If we really want to walk in love, we will _do_ what is right.

For quite some time, I have been challenging people around the world with the challenge I want to present to you today: Would you make a commitment before God and sincerely in your heart to do at least one thing for somebody else every day? It may sound simple, but to do it, you will have to think about it and choose to do it on purpose. You may even have to move beyond the normal group of people in your life and do things for people you would not normally reach out to or even strangers. That's okay, though, because there are so many people in the world who have never, ever had anyone do anything nice for them and they are desperate for some words or actions of love.

Let love be the main theme of your life and you will have a life worth living. The Bible says we know that we have passed over from death to life if we love one another (see 1 John 3:14). Remember: "Where the mind goes, the man follows." If you truly desire to excel in the love walk, you must first purpose to fill your mind with kind, loving, unselfish, and generous thoughts. This is an opportunity to practice the "on-purpose" thinking principle we talked about in the first section of the book. It is impossible to change your behavior unless you change your mind. Start thinking loving, generous thoughts today, and you'll soon have a life full of love and happiness. Take a few minutes each morning and ask God to show you what you can do for somebody else that day. You can even choose a specific person and ask Him to show you what you can do for them. It will get your mind off of you and release new levels of joy in your life as well as be a great encouragement to the people you reach out to.

Think about It

What will you do to put love into action today?

_____

_____

What about Me?

Caring about other people is the greatest thing we can ever do because, as human beings, we are so innately selfish. Selfishness and self-centeredness are inbred in us. The focus of our thoughts tends to be on ourselves, and whether we ever utter the words with our mouths or not, we constantly ask, "What about me? What about me? What about me?" This is not the way God wants us to live.

I spent many years of my life as a very unhappy, dissatisfied person, and I wasted a lot of time thinking my unhappiness was someone else's fault. Thoughts such as, *If I just had more money, I would be happy,* or *If people did more for me, I would be happy,* or *If I did not have to work so hard, I would be happy,* or *If I felt better physically, I would be happy* filled my mind. The list of reasons I thought caused my unhappiness seemed endless, and no matter what I did to entertain myself nothing worked for long. I was a Christian; I had a growing ministry and a wonderful family but my joy level was definitely affected by my circumstances. Getting what I wanted made me happy for a while, but my happiness evaporated quickly and I soon needed another "fix" of getting my way or getting what I wanted.

As I grew in my personal relationship with God, I literally became desperate for peace, stability, true happiness, and joy. That kind of hunger for change usually requires facing some truth—maybe some unpleasant truth or things we don't like to admit—about ourselves, and I have learned that if we really want truth, God will give it to us. As I began seeking God for the root cause of my unhappiness, He showed me that I was very selfish and self-centered. My focus was on what others could and should do for me, rather than what I could do for them. That was not easy for me to accept, but doing so was the beginning of a life-changing journey with God.

As God led me, I was reminded that I had grown up in a home that was not loving and kind. The people I lived with were self-focused and did not really care who was hurt as long as they got what they wanted. My role models were selfish, insensitive people.

Since these were the character traits I observed, they were the ones I developed. No one ever taught me about love, kindness, or giving until I entered a relationship with God through Jesus Christ.

God helped me begin to see myself as a person who could give and help. I had to change my thinking from, "What about me," to "What can I do for you?" I would like to say this was an easy change to make, but the truth is that it was very difficult and took a lot longer than I like to admit.

Over time, I came to understand that God is love and His nature is that of a giver (see 1 John 4:8). He gives, He helps, He cares, and He sacrifices. He does not merely do these things occasionally, but they represent His constant attitude toward us. Love is not something God does, it is who He is. He always offers us love, generosity, grace, and help. It is true that God is just and there are times when He punishes sin, but even that He does out of love, for our own good, to teach us the right way to live. Everything God does is for our good; all of His commands are intended to help us have the best lives we can possibly have. He commands us to love and be kind to others, which means taking the focus off of ourselves, silencing the voice that asks "What about me?" and learning to follow Jesus' example of being kind, generous, and loving toward others.

Think about It

Ask God to show you the root cause(s) of any unhappiness in your life. Be willing to face the truth about yourself even if you don't like it. This is the first step toward a better life!

Do It Deliberately

Jesus told us plainly what we need to do if we want to follow Him. "If anyone intends to come after Me, let him deny himself [forget, ignore, disown, and lose sight of himself and his own interests] and take up his cross, and [joining Me as a disciple and siding with My party] follow with Me [continually, cleaving steadfastly to Me]" (Mark 8:34). The "cross" we are asked to carry in life is simply one of unselfishness.

Most of us concentrate on what we can *get* in life, but we need to concentrate on what we can *give*. We think about what other people should do for us and often become angry because they do not give us what we want. Instead, we should think aggressively about what we can do for others and then trust God to meet our needs and fulfill our desires.

Please notice that I say we need to think *aggressively* about what we can do for others. Galatians 6:10 conveys the same meaning, encouraging us to "Be mindful to be a blessing." Simply put, to "be mindful" means to be intentional, to be purposeful and deliberate. God wants us to think on purpose and to make a point of being a blessing to others.

I do my best to be aggressive in my thinking about who I can bless, and realizing that I must give and help on purpose has been very beneficial to me. It did not come naturally. I had to learn to do it, but it has been one of the greatest, most rewarding lessons of my life. There are certainly times when I "feel" like being a blessing, but there are many times when I don't. Sometimes I may also feel that people should be doing more for me, and in reality perhaps they should be, but that cannot be my concern. I have learned to trust God to get to me what He wants me to have and to personally continue reaching out to others. We cannot live by what we feel and ever have consistency and stability. Our ability to choose is greater than how we feel and it is that ability we must activate. Be deliberate about love!

I remember one specific morning when I sat and thought, *Okay,*

God, I want to bless someone today. I was not talking about blessing someone by preaching or teaching, but in my personal life, in my own little corner of the world. I always want to make sure I am living the same way I encourage other people to live so I thought through the various people I would be around that day.

About thirty seconds later, God showed me something I could do for a specific person. He impressed upon me the fact that being a blessing to that person by simply telling her how much I appreciated her would really mean a lot to her and give her fuel for the day. All I needed to do was say, "I just want you to know I really appreciate you." It didn't take long, and it didn't require much effort, but I did have to think about it. I had to choose to do it on purpose; I had to be intentional about wanting to bless someone.

I encourage you to begin to think on purpose about how you can be a blessing to the people around you. Remember, it does not have to cost money although at times it may; it does not always have to take much time; and it does not have to take an enormous amount of energy. Blessing people can be quick and easy, but it won't just happen. You have to do it deliberately. At times what God asks us to do may be more costly to us in time, effort, or finances than at other times, but either way we need to be ready to be God's ambassador on Earth. Use what you have in the service of God and man and your needs will always be met.

Think about It

How will you deliberately be a blessing to someone this week?

_____

_____

Be a Blessing Dispenser

The love of God is in us because God puts His love in our hearts when we accept Jesus as our Savior, but it needs to get *through* us in order for it to help anyone else. In Genesis 12:2, God told Abraham He would bless him and make him a person who dispensed blessings everywhere he went. When I read that story, I am reminded of a bottle of hand lotion I have, one that has a pump on it. When I press the pump, it dispenses hand lotion. That's the way I want to be with blessings. When people come near me, I want to dispense something good, something that will benefit them.

I want to encourage you to use what you have to meet needs for other people, and to have what I call "prosperity with a purpose." Don't pray to be prosperous so you can have more and more for yourself, but make certain you use a good portion of what you have to bless others. I am not talking about only putting money into an offering at church on Sundays. I am talking about doing things for people in your daily life—people you work with, people in your family, people you like and people you may not particularly like, people you know and people you don't know, and those you think deserve it as well as those you don't think deserve it. This is an exciting way to live, as I have learned from personal experience.

I was out shopping one day and felt God wanted me to pay for another customer's earrings. I didn't know who the lady was; I had never seen her before; and I thought she might think I was a bit unusual because I wanted to buy the earrings for her. But the sense that I needed to pay for her earrings just wouldn't go away. So I finally walked up to her with enough money in my hand to cover the earrings and said, "Listen, I'm a Christian and I just feel that God wants you to be blessed today. He wants you to know He loves you, so here's the money to pay for your earrings."

I got away as quickly as I could because if she thought I was crazy, I didn't want to know it! Months and months later, I heard that the lady actually was out shopping that day with someone who recognized me and watched me on television. That person had a neighbor, a man who tended to poke fun at me and did not speak nicely about me. The woman from the store told the man what had happened and it changed his attitude. That man who once made fun of me ended up watching our television broadcast regularly and receiving salvation!

You never know what God has in store when He puts something on your heart to do—even when it may not make sense to you or when it seems silly or embarrassing. If He asks you to do something, do it. I assure you, He always knows what He is doing, so even when you don't understand, go ahead and obey.

When I paid for the woman's earrings during my shopping trip, I was blessed, the lady who got the earrings was blessed, the woman who witnessed it was blessed, God was honored, and the man who became a believer was blessed. I am thankful I was obedient in that situation. In many Scripture passages, the Bible teaches that when we obey God, we are blessed and when we don't, we aren't. It's that simple. I do my best to obey God when I sense He wants me to do something to bless someone, but I have certainly "missed it" at times and removed myself from being able to receive a blessing. Let me explain.

I was once in a large discount shoe store and the customer in front of me in line had several pairs of shoes she intended to purchase. I began to sense that God wanted me to pay for her shoes, but I thought she would think I was crazy, so I fiddled around long enough to keep from doing it and I didn't say anything to her. When the clerk told her the total amount of her purchase, she didn't have enough money to pay for her shoes. I felt so bad! Not only was I unwilling to be embarrassed in front of her, I was also ashamed before God because I disobeyed Him. Take my word for it, obedience is better than disobedience. I don't always get it right, and you probably won't either, but I am moving forward—and you can too. That's what God wants from us.

I encourage you to develop a new mind-set, one that says, "I love people; I enjoy helping them and being generous." Then purpose to spend some time each morning thinking about what you can do for someone else that day. Lie in your bed before you get up in the mornings and pray, "God, who can I bless today?" Don't ask, "How can I be blessed today," but "Who can I bless today?" In the evening take a "blessing inventory" by asking, "What did I do today to make someone else's life better?" As I started learning to bless others, I found that I often made plans in the morning to bless people later that day, but then became busy and did not follow through. Taking the evening inventory really helped me because I did not want to have to answer, "Nothing, I did nothing to improve someone else's life today."

Decide to use the blessings in your life to be a blessing to others everywhere you go. You can do this in big ways or in small ways, but just do it. You'll be amazed at the results.

Another way you can be a blessing is just by being friendly. Make a real effort to be friendly with people everywhere you go and show a genuine interest in them. Try to make shy people feel comfortable and confident. Try to make anyone that is handicapped in any way feel just as "normal" as anyone else. There are countless ways we can be a blessing if we think about it creatively.

Think about It

Who do you intend to bless this week and how will you do it?

_____

_____

A Great Big Happy Life

Since being good to people has been one of my personal goals, my "joy tank" never runs dry for very long. I have even discovered that when I do get sad or discouraged, I can begin to think on purpose about what I can do for someone else and before long I am joyful again.

We all experience times in our lives when things are not going great for us. We may even be in the midst of personal loss or pain, but we cannot only be good to people when things are going well for us; we also—and especially—need to bless others when times are difficult for us. The reason I believe we need to be especially diligent about blessing others when we are struggling is that when we concentrate on giving, being kind, expressing love, and blessing other people, it gets our minds off our problems and we experience joy in the midst of our trouble. Why? Because givers are happy people!

You may have heard many times that the Bible says, "It is more blessed to give than to receive" (Acts 20:35 NKJV). The *Amplified Bible* renders that verse this way: "It is more blessed (makes one happier and more to be envied) to give than to receive" (Acts 20:35). You may know that verse, but do you really believe it? If you do, then you are probably doing your best to be a blessing everywhere you go. I must admit that, for many years, I could quote this verse, but I obviously didn't really believe it because I spent my time trying to be blessed rather than being a blessing.

I have now learned that we do not even know what "happy" is until we forget about ourselves, start focusing on others, and become generous givers. In order to be generous, we have to do more than simply plunk some change in a bucket during the holidays or give to the church once a week. Actually, I think learning to give in church should simply be practice for the way we should live our everyday lives. I do not just want to merely give offerings; I want to be a giver. I want to offer myself every day to be used for whatever God chooses. For this change to take place in my life I had to change my thinking. I had to think and say thousands of times, "I love people and I enjoy helping them." This power thought will be life-changing for you if you put it to work in your life.

As you become a generous giver, you will be amazed at how happy you will be and how much you will enjoy life. In contrast, stingy people are unhappy. Those who are not generous live little bitty, pathetic lives. They just do what they have to do; they look out only for themselves; they don't like to share; and they only give when they feel they must—and then, they often do so reluctantly or grudgingly. These attitudes and actions run contrary to the way God wants us to live because they do not result in blessings for anyone. In fact, Proverbs 1:19 says being greedy will drain the life out of a person:

> So are the ways of everyone who is greedy of gain; such [greed for plunder] takes away the lives of its possessors.

God is a giver. Paul writes, "Now to Him Who, by (in consequence of) the [action of His] power that is at work within us, is able to [carry out His purpose and] *do superabundantly, far over and above all that we [dare] ask or think [infinitely beyond our highest prayers, desires, thoughts, hopes, or dreams]*—to Him be glory in the church and in Christ Jesus throughout all generations forever and ever," (Ephesians 3:20, 21, emphasis mine). These words describe God, and if we want to be like He is, we need to always go the extra mile, always do more than we have to, always give more than enough, and always be generous.

Think about It

In what ways can you become more generous?

_____

_____

If You'll Listen, You'll Know

Because human nature is selfish and self-centered, generous giving does not come naturally to us. We have to build into our thinking the mind-set that we are generous. Begin to think and say, "I am a very generous person. I look for opportunities to give."

I have found that opportunities to give are all around me—and they are all around you too. Finding out how you can bless another person is as easy as using your ears. If you simply listen to people, you'll soon know what they need or would like.

In casual conversation, a person who works for me once mentioned she liked things produced by a certain company. I asked someone to go get her a gift certificate and gave it to her with a note telling her how much I appreciate all her hard work. She began to cry and said, "It's not the gift certificate that means so much to me. It's the fact that you actually heard me and remembered what I said."

I encourage you to begin listening to others and paying attention to what they say more than ever before. People want to know you're listening to them; they feel loved and valued when you listen to them. If you don't know what to do for someone, you're not listening to them because people tell you what they want, need, and like—and you'll know if you listen. You could start a list of things that you hear people say they want or need, and if you cannot provide it for them now, you can pray that God will give you the ability to do so. If you act on what you hear and bless people accordingly, you'll see that blessing others really is better than receiving anything for yourself. I assure you, the more you give, the happier you will be.

Think about It

What have you heard recently that let you know what someone needs or wants? What will you do about it?

How Generous Are You?

I want to close this chapter with several questions for you to ask yourself to help you see how generous you are or, perhaps, are not.

- How well do I tip? If I were a waiter or waitress, would I want to wait on myself, based on the way I tip?
- What kinds of gifts do I give? Do I give the cheapest things I can find? Do I get anything just to meet an obligation or do I sincerely look·for what I believe the person receiving the gift would enjoy?
- Do I freely and frequently encourage and compliment other people?
- Am I willing to share what I have?
- Do I hoard possessions or do I give away what I'm·not using?
- How many things do I have hidden in drawers in my home—things I have not used in years that I am keeping just because I like having possessions?
- When I have opportunities to give to those less fortunate than I am, do I give generously? Do I do as much as I can or as little as I can?
- If I'm with someone who has a cold and runny nose, and I have been carrying around a package of tissues for weeks, do I give that person only one tissue, or do I offer the entire package so they will have plenty?
- Do I give someone else the best-looking steak at dinner or do I keep that one for myself?

We could ask ourselves all kinds of questions like these that would help us locate our level of generosity. I believe you want to be as generous as you can possibly be so meditating on this power will certainly help you reach your goal. Think and say, "I love people and I enjoy helping them."

Power Pack

"Be mindful to be a blessing...."
. *Galatians 6:10*

"If anyone intends to come after Me, let him deny himself [forget, ignore, disown, and lose sight of himself and his own interests] and take up his cross, and [joining Me as a disciple and siding with My party] follow with Me [continually, cleaving steadfastly to Me]."
Mark 8:34

"Let us not love [merely] in theory or in speech but in deed and in truth (in practice and in sincerity)."
1 John 3:18

"We know that we have passed over out of death into Life by the fact that we love the brethren (our fellow Christians). He who does not love abides (remains, is held and kept continually) in [spiritual] death."
1 John 3:14

POWER THOUGHT

6

I trust God completely; there is no need to worry!

"Lean on, trust in, and be confident in the Lord
with all your heart and mind and do not rely
on your own insight or understanding."
Proverbs 3:5

Worry does no good and can impact our lives in negative ways. I'm sure you have noticed how absolutely powerless you feel when you worry or feel anxious and troubled, because worry is indeed completely useless. It is a waste of time and energy because it never changes our circumstances. Worry and anxiety do, however, change us. It can make us sick and grouchy. A medical researcher recently told me that 87 percent of all illness is connected to wrong thought patterns. Worry would come under the heading of "negative thinking" and all negative thoughts actually release chemicals from the brain that affect us adversely. In her popular book *Who Switched Off My Brain?* Dr. Caroline Leaf states that we think thirty thousand thoughts per day and through an uncontrolled thought life, we create conditions that are favorable for illness; we make ourselves sick!

Despite the fact that worrying does us no good and is actually detrimental to our health and well-being, it seems to plague multitudes of people, maybe even you. It's human nature to be concerned about the bad situations in our world and in our personal lives, but if we're not careful, we can easily become worried or fearful, and we can end up in sin because worrying will keep us from trusting God. Worse than that, by worrying we end up helping the devil in his goal of tormenting us. I find it is easier for me to avoid worry if I keep reminding myself that it is a total waste of time and does absolutely no good at all.

I like to say worry is like sitting in a rocking chair, rocking back and forth; it's always in motion and it keeps us busy, but it never gets us anywhere. In fact, if we do it too long, it wears us out! Worry keeps us from living in faith and steals our peace. When we worry, we are actually saying, "If I try hard enough I can find a solution to my problem," and that is the opposite of trusting God.

The cause of worry is simple: It's the failure to trust God to take care of the various situations in our lives. Most of us have spent our lives trying to take care of ourselves, and it takes time to learn how to trust God in every situation. We learn by doing it. We have to step out in faith and as we do we will experience the faithfulness of God, and that makes it easier to trust Him the next time. Too often we trust our own abilities, believing we can figure out how to take care of our own problems. Yet most of the time, after all our worry and effort to go it alone, we come up short, unable to bring about suitable solutions. God, on the other hand, always has solutions for the things that make us anxious and worried.

Trusting Him allows us to enter His rest, and rest is a place of peace where we are able to enjoy life while we are waiting for Him to solve our problems. He cares for us; He will solve our problems and meet our needs, but we have to stop thinking and worrying about them. I realize this is easier said than done, but there is no time like the present to begin learning a new way to live—a way of living that is without worry, anxiety, and fear. This is the time to begin thinking and saying, "I trust God completely; there is no need to worry!" The more you think about this truth, the more you will find yourself choosing trust over worry.

Think about It

What do you worry about most?_____
How can you release your worry and concern to God?

_____

_____

It's a Matter of Focus

When our daughter Sandra was a teenager, she occasionally got blemish breakouts on her face. She hated them and was extremely insecure about them. She focused on the blemish so much that she actually called attention to it. She talked about it excessively and by doing so, drew attention to it and others began to notice it. She squeezed it and picked at it and then tried so hard to cover it up with makeup that she actually made it worse. She was a pretty girl, had nice hair, and was lean and thin. She was smart, athletic, and had a great personality, but every month for a week all she focused on was the couple of pimples she got. This is a good example of how we magnify things simply by focusing on them excessively.

Just as it was natural for Sandra to do what she could to try to fix the problem, it is only natural to do the same thing with our problems. We would not be responsible if we did not look for solutions at all. Considering our situation and what to do about it is one thing, but focusing on it is quite another. We can concentrate on our problems to the point that we often fail to notice or consider other things that we should notice. For example, it is important to count our blessings during challenging times because it keeps us from getting discouraged. We can focus on what needs to be done so much that we fail to see what God has done. If you are being tempted to worry about something right now, take time to write down all your blessings you can think of and it will help you not get overwhelmed by the problem.

When we have problems, we should do what we can do and not worry about what we cannot do. As my husband always says, "Do your responsibility and cast your care."

Whatever we focus on becomes bigger and bigger in our minds. It is possible for a thing to seem much larger to us than it really is. When we worry, we focus on our problems; we continually roll them over and over in our minds, which is like meditating on them. When we are anxious about things, we also talk about them incessantly because what is in our hearts eventually comes out of our mouths (see Matthew 12:34). The more we think and talk about our problems, the larger they become. A relatively small matter can grow into a huge issue merely because we focus on it too much. Instead of meditating on the problem, we can meditate on the faithfulness of God and remind ourselves there is no need to worry.

We can spend all our time thinking and talking about what is wrong in the world or we can choose to concentrate on good things. We can focus on what is wrong with a family member, friend, or coworker or we can purposely look for and highlight what is right. If ten things are wrong and we only see two we feel are right, we can make the two seem larger than the ten by what we choose to concentrate on. This is a good time to remind yourself that you can choose your own thoughts. I have heard many people say, "I just can't help it; I am a worrier." The truth is that they chose to worry because they did not know how to trust God. We become good at worrying because we practice it and we can also become good at trusting God if we practice it. Let your first response in any situation be to trust God, not to worry. Speak out loud and say, "I trust God completely; there is no need to worry!"

Satan, the enemy of our souls, does not want us to grow in faith; he wants us to be filled with worry, anxiety, and fear. He works hard to distract us from God by encouraging an excessive focus on our circumstances. We should develop a habit of letting what is in our heart become more real to us than what we see, think, or feel. My heart knows I can trust God completely, but my head often tells me to worry. If Satan can get us to think about what is wrong or what could go wrong with a situation, he can keep us from being able to focus on trusting God. This is why Hebrews 12:2 instructs us to look away from all that distracts us to Jesus, who is the Author and Finisher of our faith. If we look to God, think about Him, and speak of His goodness, we focus on faith and as we use our faith, we find that it grows. Little faith can become great faith through use. As we take steps to trust God, we experience His faithfulness and that, in turn, encourages us to have greater faith. As our faith develops and grows, our problems have less power over us and we worry less.

We can choose to think about what God can do instead of what we cannot do. If we continually think about the difficulty of our situation we may end up in despair and that means we feel unable to find a way out. We feel trapped and then it is easy to panic and begin to do irrational things that only make the problem worse. The Bible tells us that God always provides the way out (see 1 Corinthians 10:13). Even though you might not see the way out right now, one does exist and God will reveal it as you trust Him.

Think about It

What situation are you facing right now that you can choose to trust God with instead of worrying?

_____

_____

Another Form of Worry

Most of the time, we think of worry as another word for "anxiety" or as a way of describing excessive concern that often involves a good deal of emotion. But worry in its commonly understood sense is not the only expression of anxiety. Another form of worry is called reasoning, which takes place when we think about something over and over, trying to figure out what happened, trying to understand what people were thinking, or trying to decide what to do in a situation. Reasoning causes confusion and can easily make us vulnerable to deception. Trust requires some unanswered questions, and being satisfied to know that God knows what we don't know. We know in part, but God knows everything. He is never surprised or without a solution.

I find that I can ponder a situation and sometimes find answers or arrive at conclusions by doing so. However, if I think about it so long that I start feeling frustrated and confused, I know I have gone too far. It is even possible through reasoning to come up with a plan you *think* is right but, in fact, will never work. The Bible calls these man-made plans "works of the flesh." They take up our time, but keep us in the realm of self-effort and pride. They produce no good fruit, but they certainly keep us busy. We can literally spend years of our life with such man-made plans and never get around to realizing that only God can do what needs to be done. Don't waste your think time, but instead use it on power thoughts that agree with God's Word. God will not go to work until we turn our problems over to Him. He is a gentleman and does not interfere without invitation. The Bible refers to this simply by saying that we "have not" because we "ask not" (see James 4:2).

When I write about the uselessness of reasoning, I am not suggesting we become passive and never try to do anything to help ourselves solve our problems. A passive mind is one that is open ground for the devil to occupy. We need to be active in the right way. Ephesians 6:13 teaches that when we face problems, we are to do all the crisis demands and then stand firmly in our place. We certainly need to do what we believe is right and what we have peace about doing, but we shouldn't frustrate ourselves trying to do what we cannot do.

For example, when we want to see changes in someone we love, the best policy is to pray first and only take action if and when God directs us to. We can do a lot of damage to relationships by trying to change people. We may feel we are just trying to help but if the person doesn't see what you see or if they don't want to change, they may feel pressured and rejected. Timing is very important when discussing potentially touchy subjects, so if we pray first and wait on God, it always works out better. I can pray, but I cannot make a human being want to change. Only God can work inside a person's heart. If I continue trying to do what only God can do, I will make myself miserable.

I was a person who wanted to understand everything because it made me feel that I was in control. I was not good at "not knowing." My mind went on and on all day with thoughts like, *Why did I act like that? I wonder what so-and-so is thinking about my decision to buy a new car? Why hasn't God answered my prayer yet for a promotion at work? I wonder if I am doing something wrong or don't have enough faith?* The whys in my mind seemed to never cease and they made me miserable. My mind was home to all sorts of uninvited guests (tormenting thoughts) simply because I never said "no" to them.

I wondered, reasoned, worried, fretted, imagined, and was anxious to the point where it left me completely exhausted at the end of most days. God actually showed me that I was addicted to reasoning and that I had to give it up. It didn't happen overnight, but each time I started my mental gymnastics I said, "I will not worry or try to figure this out," and gradually I was able to trust God with my life.

Think about It

Are you prone to reasoning? Remember, reasoning is a form of worry, so next time you start to reason, stop and decide to trust God to figure out everything for you.

Get Some Rest

In Matthew 11:28, Jesus said, "Come to Me, all you who labor and are heavy-laden and overburdened, and I will cause you to rest. [I will ease and relieve and refresh your souls.]" Jesus wants to ease our burdens and give us rest. *The Message* says it this way: "Are you tired? Worn out? Burned out on religion? Come to me. Get away with me and you'll recover your life. I'll show you how to take a real rest. Walk with me and work with me—watch how I do it. Learn the unforced rhythms of grace. I won't lay anything heavy or ill-fitting on you. Keep company with me and you'll learn to live freely and lightly" (Matthew 11:28–30).

Living freely and lightly in the "unforced rhythms of grace" sounds good, doesn't it? I'm sure you have had enough "heavy stuff" in your life. I have too, and I want to be free. It's nice to know we don't have to worry about things, figure out everything, or carry the burdens in our lives. It is actually quite refreshing to realize that I don't need to know everything about everything! We need to get comfortable with saying, "I don't know the answer to this dilemma and I'm not going to worry about anything because God is in control, and I trust Him. I'm going to rest in Him and live freely and lightly!" When we're overloaded with the cares of life— struggling, laboring, and worrying—we need a mental and emotional vacation. Our minds need to rest from thinking about how to take care of problems, and our emotions need to rest from being upset. Worry isn't restful at all. In fact, it steals rest and the benefits of rest from us. So next time you feel you are carrying a heavy load in your mind or you find yourself worried and anxious, remember, you can live freely and lightly. All you have to do is rest in God. If someone should ask you what you are going to do about your problem, you can tell them that you are letting your mind have a break and you're not thinking about it right now.

Think about It

Do you need a mental and emotional rest? How can you put your mind at rest today?

_____

_____

Release the Weight of Worry

It is one thing to know that we should not worry, but it is quite another to stop worrying. One of the things that helped me let go of worry was finally realizing how utterly useless it was. Let me ask you some questions: How many problems have you solved by worrying? How much time have you spent worrying about things that never even happened? Has anything ever gotten any better as a result of your worrying about it? Of course not! The Bible is full of sound, proven advice for dealing with worry. For example, the apostle Paul teaches us to be anxious for nothing, but in all circumstances to let our prayer requests be known to God with thanksgiving (see Philippians 4:6). He then encourages us by saying that the peace of God will fill our hearts and minds (see Philippians 4:7).

The instant you begin to worry or feel anxious, give your concern to God in prayer. Release the weight of it and totally trust Him to either show you what to do or to take care of it Himself. Prayer is a powerful force against worry. I'm reminded of an old gospel chorus called, "Why Worry When You Can Pray?" When you're under pressure, it's always best to pray about it instead of fret about it or talk about it.

Prayer is the blueprint for a successful life. During His time on Earth, Jesus prayed. He entrusted everything to God—even His reputation and life. We can do the same. Don't complicate your communication with God. Just have confidence in simple, believing prayer.

Think about It

What do you need to be praying about instead of worrying about in your life right now?

_____

_____

You Have a Choice to Make

Worry can easily be a bad habit—one that is deeply rooted and won't be easily gotten rid of. For this reason, people tend to think, *I have tried not to worry and I just cannot seem to help it.* I've had that thought before, and have found that filling my mind with good thoughts is easier than trying to empty it of negative ones. If you follow the power thoughts plan and keep your mind full of good thoughts, there will be no room for the bad. I am very excited for you to see what will happen in your life as you change your thinking. Paul encouraged believers in Christ to "walk in the Spirit" so we will not fulfill the lusts of the flesh (see Galatians 5:16). In simple terms, this means that if we stay busy doing what is right, there will be no room to do what is wrong. As humans, we tend to fight with the negative rather than embrace the positive, but that can easily be changed as we walk in the Spirit. Say it right now: "I trust God completely; there is no need to worry!"

Another thing that is very helpful to me is to take action quickly. As soon as I start to worry about a situation, I say, "No, I am not going to worry, because it does no good." Remember to resist the devil at his onset. The longer you wait the more difficult it may be. Once a wrong thinking pattern takes root in your life, it is more difficult to change it, so "action" is the secret to success. Knowledge alone does no good, we must take action and do what we know to do.

You may be wondering how to "walk in the Spirit" in your practical, everyday life. Let me help you by providing you with four sets of choices you can make. In each instance, worry represents walking in the flesh and the other option represents walking in the Spirit. If you want to walk in the Spirit, you have to make a choice. Will you worry or will you worship? Will you worry or will you put your faith and trust in God? Will you worry or will you obey God's Word? Will you worry about yourself by thinking, *What is going to happen to me,* or will you deposit yourself with God and purposely be a blessing to someone else?

Worry or Worship?

Worry and worship are polar opposites, and we would be much happier if we learned to become worshippers instead of worriers. Worry creates an opportunity for the enemy to torment us, but worship (reverence and adoration of God) leads us into His presence, where we will always find peace, joy, and hope. God created us to worship Him, and I don't believe we can overcome the pressures and temptations in our lives if we don't become worshippers.

God is good even when our circumstances are not! He doesn't always give us our hearts' desires immediately after we ask, but He knows the right timing for everything and we can trust Him. He wants us to develop a deep, personal relationship with Him and an outrageous love for Him—so much so that we realize we can't live without Him. This kind of relationship and love brings the worshipful attitude that God wants us to have. Knowing God intimately is more important than getting what we want immediately.

So stop worrying; give your concerns to God, and live in grace. Grace isn't just divine favor; it's power! Don't waste another day of your life worrying. Determine what your responsibility is and what it is not. Don't try to take on God's responsibility. When we do what we can do, God steps in and does what we can't. So give yourself and your worries to God, worship Him, and begin enjoying the abundant life He has for you. The minute you realize you are worrying, you can interrupt the wrong thought pattern by saying, "I will not worry. I worship You, Lord. You are good and I completely trust You."

Think about It

Are you a worshipper or a worrier?

_____

_____

Worry or Faith?

In years past, soldiers often protected themselves with shields, and in Ephesians 6:16, the Bible speaks of "the shield of faith." Since shields provide protection, faith must be a way to protect ourselves when the enemy attacks. However, a shield is only effective when it is raised; it won't help a soldier while it is on the ground or at his side. He must lift it up and use it to cover himself from attack. When the devil attacks us with unpleasant circumstances or thoughts that cause us to worry and be afraid, we should immediately lift up the shield of faith. The way we do that is by deciding right away that we will trust God instead of trying to worry our way to victory. It is very helpful to say out loud, "I trust God in this situation!" Say it firmly with conviction. Jesus talked back to Satan by saying, "It is written," and quoting Scripture (see Luke 4), and we can do the same. God's Word is powerful, and it is effective against everything the enemy tries to do in our lives.

Throughout the Bible, we see wonderful accounts of men and women of faith who totally trusted God in situations that appeared impossible to solve, and they experienced God's delivering power. Each of them had to release their faith and confidence in God and refuse to worry or be anxious.

If you're a Christian who goes around burdened or weighed down all the time, something is wrong. You may have had faith in Christ for salvation, but that doesn't mean you are living by faith. The most difficult burden we have to carry in life is self. Managing self, our daily living, feelings, temptations, temperament, and inward affairs all can become a heavy burden if we do not place ourselves entirely in God's hands by faith.

Next, we must lay aside the burden of health, reputation, work, home, children, and everything else that concerns us. The Bible tells us that God is faithful (see 1 Thessalonians 5:24); that's one of His major characteristics. We can count on Him to come through for us, so we should trust Him totally and completely. When we do, we'll be ready for anything that comes our way.

There will always be situations that cause you concern, but with

God's help, you can live above all of them and enjoy life. Learn to say with your mouth and with sincerity in your heart, "God, I trust You completely; there is no need to worry!"

One woman had a heavy burden that kept her from sleeping, took her appetite, and endangered her health. One day she found a Gospel tract telling the story of Hannah, a woman who also had very heavy burdens in life, but eventually learned to give them all to the Lord. Hannah said she was finally able to realize that she could not bear her burden, but had to let God bear it for her. She shared that we must take our burdens to Him, leave them, come away, and forget them. If the worry comes back, we should take it to Him again; continuing to do this over and over until at last we have no worries and we have perfect peace. Persistence is the key to defeating Satan. You must show him that you mean business. Keep your shield of faith lifted at all times and you will have the victory.

I had to learn that God would not work as long as I worried, but the moment I trusted Him, He put His plan into action, and through faith and patience, I enjoyed the thrill of watching God work miraculously in my life.

Think about It

Are you going to worry or pray and release God to go to work?

_____

_____

How can you demonstrate your faith in God in a situation you might otherwise worry about today?

_____

_____

Worry or Obedience to the Word?

I firmly believe that when we have problems, we must not worry, but we also need to continue doing the things we know to do. For example, if you have commitments, be sure that you keep them. Quite often when people are encountering personal problems they withdraw from normal life and spend all their time trying to solve the problem. They talk about their problems to anyone who will listen and worry continually. All of this unproductive activity prevents them from doing what they should be doing, which is "doing good."

Psalm 37:3 says that we should trust in the Lord and *do good* and we will feed on His faithfulness. I have discovered that if I continue my study of God's Word, continue praying, keep my commitments, and help as many people as I can, I experience breakthrough much faster. Helping others while we are hurting is actually a very powerful thing to do. It keeps your mind off of you and your problem, and you are sowing seed that ultimately brings a harvest. Sinking into self-pity, worrying, being anxious, and speaking negatively prevent God from helping us, but trusting Him and continuing to do good releases Him to work mightily.

We may know it is wrong to worry and yet continue worrying. We must realize that none of God's promises work for us until we actually obey His Word. Knowledge alone won't solve your problems, you must take action to be obedient no matter how you feel. You might not feel like keeping a commitment or doing something to help someone else, but do it anyway.

God's Word Teaches Us to Show Love at All Times

We must not use our personal problems as an excuse to be grouchy and unloving with other people. Always remember that we overcome evil with good (see Romans 12:21). So my advice is to trust God and do good, do good, and do good!

In the Bible Paul shares how even though he was suffering he was persuaded that God would take care of those things that he had entrusted to Him. Paul gave his problems to God and refused to worry. He encouraged the people to hold fast to what they had learned and to guard and keep the precious truth that had been entrusted to them by the Holy Spirit (see 2 Timothy 1:12–14). In other words, Paul said that we should trust God and keep doing what we know to do during hard times. The obedient person always experiences victory in the end. My simple formula for victory is trust God, don't worry, do good, and keep meditating on and confessing God's Word because it is the sword of the Spirit. With that sword, you will defeat Satan.

Many resources are available to help you find the Scriptures you need to meditate on and confess, including my book *The Secret Power of Speaking God's Word*, and the section titled "The Word for Your Everyday Life" in *The Everyday Life Bible*.

Think about It

What specific verses or passages from God's Word will you meditate on to help you stop worrying?

_____

_____

What commitments will you keep even though you might not feel like doing so?

_____

_____

Who do you know that you can help so you are "doing good" during your challenging times?

_____

_____

God Is Trustworthy

By confessing and meditating on this power thought, "I trust God completely; there is no need to worry," you will eventually form a new mind-set that will enable you to put your trust in God with ease. You will habitually look for what is good and magnify it. Life is very enjoyable when we learn to pray about everything and worry about nothing.

I want to encourage you not to get discouraged if forming new mind-sets seems difficult in the beginning. You may have to say that you will trust God and not worry one thousand times before you start to feel the effects of doing it. Just remember that each time you think and say the thing that agrees with God, you are making progress. Satan will relentlessly try to get you to give up, but if you will relentlessly keep doing what I am suggesting in this book, I guarantee that you will see the result in due time.

Most of us have practiced doing things the wrong way for years, and we must not expect everything to turn around in a few days or weeks. Renewing our minds is like reprogramming a computer. Two times in the past ten years we have had to install an entirely new computer system and I can tell you that it was not easy. It was vitally necessary in order for us to make progress as a ministry, but it was probably one of the most difficult times ever for our employees. They had to learn entirely new ways of processing information and it didn't always seem to work right immediately. Eventually the old ways were gone and the new was comfortable and much, much better—but everyone had to be patient!

We inherit the promises of God by faith and patience (see Hebrews 10:36). No matter how long it takes for you to renew your mind with these power thoughts, just keep at it. You are training your mind to work for you instead of against you. Don't forget that where the mind goes, the man follows.

Think about It

What specific situation(s) do you need to trust God with today?

_____

_____

Power Pack

"Come to Me, all you who labor and are heavy-laden and
overburdened, and I will cause you to rest.
[I will ease and relieve and refresh your souls.]"
Matthew 11:28

"But I say, walk and live [habitually] in the [Holy] Spirit
[responsive to and controlled and guided by the Spirit];
then you will certainly not gratify the cravings and
desires of the flesh (of human nature without God)."
Galatians 5:16

"Therefore humble yourselves [demote, lower yourselves
in your own estimation] under the mighty hand of God,
that in due time He may exalt you, casting the whole of
your care [all your anxieties, all your worries, all your
concerns, once and for all] on Him, for He cares for
you affectionately and cares about you watchfully."
1 Peter 5:6, 7

"And who of you by worrying and being
anxious can add one unit of measure (cubit)
to his stature or to the span of his life?"
Matthew 6:27

POWER THOUGHT

7

I am content and emotionally stable.

"Godliness accompanied with contentment
(that contentment which is a sense of inward
sufficiency) is great and abundant gain."
1 Timothy 6:6

One of the greatest things God has done in my life is help me become emotionally stable and consistently content. It was a long journey and I admit that it was not easy, but nothing is more tormenting than being controlled emotionally by outside forces. I look back and realize how much time and energy I wasted over the years being upset over things that I could not do anything about.

Dave and I spent many years with very limited finances and each time something happened that was unexpected, like an appliance repair, car repair, medical bill, or higher than usual utility bill, my first response was always to get upset and start saying all kinds of foolish things. I said things like, "We will never have any money, because something always happens to steal it," or "Nothing ever works out for us so why even try?" Dave, who is Mr. Content and Stable, tried to encourage me, but I always let my emotions rule.

Dave said things like, "Thank God we had the money to take care of this unexpected bill," or "Everything will be okay because God loves us and has a good plan for us." Deep down inside I knew he was right and that my behavior was childish, but I had very bad habits that ruled me in this area.

I grew up in an unstable household with people who always let circumstances control their moods, but Dave grew up with a godly mom who remained positive in the midst of great trials. Dave's mom gave me my first Bible and in the front cover she wrote Psalm 37:5, "Commit your way to the Lord, trust also in Him and He will bring it to pass." She obviously knew the value of remaining calm and letting God work.

Interestingly, my family's natural circumstances were much better than Dave's were, but our attitudes were much worse.

My parents owned their home, both had good jobs, their health was good, and they saved a little money. In comparison, Dave's circumstance was very needy. Most of their clothing was given to the family by people that Dave's mom cleaned house for. His dad died when he was sixteen and left his mom with eight children to provide for. They lived in a three-room apartment that had a basement room, but they knew God's love and their mom gave them a great example of contentment and stability. We don't have to let our circumstances control our moods unless we choose to.

In every aspect of life, Jesus is our example—and Jesus was emotionally stable. The Bible actually refers to Him as "the Rock," and we can depend on Him to be solid, steady, and stable—the same— all the time, always faithful, loyal, mature, and true to His Word. In fact, Hebrews 13:8 tells us that He is the same "yesterday, today, and forever." In other words, He is not in one kind of mood one day and in another mood the next day. We can count on Him to be the same today as He was yesterday and the same tomorrow as He is today. Being able to depend on Jesus' stability and consistency is part of what makes a relationship with Him seem attractive to us.

Part of the appeal of stability and contentment is the fact that they enable us to enjoy our lives. None of us really like to have moments or days when emotions sink and we sit around in self-pity, filled with negative thoughts. We don't enjoy ourselves when we are in that condition and no one else enjoys us either. Being in close relationship with anyone who is discontent, not dependable, and moody is extremely difficult. We can spend all of our time trying to keep them happy instead of being free to enjoy our own lives unless we realize we are not helping them by catering to their moods.

I have discovered that I like myself better when I am stable and consistent, and I believe the same is true for you. Becoming emotionally stable and consistent are so important to a powerful life, and as you grow in these qualities, you'll find yourself strengthened as never before.

The pathway to change is to renew your mind. I had to begin believing that I could be content and stable before I actually saw the fruit of it in my life. I studied contentment quite often and read a lot of material on emotions. I began to think and say that I was content and emotionally stable. God's Word states that we can and should call things that are not as if they already existed (see Romans 4:17). When we have faith in our heart, we think and talk faith. We see the thing done by faith before we see it in reality. In this way we cooperate with God in the spiritual realm. We reach into the realm of the Spirit with our thoughts and words and draw things out of it into the realm we live in.

Think about It

On a scale of 1 to 10 how would you rate your own emotional stability and contentment?

Emotions Are Here to Stay

We all have emotions, and we always will. They are part of being human. Since that is true, I believe emotional stability should be one of the main goals of every believer. We should seek God to learn how to manage our emotions and not allow them to manage us. An excerpt from the *Random House Dictionary* states that *emotions* are "any of the feelings of joy, sorrow, hate, love, etc." Think about this: You're out shopping for a specific item you're in need of. You've made a commitment to get out of debt. You've agreed to discipline yourself in the area of your spending and not purchase things you don't need. But while shopping, you discover that the stores are having a big sale—50 percent off merchandise that is already marked down. What do you do? You get excited. The more you look around, the more excited you get. Emotions are rising higher and higher. They begin to move out—because part of the devil's plan to ruin your life is for you to follow your emotions.

An emotional person is defined as: "one easily affected with or stirred by emotion; one who displays emotion; one with a tendency to rely on or place too much value on emotion; one whose conduct is ruled by emotion rather than reason." I couldn't agree more with that definition, and I want to add several personal observations I have made about people who are not stable emotionally:

- A person who lives by emotions lives without principle.
- You cannot be spiritual (walk in the Spirit) and be led by emotions.
- Emotions won't go away, but you can learn to manage them.
- You can have emotions, but you can't always rely on them.

I urge you to make emotional maturity a priority in your life. If you do not believe you are doing a good job managing your emotions, begin to pray and seek God for emotional maturity. I also encourage you to learn what upsets you the most or prompts you to behave emotionally and watch out for those temptations.

To help you get started, let me mention several Scriptures:

- Jeremiah 17:8 and Psalm 1:3 both instruct us to be like trees firmly planted.
- First Peter 5:8, 9 teaches us to be well-balanced and temperate (self-controlled) to keep Satan from devouring us. According

to these verses, if we want to withstand him, we need to be rooted, established, strong, immovable, and determined.

- Philippians 1:28 tells us to be constantly fearless when Satan comes against us.
- Psalm 94:13 says God wants to give us power to stay calm in adversity.

All of these Scriptures are referring to being stable, so I encourage you to read them, meditate on them, and allow them to become ingrained in your thinking.

Think about It

In what ways can you begin to become more stable emotionally?

_____

_____

Level Out Your Ups and Downs

I'm sure you can tell by now that I believe some of life's greatest challenges involve or result from the ups and downs of our emotions. Think about roller coasters. If you measured the length of a roller coaster track, you'd find that the distance it covers is far greater than the distance between where you get on and where you step off. By the time the ride is over, you've spent a great deal of time speeding to great heights and swooping to deep lows. On a roller coaster many people think that is entertaining, but if we let our emotions do that in everyday life, I can assure you that it is exhausting.

Instead of riding the emotional roller coaster, which only exhausts us, we need to become stable, solid, steadfast, persevering, determined people. Renewing your mind to think and believe that you are stable and content will help you get started. We can never enjoy any of God's promises until we believe them for ourselves. In the world, we believe what we see, but in God's kingdom we believe and then we see.

If we continue to let our emotions rule over us, there's no way we'll ever be the people we were meant to be. It does no good to merely *wish* that you were not so emotional. A choice must be made to change by completely renewing your mind. None of us will ever be totally rid of emotions and we don't need to eliminate them from our lives, but we must learn to manage and control them—not allow them to control or have power over us. Emotions are not all bad, some of them are very enjoyable but they are rather fickle. You can feel one hundred ways in thirty days about the same thing.

Feelings change from day to day, hour to hour, sometimes even moment to moment. Not only do they change, they lie. For example, you may be in a crowd of people and *feel* everybody is talking about you, but that doesn't mean they are. You may *feel* nobody understands you, but that doesn't mean they don't. You may *feel* you are not well liked, unappreciated, or even mistreated, but that doesn't mean it is true. If you want to be a mature, disciplined, well-balanced person, you must be *determined* not to walk according to what you *feel*. If I am having a "touchy" day, I might feel people are not treating me very well, but in reality they are not treating me any differently than they always do—I am just more emotionally sensitive that day and things affect me differently than normal.

People often ask me, "How can I learn contentment and stability?" There are actually two answers and they are both straight out of the Bible. What are they? Patience and self-control!

Patience

God wants us to use wisdom, and wisdom encourages patience. Wisdom says, "Wait a little while, until the emotions settle down, before you do or say something, then check to see if you really believe it's the right thing to do." Emotions urge us toward haste, telling us that we must do something and do it right now! But godly wisdom tells us to be patient and wait until we have a clear picture of what we are to do and when we are to do it. We need to be able to step back from our situations and see them from God's perspective. Then we need to make decisions based on what we *know* rather than on what we *feel*.

Self-control

God has given us a free will and that means we have the privilege to choose what we will do and what we won't do. As believers in Jesus Christ, God has given us a new nature, but at the same time we also have to deal with the old nature. The Bible states that we are to "put off" the old nature and "put on" the new nature. That is actually another way of saying we have choices to make. When we allow the old nature to rule, we will follow feelings when in reality we should operate in self-control. Self-control is a fruit of our new nature and all we need to do is develop it. We can develop self-control by using it, just as we can develop muscles by using them.

Exercising self-control is a form of freedom, not a type of bondage. You don't have to do what you feel like doing. You're free to do what you know is wise. Discipline and self-control will help you be what you say you want to be, but never will be without the help of self-control.

Practicing self-control will help you feel better about yourself; you will have more self-respect. You will also have more energy when you don't allow your emotions to control you. When I was experiencing so many ups and downs, it actually made me physically tired. Going through all kinds of emotional changes takes a lot of energy. As God helped me learn to manage my emotions, I noticed that I also had more energy. If you have been tired lately, maybe you should stop and ask the Lord if the reason could be that you allow your emotions to manage you rather than you managing them.

Let me share a simple, everyday example about patience and self-control from my life. One time, I had saved up money to buy a good watch. I wanted a nice watch so the band wouldn't change colors and turn my wrist green. One day, Dave and I were in the mall and happened to stop at a jewelry store, where I saw a watch that was very pretty. When we looked at it, we discovered that it was gold-plated. We knew it would probably eventually discolor, but it was pretty and sparkled a lot and I really liked it. Not only that, but the clerk offered to lower the price. So my emotions said, "Yes! That's exactly what I want!"

But Dave said, "Well, you know it's gold-plated, and it will eventually discolor."

I said, "I know but I really like this watch. What should I do?"

"It's your money," he answered.

"I'll tell you what I'm going to do," I said to the clerk. "I'd like for you to hold the watch for me while I walk around the mall for a bit. If I want the watch, I'll come back for it within the hour."

So Dave and I walked around the mall for a while. As we did, we passed a dress shop. Because I needed a couple of new outfits, I went in and found a really nice suit. I tried it on, and it fit perfectly. I loved it.

"That's a nice suit," Dave observed. "You ought to get it."

I looked at the price tag and thought, *It costs a lot more than I thought it would.* But I really wanted the suit! Actually there were three things I wanted right then. I wanted the watch; I wanted the suit; and I wanted *not* to be broke. What did I do? I applied wisdom and decided to wait. The watch—which really wasn't of the quality I wanted—would have taken all of the money I had saved. The suit was beautiful, but again I would have needed to use most of my money. I decided that the best thing was to keep my money and wait until I was sure of what I wanted most. Had I made an emotional decision, I would have bought the watch when I saw it, rather than take time to think over my purchase and exercise self-control by not buying it impulsively. Usually the wisest course is *when in doubt, don't!* The excitement you feel in the shopping mall will fade away once you get the item home, so that had better not be the basis of your purchasing decision.

When faced with decisions, especially major ones or difficult ones, practice self-control and wait until you have a clear answer before taking a step you might regret. Remember to be led by peace, not excitement. Emotions can be wonderful when managed and handled in a godly way, but they must not be allowed to take precedence over wisdom and knowledge. Let me say again, "Control your emotions and don't let them control you." Start thinking and saying, "I am content and emotionally stable."

Think about It

In what area do you need to practice patience and exercise self-control in your life right now?

_____

_____

Stable People Get Promoted

Many people feel able and qualified to do a particular thing, and yet they live frustrated lives because the right doors don't ever seem to open for them. Their opportunities never come. Why? While there is no single, succinct answer, I do want to offer some insights I believe God taught me that I hope will be helpful to you.

I believe many people are "able but not stable." God has given them abilities, but they have not made the effort to mature in stability of character. Moses was a wonderful man of God; but he had an anger problem. Eventually God refused to let him lead the Israelites into the Promised Land because of his lack of stability in that area. So, I believe it is fair to say that his instability blocked his ability.

God must be able to trust us; and other people must be able to depend on us. When we are stable and mature in character, we do what we say we will do no matter how we happen to feel. Even if we feel grouchy, we don't behave in unpleasant ways. We realize taking out a foul mood on the people around us is not right or mature. We continue to operate in the fruit of the Spirit even when we must endure circumstances and people that are not what we would like them to be. The apostle Paul said he had learned to be content whether he was getting what he wanted or not (see Philippians 4:11). I think he learned that being upset and cranky did no good, so he simply made the decision to trust God and go ahead and enjoy the day, regardless of his circumstance.

Life is not problem free, and it never will be. You will only find one group of people who are problem free, and you have to go to your local graveyard to find them. As long as we are breathing, we are going to have times of abundance and times when we struggle, times when circumstances are up and times when they're down. Let circumstances do what they will—and as far as you're concerned, be determined to remain stable.

Think about It

Do you have an area of instability that could be hindering your promotion in life?

_____

_____

Sources of Discontent

I often think about why so many people in the world, especially Christians, are discontent. Discontentment and emotional instability go hand in hand. I have found that if I am discontent, then I easily get upset, but if I choose to be content no matter what is going on, then my emotions are balanced also.

We have periods of contentment, but being *consistently* content is another matter entirely. I think it is safe to say that I only know a small group of people I would consider to be consistently peaceful and joyful and consistently content. I believe our thoughts have a lot to do with our moods. Some thoughts improve our moods and increase our level of contentment, and others send them spiraling downward, making us unhappy and discontent. We can think ourselves happy and we can think ourselves sad! Since this book is about the power of meditating on certain thoughts, let's apply the principle to contentment. How we talk to ourselves definitely affects our emotions, so if I talk to myself properly, I can stay content and emotionally stable.

One of the main thought patterns that causes discontentment is focusing on what we don't have and what people are not doing for us. When we think about what we are not and begin to compare ourselves with other people, we also become discontent. On the other hand, when we get ourselves and our needs and desires off of our minds, life always looks brighter.

We must choose to think about how blessed we are. Just a few days ago I was talking to the Lord and pondering my blessings in life and I had a fresh revelation of how blessed I really am and of all God has done for me in my life. Had I been thinking about what I did not have, and what I still need, that moment of realization would have evaded me.

The apostle James writes about another source of discontentment when he states that we are discontent because we try to get what we want for ourselves rather than asking God for it and trusting Him completely. We see what others have and become jealous, which creates discontentment in our hearts. We should only want what God wants us to have and we should trust Him enough to believe that if we ask for something and don't get it, the only reason is that He has something better in mind for us. When we pray, we also need to realize that a delay is not always a denial.

The apostle Paul told Timothy that godliness with contentment is great gain, something to be desired and sought after (see 1 Timothy 6:6). I fear that we seek many things that do us no lasting good and often fail to seek the things that will truly satisfy us. The Bible says in Psalm 92:14, 15 that the righteous will bring forth fruit in old age—the fruit of trust, love, and contentment—and that these fruits will be living memorials to show that the Lord is upright and faithful. I believe that totally trusting God and loving people is the pathway to contentment, so it is interesting to me to find them linked together in this passage. Clearly, not trusting God and not loving people are sources of discontentment and will make us unhappy.

I have seen people who at the end of their life only had regret about the way they had lived and felt no satisfaction and contentment, but I think it is beautiful to see an elderly person who says, "My life has been good. When it is time for me to die, I can die happy." People who are discontent have never developed a habit of being appreciative and thankful. Honestly, just to be able to walk, see, and hear is a great blessing and one that people who are crippled, blind, or deaf would be extremely content with. If you were in the hospital you would be content just to sit in your own home in your favorite chair. We always think we will be content when... but why not choose to be content right now?

Even if you don't have what you want or need right now, keep a positive attitude and remain hopeful. "Hope deferred makes the heart sick" (Proverbs 13:12), but those who refuse to give up hope remain joyful. Be content with what you have, refuse to focus on what you don't have; love others; and stay hopeful concerning what you want and need.

Think about It

What are your blessings? List five.

_____

_____

What have you been complaining about lately?

_____

_____

Are you jealous of anyone or anything they have?

_____

_____

Make a List

To help you achieve and maintain a new level of contentment in your life, I encourage you to make a list of everything you have to be thankful for. It should be a long list, one that includes little things as well as big things. Why should it be long? Because we all have a *lot* to be thankful for if we just look for it.

Just the other day I was thinking about my elbow, which has been hurting for quite a while. I thought about how tired I am of the physical therapy I have had to take for it and of the doctor visits concerning it. But, then I thought about my age, how well I feel most of the time, and how many of my body parts have absolutely nothing wrong with them. I thought of all the really desperately sick people in the world and of all of the hospitals that are filled with people who have pain and disease—and I started to feel very blessed indeed. You see, it is simple, when I focused on what hurt, I felt sorry for myself; but when I focused on what works well and what is pain-free, I suddenly felt very blessed. I was aggravated about needing to get physical therapy for an elbow, but then I remembered that at least I wasn't receiving chemotherapy or radiation to fight cancer, and suddenly I felt much better. I wasn't happy about my elbow, but my level of contentment increased dramatically. I know the elbow will get well and that God will give me the ability to do whatever I need to do in the meantime because I have meditated on the power thought suggested in this book, "I can do whatever I need to do in life."

Deborah Norville tells a story in her book *Thank You Power: Making the Science of Gratitude Work for You* about a man named David, who found himself discouraged. He had moved to Manhattan with high hopes of landing a well-paying job and living in a nice apartment, only to end up with a meager salary as an assistant and living with a friend because he couldn't afford a place of his own.

One Saturday morning, while out on a job assignment, David decided to start counting things that made him happy. He started by smiling at the sight of a mother walking her baby, then realized seeing a jet make its way across the sky made him happy. He noticed fabulous aromas from cafés he passed, and enjoyed bright, colorful displays in store windows. By the time he completed his assignment, he was once again happy—and he was actually thankful he had moved to New York.

More than twenty years later, David is a successful entrepreneur, but he's never forgotten the day that turned his life around—the day he learned about the power of being thankful.[1]

Get out a piece of paper right now and start listing things you have to be thankful for. Keep the list and add to it frequently. Make it a point to think about the things that you're grateful for when you're driving the kids to an activity or waiting in line at the post office. You can only learn the "power of thank you" by practicing it. The Bible says we are to be thankful and say so. Meditating on what you have to be thankful for every day and verbalizing it will be amazingly helpful to you. Next time you have lunch or coffee with a friend, purpose to talk about the things you are thankful for instead of recounting all of your problems. Or, at the very least, if you do need to talk about a problem, be sure to follow up with things you are thankful for. By doing this you will at least keep things somewhat balanced and in perspective.

Think about It

In what specific situation do you need to begin to practice the power of thank you?

Sounds Good, Doesn't It?

Do you want to be emotionally stable and consistently content? If that sounds good to you, you can think yourself into it. Stop meditating on wrong things, getting upset and then thinking and talking about how unstable and discontent you are and repeating that cycle over and over again. Start thinking and saying, "I am emotionally stable and consistently content. No matter what is going on in my circumstances, I am able to remain calm and loving while I trust God to take care of it."

How do you see yourself? What do you want to be? Where do you want to be this time next year in spiritual growth? Make some decisions and start ordering your life instead of letting it order you. Come into agreement with God and His Word. Think what He thinks and say what He says. Will it be easy? Probably not, but it will be worth it. Will you ever backslide in your commitment to think and say positive things? Yes, you probably will, but always remember that when babies are learning how to walk, they may fall down and cry but they always get back up and try again. We are like babies any time we try something new. Thinking your own thoughts and choosing them carefully and purposefully may be new for you. If so, then you are in the baby stages. Just remember, when you fall, all you have to do is get up and try again.

Meditating on this power thought for at least one week will help renew your mind to the idea that stability and contentment are important and to be desired. It may (and probably will) take longer than one week for this principle to become rooted in your life, but start with one week and after you finish the twelve power thoughts, go back through them again and again until you find yourself with a new life that you enjoy much more than you did the old one. First we realize we should be stable and content, and then we begin to believe that we can be, and then we actually become what we believe.

Think about how wonderful it will be to get off the roller coaster of emotions that make us joyful one day and suddenly steal our joy the next. Up one moment and down the next...up and down...up and down! It is not the way Jesus wants us to live. It is not the life He died to give us. Take steps today to embrace and enjoy the life He has for you—and that includes being content and emotionally stable.

Think about It

In what specific ways do you want to grow in emotional stability? For example, do you want to become more patient, more peaceful, more secure in who you are? Do you want to learn to remain calm and respond appropriately to crises, instead of overreacting?

Power Pack

"[And it is, indeed, a source of immense profit, for] godliness accompanied with contentment (that contentment which is a sense of inward sufficiency) is great and abundant gain."
1 Timothy 6:6

"I have learned how to be content (satisfied to the point where I am not disturbed or disquieted) in whatever state I am."
Philippians 4:11

"Thank [God] in everything [no matter what the circumstances may be, be thankful and give thanks], for this is the will of God for you [who are] in Christ Jesus [the Revealer and Mediator of that will]."
1 Thessalonians 5:18

POWER THOUGHT

8

God meets all my needs abundantly.

"Beloved, I pray that you may prosper in every
way and [that your body] may keep well, even as
[I know] your soul keeps well and prospers."
3 John 2

I believe it is important to develop what I call an abundant mind-set—one that believes God will always provide whatever we need in every situation. This is God's promise throughout Scripture, and part of His nature is to provide for His children. In fact, in the Old Testament, one of the Hebrew names of God is "Jehovah-Jireh," which means, "The Lord Our Provider."

You and I are God's children. He is our Father, and He delights in providing for us just as natural parents delight in helping their children. Dave and I have four children. They love us; we love them; and so we share all we have with them. We could not even imagine leaving them in need while we enjoy abundance—and God is certainly much better at parenting than we are.

God owns everything and is able to do anything. Psalm 24:1 says, "The earth is the Lord's, and the fullness of it" and in Psalm 50:10–12, He Himself says, "For every beast of the forest is Mine, and the cattle upon a thousand hills or upon the mountains where thousands are. I know and am acquainted with all the birds of the mountains, and the wild animals of the field are Mine . . . If I were hungry, I would not tell you, for the world and its fullness are Mine." Clearly, all the resources of heaven and earth are at His disposal, so there is nothing we need that He cannot provide. He loves us and wants to take care of us. If we love Him and do our best to progressively learn and obey His ways, He will make sure our needs are met. In fact, there is no one He would rather share His blessings with than His children.

Think about It

Do you believe God loves you and wants to provide for you?

_____

_____

How has He provided for you in the past?

_____

_____

More than Money

Paul promised the believers who were partners in his ministry that God would liberally supply all of their needs according to His riches in glory in Christ Jesus (see Philippians 4:19). He didn't promise God would give them everything they wanted, but he did assure them God would meet their every need.

Many times, we think of needs in terms of the basic necessities of life—food, shelter, clothing, and finances to purchase these things. These represent our physical needs, but I believe God created us to need more than these essentials. Our needs are varied. We don't simply need money, nourishment, a roof over our heads, and clothes to wear. We also need wisdom, strength, health, friends, and loved ones; and we need the gifts and talents and abilities to help us do what we are supposed to do in life. We need many things, and God is willing to meet *all* of our needs as we obey and trust Him. We must believe that He wants to provide for us. We should develop an expectant mind-set in this area.

The people Paul wrote to in Philippians were partners in his ministry and they helped him financially. They were obeying the law of sowing and reaping (see Galatians 6:7). We cannot expect to reap where we have not sown, but when we do sow good seeds, we should indeed expect good results. This is true in every area of our lives, including health, finances, abilities, relationships, and everything else that pertains to our well-being.

If we sow good seeds by respecting our physical bodies, feeding it nutritious food and drinking ample water, giving it plenty of sleep, and eliminating excessive stress, we can expect to reap a harvest of good health. If we sow mercy, we will reap mercy; if we sow judgment, we will reap judgment. If we forgive, we will be forgiven. If we are friendly, we will have friends. If we are generous, we will experience generosity returned. The law of sowing and reaping is one of the most simple to understand and one that produces great power in our lives. Just think about it...if you need friends all you have to do is be friendly!

What Is Prosperity?

John D. Rockefeller, Jr., once said, "I know of nothing more despicable and pathetic than a man who devotes all the hours of the waking day to the making of money for money's sake."

The truth is a person is never truly prosperous if all he has is a lot of money; real prosperity requires far more than that. The apostle John writes, "Beloved, I pray that you may prosper in every way and [that your body] may keep well, even as [I know] your soul keeps well and prospers" (3 John 2). Obviously, John had a holistic approach to prosperity, and so should we. He didn't even mention money, but focused on the body and the soul. When our bodies prosper, we are strong and physically healthy. Even if we currently have a physical ailment we can pray for and expect healing, but we need to sow good seed by taking care of ourselves and not abusing our bodies.

When our souls prosper, we flourish on the inside. We are at peace; we are full of joy; we are content; we live with a sense of destiny and purpose; we are growing spiritually; and we have strong, loving relationships with others.

God is a god of abundance and He wants us to live abundant lives. Jesus said that He came so we could have and enjoy life in abundance and to the full (see John 10:10).

Is It Wrong to Want Money?

We need money! We need it for housing, clothes, education, food, automobiles, entertainment, and many other things. Actually, if I think about it, most of the places I go, money is exchanged for some goods or services. It is not wrong to want money. It is not evil; it is the love of money that is a root of all evil (see 1 Timothy 6:10). Not only does money meet our needs, but it can be used to bless others, especially those who have needs and no way to meet those needs. People contribute money to our ministry and it enables us to preach the Gospel in thirty-eight languages in approximately two-thirds of the world. It also enables us to feed the hungry, provide safe drinking water, fund orphanages, visit prisons, and hundreds of other things that help people.

It is not God's will for wicked people to have all the money in the world while His people are constantly needy. We should be good stewards of what God gives us, and good investors. I believe we should respect money and never waste it. Proverbs says over and over that we should be prudent and that means being good managers.

There is a well-known Bible story about three men who were given talents (money) according to their ability to handle them. The man who received the most was given about five thousand dollars. He invested it and returned to his master the original five and five more besides. His master complimented him, telling him that he did a good job and would be put in charge of much (see Matthew 25:14–28). As I read this story it is obvious to me that God expects us to be wise investors and if we are He rewards us. We should never love money or be greedy for gain, but we should do the best we can with what we have. Use money in the service of God and man and never try to use God or man to get money! Money is only a small portion of prosperity, but we do need it and it is not wrong to ask God to supply it abundantly.

Think about It

Do you have a healthy, well-balanced attitude toward prosperity?

No More Needy Mind-sets

Many people fail to enjoy the abundance God has for them because they have an "I'm needy" mind-set. They are constantly afraid they won't have enough of whatever resources they need. They don't believe they are strong enough to do what they need to do; they don't believe they will have enough money to meet their financial obligations; they don't believe anyone will care for them in their old age. They are afraid they will lose their jobs and not be able to find another. In fact, most of their thinking may be dominated by fear. They feel they need more friends; they need more love, and they need more energy. People with this "I need, I need, I need" mentality feel deprived spiritually, mentally, physically, financially, and socially. Sometimes people who are plagued by feelings of neediness have truly been needy at some point in their lives. These experiences cause them to be fearful of lack or loss, and that fear causes them to think they will never have enough, so they may even begin to live narrow, stingy lives.

The Great Depression in the 1930s produced an entire genera-
tion of people who were terribly fearful of loss and lack. This tragic
period in history made an almost irreversible impression on some
people, who spent the rest of their lives doing things like saving
little pieces of aluminum foil because they remembered times
of frightening scarcity, times when what they used could not be
replenished. When days of prosperity returned, many people failed
to renew the mind-sets they formed during the Depression. Anytime we go through a season of lack, it is easy to become fearful,
but it is during those times that we can trust God to meet our
needs. If you are in a season of economic downturn right now, I
strongly encourage you to realize that it will eventually pass and
you will enter a new season. Keep trusting God to help you and
boldly expect to prosper in all areas of life. If you need employment, then expect God to favor you when you look for a job.

Some people feel needy because of the conditions or attitudes
of the families in which they grew up; others feel needy because
of personal experiences in which they suffered loss. All of these
circumstances and others cause people to be afraid they will not
have enough—and this is not what God wants. He doesn't want
us to live in fear of losing what we have or being without what we
need. In fact, I think acting as if God will not meet our needs or
doesn't want us to have our needs met is rather insulting to Him.
We should compliment Him by believing He is good and by expecting Him to meet our needs according to the promises in His Word.

Fearing we will not have what we need is exactly what Satan
wants. We can open the door to his will through fear just as we can
open the door to God's will through faith.

Throughout my teenage and young adult years, I had to take care
of myself. I could not ask my parents for any more than I absolutely
had to because of the sexual abuse I was experiencing. If I asked
my father for anything, there was always "payback" of some kind
demanded, so to avoid that situation I either provided for myself
or I did without. This period of time in my life left me with a fear
of not having enough, so when I did have anything, I was afraid to
use it for fear it would not be there in case of a real emergency. You

might say that I lived in great fear. I was afraid I would never have what I needed and even when I did have it, I was afraid to use or enjoy it. Coming to the realization that God delighted in providing for me and that He wanted me to enjoy what He gave me was quite amazing to me and I must admit that it took me a while to be able to develop a new mind-set in this area.

Remember, the mind is the battlefield and Satan loves to put wrong thoughts into our minds, thoughts that are not in agreement with God's Word, hoping we will meditate on them long enough for them to become reality in our lives. Cast down those wrong thoughts and bring every thought captive into the obedience of Jesus Christ (see 2 Corinthians 10:5). Instead, think of yourself as a child of God, a person God loves and is glad to provide for. Sow good seed by helping others in need, and say things that build within you the image of a person whose needs are met instead of the image of someone who is always needy. Here is a list of things you might consider thinking and saying to yourself:

- All of my needs are met according to God's riches in Christ Jesus (see Philippians 4:19).
- God blesses me and makes me a blessing to others (see Genesis 12:2).
- I give and it is given unto me, good measure, pressed down, shaken together and running over (see Luke 6:38).
- God richly and ceaselessly provides everything for my enjoyment (see 1 Timothy 6:17).
- I serve God and He takes pleasure in my prosperity (see Psalm 35:27).

We receive from God according to our faith so it is vital for us to develop a correct mind-set in the area of God's provision for us. Don't settle for lack in your life, but instead expect abundance according to God's Word.

Think about It

Has being needy at some time in your life developed a fear in you that you will never have enough?

Great Expectations

I like the old German proverb that says, "Begin to weave and God will provide the thread." Making sure we are confident in God, eliminating any "needy" mentalities we might have, developing an abundant mind-set, and aggressively expecting God to be faithful to His nature and to meet our needs opens the door for Him to work in our lives. The Bible teaches us that God is waiting to bless people, but He is looking for someone who is expecting His favor (see Isaiah 30:18).

Sometimes we expect nothing; we merely wait to see what happens. At other times, we may fall into the trap of expecting to be disappointed because we have been disappointed time and time again in the past and we are afraid to hope for anything good. Because of the traumas I experienced early in life, I became extremely negative as an adult in my outlook on life. I was always waiting for the next disaster, and I expected it to be right around the corner. I am so glad God has taught me to aggressively expect good things to happen in my life. My life is not without challenges, but I enjoy a lot more good things than bad ones. When I expected trouble, I often got it, but now that I expect good, I often get that. Sometimes I even get better than what I have hoped for or expected because that's the way God is. He gives us exceedingly, abundantly, above and beyond all that we dare to hope, ask, or think (see Ephesians 3:20).

Let me share with you a story I hope will encourage you to believe God can do more for you than you think. Prior to the Civil

War, a man named Edmund McIlhenny ran a salt and sugar business on Avery Island, Louisiana. A Union invasion in 1863 forced him to leave his home and business, and when he returned in 1865, he found his sugar fields and saltworks completely devastated. He had almost nothing left—except some hot peppers that still grew in his garden. McIlhenny began to experiment with the peppers, to see if he could make a sauce to add taste to the bland foods he had left to eat. His sauce is now known as Tabasco® and in 2008, the sauce, still produced by the McIlhenny family, celebrated its 140th anniversary.

McIlhenny lost everything in the war; his life could have been ruined. But it wasn't. God took care of him, and God will take care of you too if you won't give up.

Begin to meditate on and say, "God abundantly meets all of my needs. I expect Him to provide for me in every area of my life. He has a good plan for me and I am expecting a great future." See yourself as someone who operates in wisdom and has the answers that are needed to make proper decisions in life. See yourself as a healthy person who is filled with energy and vitality. Believe that you are creative and have lots of good ideas. Expect to be invited to social gatherings and have many good friends, as well as a loving family. God wants you to expect good things from Him. He promises in Jeremiah 29:11 that He has thoughts and plans toward you that are good and not evil. Take Him at His Word, and have great expectations of Him.

Think about It

What are you expecting?

God Wants to Bless You

Some people have been taught that suffering and being needy are virtues in the Christian life. Being able to maintain a good attitude during times of suffering is a virtue and it is very important, but continual suffering is not God's will for anybody. The apostle Paul stated that he had times of being abased and times of abounding. We will go through difficulties in this life but we can and should expect God's deliverance and a return to an abundant life.

We must never see God as a stingy god who would withhold anything we need. Certainly, there are times when we don't get what we want when we want it, but if that happens, God has a good reason. Perhaps the timing isn't right, or we are not mature enough to handle it yet or He has something better in mind, something we don't know how to ask for, but it is never because He doesn't want us to be blessed. That thought simply isn't consistent with who He is.

If you have any doubts or questions about the fact that God wants to bless you, I want to help you because I want you to agree with Him in this area of your life. The best way to do that is to show you what God Himself says. His words are anointed to bring transformation to your thinking and change to your life, so take a look at them and ask Him to use them to shift you into a place of complete confidence in His desire to provide for you and to bless you abundantly.

- "This Book of the Law shall not depart out of your mouth, but you shall meditate on it day and night, that you may observe and do according to all that is written in it. For then you shall make your way prosperous, and then you shall deal wisely and have good success." (Joshua 1:8)
- "Blessed (happy, fortunate, prosperous, and enviable) is the man who walks and lives not in the counsel of the ungodly... but his delight and desire are in the law of the Lord, and on His law (the precepts, the instructions, the teachings of God)

he habitually meditates...everything he does shall prosper [and come to maturity]." (Psalm 1:1–3)

- "The Lord is my Shepherd [to feed, guide, and shield me], I shall not lack." (Psalm 23:1)
- "The young lions lack food and suffer hunger, but they who seek (inquire of and require) the Lord [by right of their need and on the authority of His Word], none of them shall lack any beneficial thing." (Psalm 34:10)
- "Let the Lord be magnified, Who takes pleasure in the prosperity of His servant." (Psalm 35:27)
- "He will bless those who reverently and worshipfully fear the Lord, both small and great." (Psalm 115:13)
- "And why should you be anxious about clothes? Consider the lilies of the field...they neither toil nor spin....If God so clothes the grass of the field, which today is alive and green and tomorrow is tossed into the furnace, will He not much more surely clothe you, O you of little faith?" (Matthew 6:28–30)
- "The thief comes only in order to steal and kill and destroy. I came that they may have and enjoy life, and have it in abundance (to the full, till it overflows)." (John 10:10)

Think about It

Which of the Scriptures in this section speaks most to your heart or seems most appropriate for you right now?

_____

_____

I encourage you to memorize and meditate on it.

I Learned a Lesson

I know firsthand the power of God's Word and Scriptures like those mentioned above to completely change the way we think. Like many other people, I needed God's Word to do a major work in my thinking in the area of blessings and provision. Before I understood the power of thoughts, words, and actions, I had what I call a "cheap spirit." I always paid the lowest possible price for everything I bought. I shopped at rummage sales, discount stores, and even dug in the "dented-can basket" at the grocery store, hoping to catch sales and find good bargains. I bought day-old bread and off-brands. You might be thinking, *So you were frugal. What's wrong with that?* The answer is, absolutely nothing. The problem is that I went way beyond frugality. I saw myself as someone who could never afford the good stuff. I lived with the fear that if I spent the money I had, we would run out and not have enough.

My husband, on the other hand, saw the situation from the completely opposite point of view. He did not spend money he didn't have, but if he had it, he certainly wasn't afraid to purchase what he needed and he always believed in getting the best quality he could afford instead of the cheapest thing he could find. We had many arguments about this particular subject and one day, while he was frustrated with me, he said, "God is never going to be able to really bless us until you get rid of this cheap attitude." What he said made me angry, but he was right! God cannot give us abundance if we have no vision for it.

On a different occasion, we had an experience that taught me another valuable lesson. We needed a new car. I wanted a certain kind, but when we went car shopping I was afraid to purchase what I really wanted. Instead, I said that I felt we should purchase a cheaper model. Dave felt strongly that I should get the car I really wanted because we could afford it. I reasoned that, even though we could afford it, we would have more money left over each month if I settled for the car I didn't like nearly as much but knew I could get by with.

The payment for the car I really wanted was about fifty dollars a month more than the one I would have settled for, and eventually Dave won out and we got the more expensive model. I loved the car and felt really good driving it. To my amazement, about two weeks after we purchased it, I received an unexpected pay raise and what I cleared after taxes was almost exactly fifty dollars a month.

The "cheap" attitude I described in this story affected every area of my life. I thought the way I thought at the car lot all the time— constantly reasoning and talking myself into buying or taking less than I wanted and could afford. The result was that I always felt deprived, but in reality, I was depriving myself. I believe God used this situation to help me break my unhealthy thought pattern. I firmly believe now that had I settled for the one I thought I could get by with, that I would have never gotten the raise I received. So often God wants to give us one of the desires of our hearts and He cannot do so because we refuse to have it. We think it is too good for us or we try so hard to take care of our own future that we live in fear and won't use what God has given us to enjoy in the present.

Let me be clear: I am not suggesting that looking for a bargain is a bad thing or that going to a garage sale means that I have a cheap attitude. I like a good sale as well as anybody, but I don't let it rule all of my purchases any longer. I have a good friend who goes to resale shops as a hobby. She and her mom will spend most of the day going from place to place and the bargains they get amaze me. They have fun and enjoy it; they don't go out of fear like I did.

I also want to be clear that I am not suggesting that people spend money they don't have or go into debt to buy things they cannot afford. Concerning our finances, we should always save some, give some, and spend some. Never spend all you have, but don't be afraid to spend what you need to in order to have some things you will enjoy. Pray about large purchases and, if you have the money and believe God approves of the item you plan to buy, then do so without fear or feeling guilty.

I strongly urge anyone with the same problem I had to begin seeing yourself in a new way. You are valuable and should have nice things. God wants to bless you, but you need a healthy self-image.

See yourself with your needs met; say that God meets them; and get ready to come up to a new level of abundance in your life.

Think about It

Do you have a "cheap attitude"?

_____

_____

How can you begin to develop a mind-set of abundance?

_____

_____

Be Equipped to Meet Needs

When I talk about prosperity, I like to say we need to have "prosperity with a purpose." As I wrote in Power Thought 5, God blesses us so we can bless others. He does not want us to be needy; He wants us to be equipped to help people who are in need, and we cannot do that if all we are experiencing is lack. When we don't have enough to meet our own needs and the needs of our families or others for whom we are responsible, then it is very difficult to help other people in need. This is one reason God promises to provide for us and to do so abundantly.

To help other people, we need strength, good health, and clarity of mind. We need money to help people who are struggling financially. We need clothes to be able to share with people who need them. In 2 Corinthians 9:8, Paul teaches us that "God is able to make all grace (every favor and earthly blessing) come to you in abundance, so that you may always and under all circumstances and whatever the need be self-sufficient [possessing enough to require no aid or support and furnished in abundance for every good work and charitable donation]." The following verses say that God gives seed to a person who is willing to sow (see 2 Corinthians 9:9, 10). This means, if you are willing to share with others and meet their needs, God will not only meet your needs, He will give you an abundance of supply so you will always be able to give.

I encourage you to develop the mind-set that you are a generous giver. Look for ways to give and for needy people to whom you can give. The more you reach out to others, the happier you will be. Jesus said that we would always have the poor with us (see Matthew 26:11), and the Bible has more than two thousand Scriptures that deal with our responsibility to the poor and needy. Study what the Bible says about God's provision and see yourself as one who meets needs rather than one who is needy.

Live with an attitude of expectancy. King David said, "[What, what would have become of me] had I not believed that I would see the Lord's goodness in the land of the living!" (Psalm 27:13). To live expectantly is not the same as living with a sense of entitlement, which is an attitude that we deserve everything without doing anything. We don't deserve anything from God, but in His mercy He wants us to live in holy expectancy so we can receive His best.

Expect bargains, but don't settle for something you don't really like just to get it for less money if you are able to pay more and get what you truly desire. Here is an example: I can remember going to buy a pair of shoes, finding what I really liked at the first store, but because they were not on sale I would spend several more hours going from store to store, trying to find them cheaper. When I finally saw what I was doing, it became apparent that my attitude was foolish because even if I found some shoes for less money, I had already spent what I saved in time and gas money looking for what I perceived as a bargain. Not only that, but I rarely liked them as much as the first pair and ended up feeling deprived. Even if you have been needy all of your life, that can change if you will do your part. Your part is to obey God, sow good seeds, have a vision of abundance and think and say right things that agree with God's Word—and be persistent. Do what you have to right now because you cannot spend what you don't have, but don't believe you are stuck there forever.

I believe this is an important area and one where Satan fights hard to keep people deceived. He wants us to feel deprived because that ultimately produces self-pity, jealousy, envy, and a general feeling of discontent. You must be ready to be persistent in developing a new mind-set in this area. Meditate on and confess, "God meets all my needs abundantly." As you continue doing this you will develop a healthy mind-set that will enable you to prosper in all areas.

I want to close this chapter with a passage of Scripture for you to meditate on, one that clearly and powerfully communicates what God wants to do for you. I urge you to read it and see it as a personal message from God to you. Let it sink into your heart and change your thinking. If you can develop a mind-set based on the truths in this verse, you'll find yourself more blessed than you ever thought possible.

> And therefore the Lord [earnestly] waits [expecting,
> looking, and longing] to be gracious to you; and
> therefore He lifts Himself up, that He may have
> mercy on you and show loving-kindness to you.
> For the Lord is a God of justice. Blessed (happy,
> fortunate, to be envied) are all those who [earnestly]
> wait for Him, who expect and look and long for Him
> [for His victory, His favor, His love, His peace, His joy,
> and His matchless, unbroken companionship]!
> *(Isaiah 30:18)*

Think about It

Do you believe God will bless you and make you a blessing to others? What do you have right now that you can share with someone in need?

Power Pack

"And my God will liberally supply (fill to the full) your every need according to His riches in glory in Christ Jesus."
Philippians 4:19

"Let the Lord be magnified, Who takes pleasure in the prosperity of His servant."
Psalm 35:27

"God is able to make all grace (every favor and earthly blessing) come to you in abundance, so that you may always and under all circumstances and whatever the need be self-sufficient [possessing enough to require no aid or support and furnished in abundance for every good work and charitable donation]."
2 Corinthians 9:8

"And I will make of you a great nation, and I will bless you [with abundant increase of favors] and make your name famous and distinguished, and you will be a blessing [dispensing good to others]."
Genesis 12:2

9

I pursue peace with God, myself, and others.

"Seek, inquire for, and crave peace and pursue (go after) it!"
Psalm 34:14

A Legacy of Peace

Being at peace with God begins with recognizing that we are sinners in need of a Savior and asking Him to forgive us. We need to simply believe that Jesus died for our sins, became our substitute, and took the punishment that we deserved and then receive Him into our heart. Be willing to turn away from a sinful lifestyle and learn to live the way God asks us to.

Peace with God is maintained by never attempting to hide sin. We must always come clean with God and keep good communication open between us and Him. When we make mistakes we should never withdraw from Him, but we should come near because only He can restore us. To repent means to turn away from sin and return to the highest place. God is not surprised by our weaknesses and failures. Actually, He knew about the mistakes we would make before we made them. All we need to do is admit them and He is faithful to forgive us continually from all sin (see 1 John 1:9).

To be at peace with God we must try to obey Him to the best of our ability. We will not arrive at perfection while we are in fleshly bodies, but we can have a perfect heart toward God and try our best every day to please Him. I like to say, "Do your best and God will do the rest."

Think about It

Are you at peace with God?

_____

_____

Are You Ready to Take a Shortcut?

I make mistakes every day but I don't make them on purpose. I am not where I need to be, but thank God I am not where I used to be. I am growing and seeing good changes all the time. It took me many years to be able to make that statement. I hope I can help you take a shortcut that I didn't know existed.

I concentrated far too long on what was wrong with me and finally learned that focusing on my faults only increased them. I had to learn how to focus on Jesus and what He had done for me, and I had to truly believe that He loved me unconditionally and would continually forgive me when He drew me into a relationship with Himself. We would do much better in our own personal relationships if we would realize that from time to time we will have to forgive; we can plan to forgive ahead of time instead of expecting perfection and always being disappointed when we don't get it. That would enable us not to pressure others just as God never pressures us! When we feel pressured, it is from Satan, not from God. God leads, guides, urges, and prompts us, but He does not pressure us.

If you have a healthy relationship with yourself, you can take a shortcut and avoid years of agony that are completely useless. I remember the day that God whispered to my heart and said, "Joyce, it is alright for you to have weaknesses." You see, I tried very hard to be strong in every area and I was constantly frustrated because I was trying to do something that I could not do. God's intention was certainly not to tell me that I could just do whatever I felt like doing and it didn't matter. He was simply showing me that if I did my best and still manifested weakness (which I always did) that He knew all about it and understood it and I did not have to be afraid. Paul said he was strong in the Lord, but he also said that he was weak in Him (see 2 Corinthians 13:4). Whether we are weak or strong we are still in Christ and nothing changes that. He does not receive us and then reject us every time we manifest weakness. If you can understand this, it will help you not only make your journey in God faster, but you will be able to enjoy it more.

Don't have unrealistic expectations of yourself or others. I have discovered over the years that what I expect from myself is what I usually expect out of people also. In other words if I receive God's mercy then I will be able to give mercy to others, but if I am demanding and never satisfied with myself I will be the same way with others. How we treat ourselves is often how we treat others. I believe we need to learn to be good to ourselves and yet not be self-centered. We should respect and value ourselves. We should know what we are good at and what we are not good at and realize that God's strength is perfected in our weaknesses (see 2 Corinthians 12:9). We stress out over our faults and yet everyone has them. If we had no faults we would not need Jesus.

You can enjoy peace with yourself but you will have to pursue it. Make a decision that since you are with you all the time, you should like yourself. God created you and He does not make junk, so start seeing your strengths and stop staring at your weaknesses.

I believe that a lot of internal stress works its way out of us and becomes external stress. In other words, if we are upset internally, we're much more likely to display upset when our external circumstances are troublesome. If you don't like yourself, you won't like much of anything. If we can relax about ourselves, then we can usually relax more about life in general. We all have a relationship with ourselves. It's important to ask yourself what kind of relationship you have with *you*! Do you enjoy spending time alone? Can you handle being with yourself or do you always need people and noise to distract you from the way you feel inside? Are you able to forgive yourself (receive God's forgiveness) when you make mistakes? Are you patient with yourself while God is changing you? How much time do you waste feeling guilty and condemned about things in the past? Do you compare yourself with other people and struggle trying to be like them? Do you feel the need to compete with others and try to be good at what they are good at? Do you let the world's standard of looks and body image become your standard? Or, are you able to freely be the precious individual that God created you to be?

It is only when we ask these questions and answer them honestly that we can begin to understand what kind of relationship we have with ourselves.

Start meditating on this power thought: "I pursue peace with God, myself, and others."

Think about It

Are you at peace with *you*?

Stress-free Relationships

Do any totally stress-free relationships exist? I doubt it, but there are definitely steps we can take that will improve all of our relationships and allow us to be at peace with others. I want to share four steps with you that I believe will help you reach the goal of enjoying peace with people.

Step 1.

Develop and maintain peace with God and peace with yourself. Then and only then will you begin to develop a mind-set that allows you to have peace with all types of people. Most of us can have peace with people who behave the way we want them to, but as I am sure you are aware, not many of those kinds of people are in our lives. It seems God purposely surrounds me with people who are not anything like what I would choose. Furthermore, it seems to me that He delights in doing so!

We often marry people who are the opposite of us and then spend years trying to change them, which never works and only frustrates us. Likewise we choose friends who are not like us and then struggle with them. We tell God that we want to love everybody, but when He surrounds us with all kinds of people, we want Him to make the ones that frustrate us disappear or we want Him to change them into what we would like them to be.

If we can manage to have balanced expectations we can increase our peace with people, so the first step is to make sure you don't have unrealistic expectations.

Step 2.

Don't expect people to be perfect, because they won't be. People who have perfectionist tendencies have a real struggle in this area. It seems that the only way they can be satisfied with anything—including themselves—is when all things are perfect. When was the last time everything was perfect in your life? Obviously these people are destined to be frustrated and discontented most of the time. Don't spend your life trying to make the impossible possible. People have faults and there is no way around it! No matter who you are in relationship with there will be times when they will disappoint you, so plan on forgiving frequently.

Think about It

Do you have unrealistic expectations and end up being disappointed because of them?

_____

_____

People will enjoy your company much more if you don't pressure them to be something they can't be. I like to be with people who know me—and love me anyway. They say that love is blind and I believe it is to some degree. My husband actually thinks some of my weaknesses are cute. For example I can be a bit snippy at times and instead of getting irritated, he usually just says, "There is that fire that I married you for." In other words, my aggressive nature was one of the things that drew him to me, so why be bothered by it now? He recently gave me a card for Valentine's Day that was a musical one. When I opened it, Johnny Cash was singing, "I fell into a burning ring of fire." We both had a good laugh!

Like most men, Dave is almost never wrong and for years I thought my mission in life was to get him to admit that he was wrong. Now we actually laugh about it. He knows and so do I that it is impossible for anyone to be right all the time. His tendency not to admit his mistakes is just one of his "things." It seems to be a "man thing." From what my friends tell me, their husbands are the same way. I have lots of "things" of my own to deal with and so does everyone else. So why not lighten up and stop being overly exacting, demanding something we are probably not going to get?

Dave is an excellent driver, but he is quite impatient with other people who make mistakes while driving, especially me. If I try to drive and he rides, he has already corrected me three times before we get out of the driveway. For years I got upset about that and it caused lots of arguments and unpleasant road trips.

Now, I just don't drive when he's with me unless I have no other choice. Dave always assures me he is only trying to help me, and

I assure him that I manage to get places all the time without his "help." I am sure you recognize the conversation, but the good news is that although I would rather he not do it, I don't let it steal my peace because I just know that is the way he is and it probably won't change. It is one of his "things." But, as I said, I have plenty of "things" of my own.

If you are going to have peace, you will have to pursue it. It won't fall on you like ripe cherries falling off of a tree. You have to be "peaceful on purpose."

Step 3.

Don't expect everyone to be like you...because they aren't. Discovering that we are each born with a temperament that is given to us by God, and that we are all uniquely different was quite an eye opener to me. Until then I just expected everyone to think and act as I did. Now, I know that sounds rather haughty but I simply did not know any better. I distinctly remember reading two different books on personality types and discovering that our personality is a combination of our temperament given at birth and the events of our life. For example, I was given a temperament that is decisive, strong, and straightforward. I have leadership qualities, want to be in charge, make quick decisions, am impatient, and always have definite opinions about what I want to do.

When I married Dave, I could not figure out what was wrong with him because he is more easygoing, takes more time to make decisions, is very patient, doesn't need to be in charge, is easily satisfied, and many things just don't matter to him. Not realizing that he was designed by God to be the way he was, I kept trying to get him to change and be more like me. Naturally, my attitude caused a lot of problems for us. He felt pressured and I was angry most of the time. God had given me exactly what I needed but I did not know it. Dave was strong where I was weak and I was strong where he was weak so the two of us made a great team. But, until I stopped trying to change him into what I thought he should be, we were both miserable.

We are what we are and although God keeps refining us to help us be a better us, we are still us! The day I realized I needed to accept and appreciate Dave for who he is changed the entire atmosphere in our home and relationship.

I deal with literally thousands of people, and had I not learned that we are all different I think I'd have lost my mind by now. At the very least I would have been frustrated all my life and been successful at making most people in my world feel rejected by me.

I highly recommend that you ask yourself how well you are able to accept people "as is." Of course, we all need to change and improve in certain areas, but the truth is that only God can change people from the inside out. When we try to change one another, it just never works well. Even if someone does try to change because I am insisting that they do, they end up resenting me and feeling pressured. The best policy is to see the strengths people have and the benefit they are to you and leave the rest to God. Realizing that we all have weaknesses is also helpful. There just are no perfect people! Let's learn to celebrate our differences rather than allowing them to be a point of disagreement and rejection.

We have four children and they are all different. Each one has things about them that I love and things I could easily do without, but they are all wonderful. I used to think I wanted everyone to be like me until I had two sons who are just like me. Then I realized that causes tension, too. The three of us all want to be the boss and as we know, that doesn't work either. Everyone in our family is very opinionated and we all tend to think we are right, so that can add a bit more tension. In other words, our family is just like any other and yet we get along great, not because it is easy, but because we have decided to. You can do the same thing, but you will have to accept each person as an individual designed specifically by God and you must give them freedom to be who they are. Without that, peace with people is next to impossible.

Step 4.

Be an encourager—not a discourager. Everyone loves to be with people who celebrate and notice their strengths and choose to ignore their weaknesses. We all love to be encouraged and made to feel really good about ourselves, and we hate to be around negative, discouraging people who tend to be faultfinders.

I used to be the kind of person who wanted to at least mention things I saw as faults or mistakes. I prided myself in thinking I was generous enough to forgive but wanted to make sure people at least knew what I was forgiving them for. For example, I might say to Dave, "I turned the light out in your closet again." In actuality I was still being discouraging by reminding him that he had not done what I wanted him to do and I had to do it for him. I had to learn that the best policy was to simply not say anything unless it was really necessary. It is a better thing to just turn the light off and hope someone will do the same for me when I leave one on. I realize that we need to train our children to do things certain ways and I am not suggesting that all training is discouraging, but when training becomes nagging, we have crossed a line that becomes a problem in relationships. The spirit of a person can be broken or bruised by excessive mentioning of faults.

The more we encourage people, the better they behave. In fact, compliments actually help people perform better, while nagging makes them behave worse. Choose a person who you would like to have a better relationship with and begin to aggressively encourage and compliment them. I believe you will be amazed at how much better they respond to you. Your first concern might be, "If I ignore their faults won't they just take advantage of me?" That of course can happen, but it usually doesn't. What frequently happens is that the person being encouraged has a change of heart and they work harder to please you than ever before. They are now doing it because they choose to and not because you are trying to force them.

Being encouraging is part of being a more positive person. Be careful of your thoughts about people. If we think uncompliment-ary or discouraging thoughts they will usually slip out of our mouth. Look for and magnify the good in every person. The Bible teaches us to do unto others as we want them to do unto us, so all we need to do is think about what we want and start to give it away. If you want to be encouraged, then be encouraging!

Peace-Peace-Peace

I have come to the place where I don't believe life is really worth living without peace, and that drives me to pursue peace in all areas.
I spent many years frustrated and struggling in my relationships
with God, myself, and other people and I refuse to live like that any
longer. In order for things to change in our lives we must pray but
we must also be willing to change. We cannot expect everyone and
everything around us to change so we can be comfortable while we
are passive and do nothing.

The Bible says that if we want to live in harmony with others
we must adapt to people and things. I can assure you that I had no
interest in adapting to anything or anyone. I did want them to adapt
to me, but in my pride I didn't even consider I needed to change, so
my life and relationships remained in turmoil. After many years
I finally became willing to do whatever "I" needed to do to have
peace, and learning how to adapt was number one on God's list for
me. I have discovered that having my way all the time is not really
as important as I once thought it was. Now, I actually enjoy the
freedom of not having to have my way. Yes, I said the *freedom of not
having to have my own way*. My flesh may be uncomfortable for a
short while when I adapt to someone or something else and it is not
really what "I" wanted, but I feel great inside because I know I have
followed the law of love and have done my part to pursue peace.

Adapting to others does not mean that we let them control us
or that we become a doormat for the world to walk on. There are
times when we need to stand firm no matter who gets upset, but
there are also many times in life when we make mountains out of
molehills and give up our peace over things that are petty. Will you
make a commitment to be a maker and maintainer of peace? Will
you examine all of your relationships—with God, yourself, and
others—and do everything you can do to live in peace?

To me the most important point in this section is that we must
pursue peace. Most people want peace, but they don't do what they
need to do in order to have it. The first step is to get a mind-set

that you are going to pursue peace with God, yourself, and others. As you meditate on that power thought and speak it over and over you will find yourself becoming more and more dissatisfied with turmoil. You will pursue peace! Think about it. What can you do to bring more peace into your relationships?

Power Pack

"Depart from evil and do good; seek, inquire for,
and crave peace and pursue (go after) it!"
Psalm 34:14

"I have told you these things, so that in Me you have
[perfect] peace and confidence. In the world you have
tribulation and trials and distress and frustration: but
be of good cheer [take courage; be confident, certain,
undaunted]! For I have overcome the world. [I have deprived
it of power to harm you and have conquered it for you.]"
John 16:33

"If possible, as far as it depends on you,
live at peace with everyone."
Romans 12:18

POWER THOUGHT

10

I live in the present and enjoy each moment.

"This is the day which the Lord has brought
about; we will rejoice and be glad in it."
Psalm 118:24

There's a saying I love that goes like this: *Yesterday is history. Tomorrow is a mystery. Today is a gift; that's why it's called the present.* We need to enjoy every moment of our lives and stay focused on the present. We can't dwell on the past or look too far into the future, but we need to realize the present moment is God's gift to us *right now,* so we need to fully live in it and enjoy it.

A friend of mine did not marry until she was forty-five years old. Her marriage was so wonderful and satisfying to her that she often said that her husband was God's present to her. One day her husband went into the hospital for a routine surgery, but due to an unexpected infection he never came home. His death was a terrible shock and a devastating disappointment, but she is very glad that she thoroughly enjoyed her husband during the years they had together. I am so glad for her that she is not living with the pain of her loss plus a lot of regret. All too often people are so busy that they put off enjoying their family and friends and then when it is too late they regret that they did not make better choices.

The only way to avoid regret is to make good choices and enjoy the present. Every moment is a gift from God. I make an effort to focus on and enjoy every moment of my life, but doing so has been a long and difficult journey for me. I've really had to work on doing so because I am a planner, and if I am not careful, I find myself planning the next thing while doing the current thing, which of course steals the present moment from me. Although being focused is a good thing, I can also easily get so focused on my work that I fail to enjoy the magic of the moment. For example, I was usually working while my children were little and found it difficult to even take a moment to stop and enjoy the cute things they said or did. I missed many of those moments and will never get them back. We should celebrate life and the people God has placed in our path. Life is to be enjoyed, not dreaded or regretted.

Through growing up in a dysfunctional home where we certainly did not enjoy life, I turned into a workaholic and tried to find my worth and value in *what I did*, rather than in *who I was*. Because my parents seemed to be more pleased with me when I was doing something and being productive than when I wasn't, I thought God was also more pleased with me when I was doing and producing.

The atmosphere in my home growing up was very intense and I experienced a lot of fear. I didn't get to have much fun during my childhood, and when I was in my twenties, I could not remember *ever* being truly happy or completely relaxed. Because of the abuse, my childhood was stolen. I became an adult, but there was no child in me, no childlikeness in me at all—and that's not healthy. Every healthy adult needs to have a healthy child on the inside. We need to know how to work and how to be responsible, but we also need to know how to play and enjoy ourselves. We should never miss an opportunity to laugh because it is like medicine. It helps us in many ways, including our physical health. And, being lighthearted makes even our work more pleasant and enjoyable.

This power thought—I live in the present and enjoy each moment—can transform your life because if you really allow it to change your thinking, you'll begin enjoying your life in brand-new ways. Even if you consider yourself a "serious" person, extremely focused or very responsible, you should still take time to enjoy what you are doing. Never be too busy to enjoy every aspect of your life.

Think about It

How much do you really enjoy and live in the present moment?
A lot_____
A little_____
Not much at all_____

How much do you enjoy the people in your life?

_____

_____

God Wants You to Enjoy Your Life

Do you believe God wants you to enjoy your life? Of course, He does. In fact, part of God's will is for you to enjoy every moment of it. How can I be so sure? Because His Word says so in many places. King Solomon, who is considered to have been very wise, wrote in Ecclesiastes 2:24, "There is nothing better for a man than that he should eat and drink and make himself enjoy good in his labor. Even this, I have seen, is from the hand of God." Solomon said to make yourself enjoy the good of your labor. That sounds like it is something we must do as an act of our will. This does not mean that all of life becomes a huge party or a vacation, but it does mean that through the power of God we can learn to enjoy all of life, even things others would consider ordinary and boring. I think a lot of people have the mentality of just trying to "endure" large portions of their life, but I believe it is tragic to live and not enjoy every moment. I admit that some things are more pleasant to our emotions than others, but we can learn to enjoy God's presence in everything we do. Try reminding yourself throughout the day that God is with you and the moment you have right now is a gift from Him.

I was struggling with the whole concept of enjoying life until I did a study on what the Lord had to say about it; now I know it is His will and something I am not only entitled to, but actually need. I need to enjoy life for myself, but also for Jesus, Who paid a very high price for me to be able to do so.

Jesus Himself, when He stated why He came to Earth, said, "I came that they may have and enjoy life, and have it in abundance (to the full, till it overflows)" (John 10:10). He also said, "I have told you these things, that My joy and delight may be in you, and that your joy and gladness may be of full measure and complete and overflowing" (John 15:11) and "But now ask and keep on asking and you will receive, so that your joy (gladness, delight) may be full and complete" (John 16:24). When He prayed to the Father in John 17:13, He actually prayed that we would have joy: "And now I am coming to You; I say these things while I am still in the world, so that My joy may be made full and complete and perfect in them [that they may experience My delight fulfilled in them, that My enjoyment may be perfected in their own souls, that they may have My gladness within them, filling their hearts]." With Jesus Himself speaking and praying such powerful words about His desire for us to have joy, how could we ever doubt that God wants us to be happy and enjoy our lives? If it is God's desire that we enjoy life, then why are so many people miserable and unhappy? Perhaps it is because we fail to set our minds to enjoy life. We can easily fall into a pattern of surviving and enduring rather than enjoying. But a new mind-set will release you to begin enjoying life like never before. The more you enjoy life the more enjoyable you will be, so get started today and don't delay. Meditate on and say repeatedly, "I live in the present and enjoy each moment."

One thing I like to do that helps me savor the day is to take time in the evening to mentally recall all that I did that day. It is amazing what we accomplish and are involved in during one day, but we often go through our days so fast and with our focus divided that we barely remember them, if at all. Meditate on your day each evening and thank God for all that He brought you through and allowed you to do. If you made mistakes, you can learn from them and if you had great victories, remembering them will allow you to enjoy them all over again.

Think about It

Does your day go by in a blur or do you truly enjoy it?

_____

_____

There's Nothing Wrong with Having Some Fun

When I began to understand John 10:10, I became angry because I realized the enemy had deceived me into thinking that enjoying things was not important. Under the influence of the devil, who is the Deceiver, I had come to believe—falsely, of course—that if I was having fun, something was wrong with it. I must not be working hard enough! I never saw my father enjoy life and it seemed to aggravate him when others did, so I just grew up thinking something must be wrong with it. I can remember being told to be quiet when I laughed out loud.

Maybe you can relate; perhaps you went through some of the same struggles in your childhood, or have been through other things that have left you too serious. Every time you try to rest, every time you try to do anything recreational, anytime you do anything besides work, you have a vague feeling of guilt, as if something is wrong with it. I realize some people may not understand this struggle, but many, many do.

I think this excessive work mentality is one reason people often backslide in their relationships with God. They mistakenly try to serve God as a job or as "work" and fail to enjoy Him. The seventeenth-century French mystic Madame Guyon said that the highest call for every child of God is to enjoy God. I remember what a heavy load lifted off of me the first time I read that. At that time I was working so hard trying to please God that the thought of simply enjoying Him had not occurred to me at all. I had never heard of such a thing! I think it is sad indeed that I had been a committed church member for over twenty years before I learned that God wanted me to enjoy Him and the life He had given me.

God has created all things for our enjoyment and it begins by enjoying Him. He also wants us to enjoy one another and He wants us to enjoy ourselves.

Next time you have a desire to take a short break from your work and go for a walk in the park, or watch a child play. Go ahead and do it without feeling guilty or unspiritual. Your work will still be there when you return. I am not encouraging you to be irresponsible, but I do want you to take the appropriate steps to enjoy life in the midst of accomplishing great things. If you have been working hard and feel you need a day off, then take it. You will be more fruitful if you take time to be refreshed. We live in the midst of a driven society but we can change if we choose to. If you don't want to end up old with all kinds of regret about things you wish you would have done, then get started today making every moment count.

Think about It

What can you do to have some fun today, even while you are working?

_____

_____

Choose one thing each day you would like to do just for the joy of doing it.

Set a New Goal

When I started my journey to learn how to enjoy life, I set a goal of purposely enjoying everything I did, even things I normally just did to get them over with or to check them off of my list. For example, instead of hurrying to get ready in the morning so I could get about my day, I purposed to enjoy the entire process. Things like choosing my wardrobe for the day, putting on makeup, and fixing my hair. Although I did these things daily, it never occurred to me that they were a part of every day of my life and I could and should enjoy doing them. I said to myself, "I am enjoying this moment in my life and the task at hand." I try to do for God's glory what I commonly did out of routine, and with no purpose except to get it done.

The Carmelite monk called Brother Lawrence, who wrote the spiritual classic *Practicing the Presence of God,* learned to do the same thing. He found kitchen work to be very distasteful, but learned that if he did it for the love of God, he was able to practice the presence of God in the midst of it. This same principle was applied to every facet of his life and practicing it enabled him to enjoy life in a superior manner. He turned what could have been a boring, mundane, miserable existence into one that was admired and coveted by many. People wanted his simplicity, joy, peace, and profound ability to converse with God while doing everything he did.

There are dozens of things that pertain to ordinary everyday life and we can enjoy them all if we just make a decision to do it. Things like getting dressed, driving to work, going to the grocery store, running errands, keeping things organized, and hundreds of other things. After all, they are the things that life is made up of. Begin doing them for the love of God and realize that through the Holy Spirit, you can enjoy absolutely everything you do. Joy doesn't come merely from being entertained, but from a decision to appreciate each moment that you are given as a rare and precious gift from God.

Keys to Enjoying the Present Moment

Please remember that any day you waste is one that you will never get back. Make sure that every day you live counts! I want to share with you some specific keys I have found to help me learn to live in the present moment and enjoy my life. I believe, if you'll put them into practice in your life, they'll help you too.

Give Yourself to What You Are Doing

When the term *multitasking* first became popular, everyone seemed to want to do it. Many job descriptions suddenly included phrases such as "must be able to multitask," and they still do. While there are certainly times a person must juggle responsibilities and handle more than one thing at a time, I am not sure multitasking serves us well in everyday life, and I don't think it should become the normal way we live. In fact, I think trying to do too many things at once creates stress and prevents us from enjoying any of them. Some people are able to do several things at once and still stay calm and focused, but even they have their limit and limits should always be honored. Whatever our abilities and work habits are, we need to be aware that stress, confusion, and frustration are not the way to enjoy the moment.

I want to challenge you to stop trying to multitask excessively and learn to give yourself to what you are doing. Commit to do one thing at a time and determine that you will enjoy it. It's certainly fine to read a book while you sit in a waiting room before an appointment, but begin to resist the urge to simultaneously do more than one thing that requires brainpower or your full attention. For example, don't talk on the phone while you try to pay bills online. Don't make a list of weekend home improvement projects while you are supposed to be paying attention in a business meeting. Don't put on your makeup while you are driving. Don't answer e-mails or text messages while driving.

The ability to e-mail and text is certainly convenient and has enabled us to communicate much faster, but if we let every little beep of the phone or message that announces "You've got mail," be the controlling factor in our lives, we will end up frustrated and often appear to be rude.

Listening requires your attention and pretending to listen when in reality your mind is on ten other things is not only rude, but it does nothing to build good relationships.

The *Amplified Bible* explains Ecclesiastes 5:1 this way: "Give your mind to what you are doing." In other words, train yourself to focus your full attention on what you are involved in at any given time. Then finish what you're currently doing before you start something else. This kind of concentration requires discipline, but it's worth it because being able to focus helps you enjoy the present moment. I recently made progress in this area when I decided that from now on if I was doing something important that I was not going to answer the phone. Usually I answer it no matter what I am doing and often find that it frustrates me and causes me to lose my focus. I look at the caller ID to make sure it is not an emergency, and I do return my calls, but I am not going to let them control me.

We will not enjoy the present moment and the gifts it contains if we don't have balanced attitudes toward work. Luke 10:38–42 tells the story of Jesus' visit to the home of two sisters, Mary and Martha. Martha was "overly occupied and too busy" (see Luke 10:40). But Mary sat down at Jesus' feet and listened to what He had to say. Martha was distracted with much serving; Mary determined not to miss the beauty of the present moment. And Jesus said that Mary made a better choice than Martha did. Jesus did not tell Martha not to work, He told her not to be frustrated and have a bad attitude while she worked. Jesus wants us to work hard, but He also wants us to be wise enough to realize when we should stop all activity and not miss the miracle of the moment.

Breaking the bad habit of excessive multitasking may sound easy, but it is actually quite difficult in our society, so be determined to form new, balanced habits in this area. This book is about learning to control your thinking, and the art of focusing on what you are doing is a vital part of that goal.

What multitasking "traps" do you most often fall into? Do the thoughts flying around in your mind make it feel like a freeway in rush-hour traffic? Take a deep breath, slow down, and be determined to only do what you can do peacefully and enjoyably.

Become Childlike in Your Approach to God

Acting like an adult is generally considered a good thing, and in most cases it is. But we are to approach God as little children—not being *childish*, but being *childlike*. One thing is for certain: little children can easily find a way to enjoy whatever they are doing. Our youngest son, Daniel, has always had a "let's enjoy life mentality," and I can remember when he was a small child how he thoroughly enjoyed all of life. I recall one day telling him to sweep the patio and noticed a few minutes later that he was dancing with the broom. Another time I made him stand in the corner to correct him for something he had done wrong and soon I noticed he was playing with the flowers in the wallpaper. I think we can learn a lot from watching little children. They find a way to enjoy everything— even chores or correction. They are quick to forgive any offense and trusting people comes easily to them.

Come to God with a childlike trust that does not always have to understand the "why" behind everything. Most parents get very weary of hearing their children ask why a hundred times a day and I believe God gets tired of it too.

Have simple faith; pray simple prayers; be quick to repent; and be quick to receive God's help. Believe God is good. If you need forgiveness, ask God for it, receive it by faith, and don't waste your time feeling guilty and condemned. With this kind of simplicity in your relationship with God, you'll find yourself growing spiritually and enjoying Him more than ever. Remember, enjoying God at all times in whatever we are doing is our goal!

Think about It

What are three childlike traits that you could practice in your relationship with God?

_____

_____

Enjoy People

We certainly cannot enjoy the present moment if we don't learn to enjoy all different types of people, because many of our moments have people in them. I recently read that most of our unhappiness is caused from people not being what we want them to be or doing what we want them to do, and I couldn't agree more. That being the case, what is the answer? How can I enjoy the day if I am going to have to deal with annoying people? I have found it helpful to realize that even though they might annoy me, God loves them very much and doesn't appreciate me having a bad attitude toward anyone.

I cannot enjoy anyone that I am judging critically, so I often say to myself, "Joyce, the way this person acts is none of your business." Being merciful in my attitude toward others actually helps me enjoy my life and I highly recommend it. I recently encountered a clerk in a shoe store who talked on her cell phone the entire time I was in the store and even when I needed help finding a right size. I was aware that she wanted me to hurry so she could get back to her conversation. She was speaking Spanish so I couldn't understand her, but as my aggravation mounted I chose to think, *Perhaps she is handling some kind of emergency or is dealing with something that is very important to her.* I was on the verge of losing my joy, but decided to be merciful and stay happy. I highly recommend it!

God has created all kinds of people with many different temperaments and personalities and I truly believe He enjoys them all. Variety seems to be something that God really delights in. If you have never given this any thought, take a little time and look around you. God created variety and He says that what He has created is good, so I urge you to accept those that are different from you and learn to enjoy them as God does.

We encounter a lot of people. Some of them are by choice, but a lot of them just end up in our life as we go through our day. You will not enjoy a lot of your "present moments" unless you decide to also find a way to enjoy the people who invade them.

Think about It

How often do you fail to enjoy your day because a person isn't what you want them to be?

Enjoy a Balanced Life

A door of opportunity is opened for Satan to bring destruction to the lives of those who get out of balance (see 1 Peter 5:8). Too much of anything is a problem, even if we are doing too much of a good thing. For example: work is good, but too much of it causes stress which can result in disease, resentment, depression, and the breakdown of relationships. Food is good, but as most of us know too much of it is not good. It is good to be organized, but if we become a perfectionist we can drive ourselves and everyone around us crazy. Sleep is vitally necessary and if we don't get enough, we don't feel good, but the other day I was talking to someone who said, "I have discovered that if I sleep too much, I don't feel good." Any area that is out of balance causes confusion and distress in our lives and steals the joy of the present moment.

I truly believe that maintaining a life of balance is possibly one of the biggest challenges we have. I encourage you to regularly examine your life and ask yourself honestly if you have allowed any area to get out of balance. Are you doing too much or too little of anything? A lack of balance could be the root cause of not enjoying life.

I have not always lived a balanced life, but I thank God for helping me reach the point where I do stay balanced now—at least most of the time. I encourage you to do the same. Balance your activities and vary your routine. Don't do the same things all the time or overdo anything. Do all things in moderation. That way, you'll avoid burnout and be able to enjoy everything.

Think about It

Do you live a balanced life?

_____

_____

Where do you need to improve and how can you do better?

_____

_____

Let Go of the Past

Your past can be an unbearably heavy load when you try to carry it into your present. The way to let go of it is to stop thinking about it. Get it off of your mind and out of your conversation. Satan will remind you of your past because he desires that you stay stuck in it, but please remember that you can choose your own thoughts. You do not have to think about everything that falls into your mind. You have the ability to choose your thoughts. Without a doubt, holding on to your past will keep you from enjoying your present and from looking forward to your future. If you struggle with guilt, condemnation, shame, blame, or regret about your past, God will forgive you and set you free if you simply ask Him. If you feel disappointment due to the mistakes of the past, it is time to shake it off and get re-appointed. Your future has no room in it for the past! I recently wrote in my journal that I was eliminating the reverse gear from my life, and I did it so I could never waste time on what was or could have been.

The apostle Paul was determined to live in the present moment. In Philippians 3:13, 14, he writes, "I do not consider, brethren, that I have captured and made it my own [yet]; but one thing I do [it is my one aspiration]: forgetting what lies behind and straining forward to what lies ahead, I press on toward the goal to win the [supreme and heavenly] prize to which God in Christ Jesus is calling us upward." Use all the keys I have given you and keep adding your own as you progress in your new life of enjoyment. And above all, keep meditating on and confessing this power thought: "I live in the present and enjoy each moment."

Think about It

When you read Philippians 3:13, 14—about forgetting the past— what situation comes to mind for you?

_____

_____

Choose Your Battles

I believe one of the best ways to enjoy the present moment and avoid undue stress is to refuse to let every little thing upset you. In other words, choose your battles, and don't make mountains out of molehills. Before you devote time, energy, and emotion to an issue or a situation, ask yourself two questions. First, ask yourself how important it is; and second, ask yourself how much of your time, effort, and energy is really appropriate for you to put into it. Know what really matters in life, and focus on those things. Learn to discern the difference between major matters and minor matters.

In Exodus 18:13–23, Moses' father-in-law, Jethro, gave him great advice. Moses was becoming exhausted because he personally handled every situation, dispute, and crisis that arose among the Israelites. Perhaps he thought he had to do so, since he was the leader of the nation. Jethro said to him, essentially, "You take care of the big things, and leave the small stuff to someone else." He went on to say, "If you will do this, and God so commands you, you will be able to endure [the strain], and all these people also will go to their [tents] in peace" (Exodus 18:23).

I'm sure your life has plenty of strain without adding anything more. When you are tempted to take on a "battle," step back first and decide if it's worth what it will require of you.

Think about It

Think about your current battles. Which ones do you need to walk away from and which ones are worth fighting?

Realize That You Cannot Meet Everyone's Expectations

We all have a lot of different relationships and most people expect something from us. Moses told his father-in-law that he was judging every matter small or large because the people were coming to him. Obviously, they were coming with an expectation of getting Moses to help them. He did not want to disappoint them so he daily exhausted himself. When we do this we are pleasing people rather than pleasing God and we become ineffective. We all want people to be pleased with us, but we must also realize that they frequently have unrealistic expectations that are selfish. We cannot enjoy the moment we have if we are disobeying God in the midst of it.

Think about It

Are you exhausted much of the time due to trying to keep too many people happy?

_____

_____

Don't Wait to Enjoy Yourself

Our ministry hosts a number of conferences each year and I do a lot of speaking and teaching at each one. I used to approach these events as work, as part of my job. Every time I did a conference, I thought, _This is my work, and when my work is over, I will enjoy myself._ After several years, I began to think about how much time I spend in the pulpit, and I realized that if I don't enjoy it, I won't have much time left to enjoy anything. So I decided to have fun while I work. This is one way I have learned to enjoy every moment.

You will need to find ways to enjoy the present moments in your life. Certainly, learning to be happy while you work may be one way, but there are many others. Begin now to think about what you can do to find more joy in every experience. The present moment is all we're guaranteed, so don't wait until later—until you get married, until you retire, until you go on vacation, until your children finish college—to enjoy life. Nobody knows what is going to happen next in their lives or in the world. You are alive _now,_ so maximize it, embrace it, and celebrate it.

Let me close this section with an anonymous writing that has been around for years and encouraged millions of people to enjoy every day and appreciate each moment. Let it inspire you to do likewise.

If I had my life to live over, I'd try to make more mistakes next time. I would relax. I would be sillier than I have been this trip. I know of very few things that I would take seriously.

I would be crazier. I would be less hygienic. I would take more chances. I would take more trips. I would climb more mountains, swim more rivers, watch more sunsets. I would walk more. I would eat more ice cream and less beans. I would have more actual troubles and fewer imaginary ones. You see, I am one of those people who lives prophylactically and sensibly and sanely, hour after hour, day after day. Oh, I have had my moments, and if I had it to do over again, I'd have more of them. In fact, I'd try to have nothing else. Just moments, one after another, instead of living so many years ahead each day. I have been one of those people who never goes anywhere without a thermometer, a hot water bottle, a gargle, a raincoat, and a parachute. If I had it to do over again, I would go places and do things and travel lighter than I have. If I had my life to do over, I would start barefooted earlier in the spring and stay that way later in the fall. I would play hooky more. I wouldn't make such good grades except by accident. I would ride on more merry-go-rounds. I would pick more daisies.[1]

Although I am not suggesting that we live riotously, I do believe the little story makes a good point. Let's be serious enough to accomplish our goals in life, but not so serious that we kill creative spontaneity.

Think about It

What are you waiting on? Get busy and enjoy your life!

Power Pack

"This is the day which the Lord has brought
about; we will rejoice and be glad in it."
Psalm 118:24

"I came that they may have and enjoy life, and have
it in abundance (to the full, till it overflows)."
John 10:10

"I have told you these things, that My joy and delight
may be in you, and that your joy and gladness may be
of full measure and complete and overflowing."
John 15:11

POWER THOUGHT

11

I am disciplined and self-controlled.

"For the time being no discipline brings joy, but seems
grievous and painful; but afterwards it yields a peaceable
fruit of righteousness to those who have been trained by it."
Hebrews 12:11

Many people enjoy watching athletic events such as the Olympic
Games, the World Series, or the Super Bowl. Even those who don't
consider themselves serious sports fans often pay attention to these
contests when a prize such as a gold medal or a championship title
is at stake. I believe the reason for this is that we all enjoy seeing
people who work hard receive rewards for their efforts. We enjoy
this on a personal level too; we like to know our training, work,
and sacrifices bring benefits into our lives. I often get tears in my
eyes when I see someone cross the finish line in a race. Why would
I cry when I don't even know the person? Because I know what it
takes to win!

Thomas Paine said, "The harder the conflict, the more glorious
the triumph. What we obtain too cheap, we esteem too lightly."
Before we can ever receive a prize or enjoy a reward, we have to do
the work required. In fact, investments of time, energy, and dedication are what make the rewards sweet. The harder we work to reach
a goal, the more we appreciate finally accomplishing it. Everything I have mentioned thus far—hard work, training, sacrifices,

investments of time and energy, and dedication—falls under the category of "discipline."

I truly believe that a disciplined life is a powerful life. Learning to be disciplined and to practice self-control will keep you from laziness and excess, and will help you stay focused and productive. It will require you to make an effort, but the reward will be worth the work. A disciplined life begins with a disciplined mind. We must be able to set our mind and keep it set concerning our desires and goals.

Think about It

Do you enjoy seeing people who work hard receive rewards?

_____

_____

Are you willing to do whatever you need to do in order to have what you say you want?

_____

_____

Liberty with Limits

The apostle Paul understood discipline and wrote about it in several of his letters. In 1 Corinthians 6:12, he observed, "Everything is permissible (allowable and lawful) for me; but not all things are helpful (good for me to do, expedient and profitable when considered with other things). Everything is lawful for me, but *I will not become the slave of anything or be brought under its power*" (emphasis mine).

Discipline is the price of freedom. It is the door to liberation. When we are not disciplined, we become slaves; we fall under the power of things that should have no control over us. For example, when we don't discipline ourselves to eat healthily, we become slaves to fats, sugars, and other substances that are detrimental to our physical health. I am acquainted with many people who know that eating a lot of sugar makes them feel tired and even sick, but they eat it anyway. They "wish" they did not want the unhealthy food, but they are not willing to discipline themselves to make better choices. When we do not practice self-control with our finances, we fall under the power of debt, and our indebtedness can literally keep us from doing what we want or need to do in life. Oppressive debt is often the root cause of anxiety, disease, and serious marital problems. When we do not discipline ourselves to get enough rest, we become slaves to fatigue, which makes us grouchy, prone to mistakes, and tired when we need to be energetic. Fatigue is one of the greatest thieves of creativity so we need to avoid it as much as possible. It seems to me that everyone is tired these days, and I am certain that is not God's will for people.

Paul echoed a similar sentiment in 1 Corinthians 10:23 when he wrote, "All things are legitimate [permissible—and we are free to do anything we please], but not all things are helpful (expedient, profitable, and wholesome). All things are legitimate, but *not all things are constructive [to character] and edifying [to spiritual life]"* (emphasis mine). Notice in this verse, Paul again states that he is technically free to do anything he wants to do, but that he restrains himself from doing things that are not character-building or spiritually edifying. The Bible says, "Discipline yourself for the purpose of godliness" (1 Timothy 4:7 NASB). Making decisions based on whether or not it will enhance your character or help you spiritually is a wise approach to practicing discipline.

We should practice discipline in what we allow ourselves to see and hear. Our eyes and ears are gateways into our soul and spirit and as such they should be guarded with all diligence. For example, if you receive a magazine in your home, and as you page through it you find the models are dressed scantily and inappropriately, the best choice is to simply throw it away. If you are surfing the channels on television you will need to discipline yourself in what you choose to watch. Another example would be to choose not to gossip or reveal people's secrets no matter how much you are tempted to. The power of life and death are in them so we should use great caution, discipline, and self-control concerning them.

Think about It

Have you become a "slave" to anything, or does anything have power over you?_____ If so, what is it? _____
Are you regularly disciplining yourself unto godliness?

_____

_____

We Need to Be Taught

It's impossible to imagine the possibility of becoming a successful doctor or lawyer without education. I wish Christians had the same understanding concerning spiritual growth. Becoming a Christian begins with surrender and a decision to believe that Jesus is God and that He did indeed die for our sins. He took the punishment we deserved, paid the debt we owed as sinners, and He rose from the dead, ascended into heaven to be seated at God's right hand. He is alive today and has sent His Holy Spirit to dwell in the hearts of those who receive Him by faith. That is the beginning of our faith and our Christian experience, but it is far from the end.

We need to be educated concerning what belongs to us by virtue of our relationship with Jesus, how to live the new life He gives us, and how to align our thinking with the truth of His Word. We need to *learn* to think and then behave according to the new nature we have, rather than the old nature that officially went to the cross with Jesus. It's so important to realize at the beginning of our journey that success will require time and effort—probably more than we would like! To think that this type of radical change will take place quickly and with no effort is pure foolishness. We have to be disciplined about it. God gives us great freedom; He allows us to choose what we want to think, say, and do. If we will be wise enough to put good limits on our liberty, we will see great results. The mind must be renewed. We must learn to think as God thinks if we want to have what He wants us to have.

God Has Given Us a Spirit of Discipline and Self-control

I frequently hear people say, "I am just not a disciplined person," or, "I just don't have any self-control," and they name a certain area like eating, exercising, or keeping things organized. If you are one of these people who believe you are not disciplined, then I want you to change your thinking. The apostle Paul stated that God hasn't given us a spirit of fear, but of power, love, and a sound mind, and a spirit of discipline and self-control (see 2 Timothy 1:7). It is time to start renewing your mind by meditating on this power thought: "I am disciplined and self-controlled." You will never rise above what you believe, and as long as you believe you are not a disciplined person, then you won't be one.

Winning the Battle in the Mind

The Roman poet Horace wrote, "Rule your mind or it will rule you," and I believe that is true. We must understand that the enemy wants our minds; he wants to control or influence as much of our thinking as possible, but we do not have to let him. Just as we have to be educated about how to think as God wants us to think, we also have to learn to resist the enemy as he tries to influence our thoughts. The key to overcoming him is learning to discipline ourselves where our thinking is concerned, and disciplining ourselves to believe we are disciplined is the beginning.

This morning I was discussing discipline with my son. We

talked about prayer, Bible reading, silence, and solitude, and then my son said, "Discipline is a discipline." I never thought of it quite like that, but it is very true.

I have taught about the benefits of discipline many times and still, no one seems to be excited when I mention the word. I believe, if we really understood the power, the liberty, the joy, and the victory discipline brings to our lives, we would embrace it eagerly. In many areas, especially in our thinking, it makes the difference between a happy life and a miserable life, a life of bondage to the enemy or a life of freedom in God. Always remember that discipline is your friend, something to be embraced and used daily. Discipline is a tool given by God to help you reach your goals. Start thinking and saying, "I am a disciplined person and I use self-control." Then apply that discipline and self-control to all of your thought patterns.

One reason disciplining our mind is so important is that the condition of it can change quickly. One day, you may be calm, peaceful, sure of yourself, and confident in God. Another day, you may be anxious, worried, insecure, and full of doubt. I have certainly experienced these kinds of ups and downs at times in my life and they are always rooted in how I think. Our thinking directly affects our emotions.

I can remember times when I was able to make a decision quickly and stick with it easily. I can also recall times I couldn't seem to arrive at a decision at all, no matter how I tried, or even worse, I made a decision but kept changing my mind. Doubt, fear, and uncertainty haunted me mercilessly as I second-guessed myself and simply could not make up my mind in a situation. When we allow ourselves to entertain self-doubt and double-mindedness, we are inviting confusion and misery. Many people struggle with this lack of ability to concentrate and make decisions. When a decision is called for, especially an important one, they lack confidence. Fear seeps into their thinking and controls all of their actions.

You can renew your mind with thinking like, *I hear from God and I am led by the Holy Spirit. I refuse to live in fear and be double-minded.* We can easily feel overwhelmed by all the decisions we need to make daily unless we have the confidence to believe that we have the ability to make right ones. Don't ever say again, "I have a hard time making decisions," because when you think and speak like that, you are setting yourself up to be confused. Instead, you can believe that when you need to make a decision, you will know what to do. Even if you have had difficulty doing so in the past, this is a new day for you and you are in charge of your thinking; it is no longer in charge of you! Remember: you are a disciplined and self-controlled person according to God's Word.

I have learned that when Satan has successfully built a stronghold in our minds, he does not give up his ground easily. We must be willing to not only start thinking right, but we must also keep it up until we have victory. If you have spent years allowing your mind to wander in all sorts of directions, it will take time to retrain it, but the effort you invest will give you amazing dividends. Lots of people struggle with indecision and similar challenges in their minds because they have not disciplined themselves concerning their thoughts. People who can't seem to concentrate long enough to make a decision often wonder if something is wrong with their mind. However, the inability to concentrate and make a decision can be the result of years of letting the mind do whatever it wants to do rather than disciplining it. As I said, this is often the sign and the result of a stronghold the enemy has constructed in a person's mind. For me, tearing down those mental strongholds took some time, but it did happen, and it can happen for you. It wasn't easy for me, so don't be discouraged if it takes time and effort for you. I feel that this is so important that I wrote a book, *Never Give Up!*, which is solely devoted to perseverance. Perseverance is what the apostle Paul called "pressing on." You can press on far beyond wherever you think your abilities end. When we run out of our own strength, God is ready to give us His if we ask for it.

Sometimes, I still have relapses in this area of concentration and while trying to complete a project, I'll suddenly realize my mind has just wandered on to something else that has absolutely nothing to do with the issue at hand. I have not yet arrived at a place of perfect concentration, but at least I understand how important it is not to allow my mind to go wherever it wishes, whenever it wants to. I have already decided that I will never give up on learning how to think properly and I strongly urge you to do the same thing. I am not where I want to be, but I am making progress!

Think about It

Does your mind wander and, if so, are you ready to discipline it?

_____

_____

Have you made a decision that you will never give up until you experience complete victory?

_____

_____

It Takes Practice

Training our minds to be disciplined takes practice. One way I learned to do it was to stop allowing my mind to wander during conversations. There are times when Dave is talking to me and I listen for a while; then all of a sudden, I realize I haven't heard one word he has spoken because I allowed my mind to wander on to something else. My body is standing there near him and many times my face is even turned toward him, but in my mind I don't hear anything he says. For many years, when this sort of thing happened, I pretended to know exactly what Dave was saying. Now I simply stop and ask, "Would you back up and repeat that? I let my mind wander, and I didn't hear a thing you said." In this way, I'm dealing with the problem. I'm disciplining my mind to stay on track. Confronting these issues is the only way to get on the victorious side of them.

I've also discovered that we all have a lot of what I call "mental roaming time"—time when we are not occupied with anything specific and our minds are free to roam around and select something to meditate on. This might be drive time, shower time, the time before falling asleep, or other similar occasions. We need to be careful to use this time in productive ways and make sure we think about things that build character and help us grow spiritually. These can be some of the best times to meditate on the power thoughts you are learning in this book. As you fall asleep at night, do so rolling these thoughts over and over in your mind:

- I can do whatever I need to do in life through Christ.
- God loves me unconditionally.
- I will not live in fear.
- I am difficult to offend.
- I love people and I enjoy helping them.
- I trust God completely; there is no need to worry!
- I am content and emotionally stable.
- God meets all my needs abundantly.
- I pursue peace with God, myself, and others.
- I live in the present and enjoy each moment.
- I am disciplined and self-controlled.
- I put God first in all things.

Remember, the mind is the battlefield. It is the place we win or lose our battles in life. Indecision, uncertainty, fear, and random "roaming" thoughts are simply results of not disciplining the mind. This lack of discipline can be frustrating and make you think, *What is wrong with me? Why can't I keep my mind on what I am doing?* But the truth is, the mind needs to be disciplined and trained to focus. You have a spirit of discipline and self-control and it is time to start developing it.

Ask God to help you, and then refuse to allow your mind to think about whatever it pleases. Begin today to control your thoughts and keep your mind on what you're doing, saying, or hearing. You'll need to practice for a while; breaking old habits and forming new ones always takes time. Developing discipline is never easy, but it's always worth it in the end. When you win the battle for your mind, you'll be much more decisive, more confident, and focused. Then, you'll also be a more effective and productive person.

Think about It

Are you able to keep your mind focused on what you are doing?

_____

_____

When You Can't Get It Out of Your Mind

Not being able to keep our minds on what we want to keep them on is one problem, but being unable to get something off of our minds is another. We might worry about a situation, or continually roll it over and over in our minds trying to find a solution. We want to get it off our minds and enjoy peace, but it appears to have taken up residence.

Does this sound familiar to you? Do you ever experience times when you know a particular line of thinking is making you miserable and doing absolutely no good, but you just cannot seem to stop? We all do, but we can learn to discipline our minds to allow other thoughts in and not focus so completely on one issue or situation. The way to stop thinking about something you don't want to think about is to simply think about something else. Even getting in a different atmosphere helps. If you are worried, don't just sit home and worry—get out of the house and go do something! Get your mind on something that will produce good fruit because worry does absolutely no good. I have discovered that even when I feel bad physically, doing something that gets my mind off how I feel makes me feel better.

I recently spent a good deal of time with a friend who was

experiencing a tremendous mental battle that was rooted in a fear of displeasing an authority figure in her life. She thought about the situation—and thought about it and thought about it and thought about it. At one point, she asked, "Why can't I get this off my mind?" Her one-track thinking caused her to be stuck in the fear she felt in the situation with her authority figure.

However, I soon noticed that when we became involved in some ministry activity together, she got her spark back and no longer mentioned her mental battle. When I asked her later that day how she was doing, she said, "I'm fine when I get involved in what God has called me to do."

What we learn from this story about my friend is the answer to the question, "What do I do when I cannot get something off my mind and I know it is making me miserable and probably displeasing God?" The answer is to get involved in something that gives you joy, something that forces you to get your mind off the troubling circumstances and onto something positive and worthwhile.

Satan was attacking my friend at a weak point. She had been abandoned by her birth mother and abused as a child, which caused her to battle with an excessive need to be accepted by authority figures. Likewise, I have struggled with insecurities and a need to be accepted by authority figures in my life. These areas were "open doors" for the enemy in my life (places where he could easily take advantage of me and gain influence over me). As God continually works in me, these doors are shrinking in size and getting more and more difficult for the enemy to get through. What was once a wide door of opportunity for the devil has been almost completely closed.

Satan often works through or takes advantage of our weaknesses at the precise time God is trying to promote us or lead us to take a step of faith that will advance His kingdom or move us closer to fulfilling our destinies. I believe this was the case with my friend, and I know it has been the case in my life and the lives of many others.

I well remember times when God was trying to get me to make a decision that would enable me to do more in His kingdom, but fear of what people would think held me captive and immobilized me. When you find yourself stuck in a thought pattern that is detrimental to you—one that plays out over and over again like a broken record in your mind—get busy doing something God has called you to do or something that will bless someone. Don't be passive and merely wish you could get it off of your mind. Be aggressive and refuse to lend your mind to the devil for his activity. Remember that bad thoughts lead to bad moods and bad decisions, so don't waste your time on anything that doesn't add to the quality of your life.

Think about It

What do you consider your weak point(s), where Satan could take advantage of you?

_____

_____

Make a Choice

In Deuteronomy 30:19, God says, "I have set before you life and death, the blessings and the curses; therefore choose life." He gives us options, but He wants us to do the choosing. A choice often means we can go the easy way or the hard way. We can go the way we feel like going or we can go the way we know is right. To make a right and a wise choice means we will probably have to discipline ourselves to do something we don't feel like doing, but know is best.

As the Bible states, discipline doesn't bring immediate joy, but it does bring lasting joy later on. The enemy is always out to destroy us and he often tries to do that by influencing us to make bad choices—to choose to do what feels good or is easy now, instead of what will be beneficial in the long run. These choices may temporarily satisfy the flesh, but they don't please God or satisfy us permanently. We should discipline ourselves to make good choices that honor God and His Word. God encourages His children to walk in the Spirit and the way we do that is by choosing to do what we know is right even if it doesn't feel good. If we know to do right and don't do it, it is sin (see James 4:17). When Dave and I have a disagreement and the air is filled with tension, I can choose to apologize and do what will restore peace or I can choose to stay angry and wait for him to apologize to me. Is it more important for me to be right or peaceful? I know that it is right for me to make peace and if I don't, then I am sinning. God is our Vindicator and if I need to be shown to be in the right, He will take care of that, but my part is to honor Him by doing what I know is right according to His Word. God can work out all the details but we need to be makers and maintainers of peace (see Matthew 5:9).

Just last week I had a situation with someone who was acting very badly. She was complaining, showing no appreciation, and being extremely difficult to get along with. We had a few heated words and I left. I hoped she would call and apologize because in reality she was wrong, but she did not call. I remembered that Matthew 5:23–24 says, "So if when you are offering your gift at the altar you there remember that your brother has any [grievance] against you, leave your gift at the altar and go. First make peace with your brother, and then come back and present your gift." Since God recalled that Scripture to my mind, I realized He was asking me to do what was right even if the other person would not. I called her and asked how she was doing and we chatted a little. I did not apologize because I had not done anything wrong, but I did reach out to her as a way of saying I am not angry at you. My peace returned and I had the satisfaction of knowing that I had obeyed God and the rest was up to Him.

I realize now more than ever that making right choices is the key to a happy life, and keeping our minds on right things is another one. Don't let your mind wander around and do whatever it pleases. Remember, you have a spirit of discipline and self-control. You have been given a sound mind.

Sometimes, when I am riding down the road looking out the passenger side window while my husband is driving, I realize my mind has drifted or wandered off onto something that is worthless and will not produce anything good in my life. That doesn't make me a bad person; it just means I have a choice to make. Will I be lazy and let it "drift," or will I once again discipline myself to stop thinking that wrong thought and find something good and noble to think about?

I mentioned that my mind sometimes wanders in conversations with Dave, but it also happens sometimes when others are speaking and what they are saying really isn't very interesting to me. It seems to be important to them, but it isn't to me. My mind begins to drift to thoughts such as, *I hope they get this over quickly; I have more important things to do. Or, This is so boring; I will be so glad when I can get out of here.* Then, I suddenly remember a message I often preach on love—the one about how one way to demonstrate love is to listen to someone to make him or her feel valuable. I am faced with a choice: do I walk in love and show respect for the person talking to me, or just keep pretending to listen while I have very unloving thoughts?

Are you surprised to learn that these types of things happen to me? I will tell you a secret: they happen to everyone. We are not bad people because bad thoughts come to us but if we don't resist them, we can become whatever we choose to focus our thoughts on.

The Bible teaches that we have to *seek* to do good (see 1 Thessalonians 5:15, emphasis mine). *Seek* means "make an attempt" (*Merriam-Webster's Collegiate Dictionary*, Eleventh Edition). We also have to seek to think right thoughts. It takes discipline and training, but we can do it. Determine today to set your mind on right things and discipline yourself to keep it set on them and you will enjoy the great and powerful life God has in His mind for you.

Think about It

What will you do in the future when your mind begins to wander?

_____

_____

Control Yourself

Self-control is closely related to discipline. If you have one, you have the other. I like to say that self-control and discipline are friends that will help you do what you don't want to do, so you can have what you say you want to have. It is obvious that God has given us the fruit of self-control because He expects us to control ourselves. It is inaccurate for a person to say, "I can't control myself." The truth is that they could if they wanted to. People cannot change unless they face the truth about where they are, so all excuses have to cease and they must take responsibility in these areas we are discussing. Begin thinking and saying, "I am a disciplined and self-controlled person."

The apostle Peter wrote about several positive qualities we need to develop, including diligence, faith, virtue, and knowledge (see 2 Peter 1:5). He then went on to urge us: "And in [exercising] knowledge [develop] self-control, and in [exercising] self-control [develop] steadfastness (patience, endurance), and in [exercising] steadfastness [develop] . . . Christian love" (2 Peter 1:6, 7). Showing love for people is the will of God and should be every Christian's goal. It is apparent from what the Bible says that the exercise of self-control is necessary in order for us to reach that goal.

To live with self-control means to exercise restraint. Restraint is not always fun, but the Bible presents it as an admirable thing to do. In Proverbs 1:15, when King Solomon writes to his son about how to live with sinners all around, he simply counsels, "My son, do not walk in the way with them; *restrain* your foot from their path" (emphasis mine). Obviously, this is good advice for the young man. Proverbs 10:19 notes, "In a multitude of words transgression is not lacking, but he who *restrains* his lips is prudent" (emphasis mine). Here, we see that restraining ourselves is part of being wise. It's also part of having good common sense, as we see in Proverbs 19:11: "Good sense makes a man *restrain* his anger, and it is his glory to overlook a transgression or an offense" (emphasis mine).

Obviously, restraint has many benefits and learning to practice it will serve us well in every aspect of our lives.

We must teach our children to exercise restraint in their lives, for if we don't, there will always be trouble. Eli, the Old Testament priest, allowed his sons to do whatever they wanted to do—and the things they wanted to do were sinful. As a result, God made this pronouncement about Eli's family: "I will judge and punish his house forever for the iniquity of which he knew, for his sons were bringing a curse upon themselves [blaspheming God], and he did not restrain them" (1 Samuel 3:13). Because Eli did not restrain his sons who were sinning, a curse came upon his house forever. That's a high price to pay, and Eli could have avoided it and had blessings upon his house, had he disciplined his children.

Many times, we fail to discipline our children because we are not disciplined ourselves. Only a disciplined parent will do what is necessary to properly discipline their children. Don't wait until your children are teenagers and then wish they were disciplined. We never get what we desire by wishing; we have to practice the disciplines that are necessary in order to obtain what we want. It is amazing the difference in children who have been regularly and properly disciplined compared with those who have not. It is actually unpleasant to be with undisciplined children for a long period of time. They constantly have to be told over and over what to do and what not to do. Undisciplined children interrupt when people are having conversation; they make messes for others to clean up, and are generally obnoxious in their behavior. As parents, we would be wise to do the work we need to do on the front end of raising our children so we can enjoy them for many, many years to come.

As the leader of a large organization, I sometimes become weary of correcting people over and over who are under my authority. Often, simply forgetting or overlooking a matter would be much easier than dealing with it. But, I discipline myself to discipline others, because I know they may not learn to be disciplined otherwise—and I know that discipline will not only solve my problem at the time, it will also reap a good harvest in the lives of those on the receiving end if they receive it with a good attitude. Of course there are always times to be merciful and just overlook mistakes, but if they are made out of negligence or occur repeatedly, that usually means it is time to confront.

Many people are not interested in restraint or self-control; and discipline certainly isn't a popular concept. People tend to prefer living by the motto, "If it feels good, do it." The problem is, that just doesn't work! I don't believe I am exaggerating to say the world could well be in the worst condition it has ever been in right now, and people enjoy more supposed "freedom" than at any other time in history. Human rights and true godly freedom is a wonderful thing, but to think that "freedom" means we can do whatever we want to do whenever we want to do it is to invite disaster into our lives. I believe God knew what He was talking about when He encouraged us to be disciplined. Discipline is a good thing. Increase the discipline in your life, and you'll see what I mean. Think of areas in your life that you want to see improve; it could be finances, health, better organization in your life, how you think or what you talk about, or any number of things. Now say, "I am a disciplined and self-controlled person and I will do my part to get my life in order."

Think about It

Do you believe you exercise appropriate self-control? In what area do you most need to improve your ability to restrain or discipline yourself?

Power Pack

"For the time being no discipline brings joy, but seems grievous and painful; but afterwards it yields a peaceable fruit of righteousness to those who have been trained by it."
Hebrews 12:11

"Everything is permissible (allowable and lawful) for me; but not all things are helpful (good for me to do, expedient and profitable when considered with other things). Everything is lawful for me, but I will not become the slave of anything or be brought under its power."
1 Corinthians 6:12

"And in [exercising] knowledge [develop] self-control, and in [exercising] self-control [develop] steadfastness (patience, endurance), and in [exercising] steadfastness [develop] ... Christian love."
2 Peter 1:6, 7

"Discipline yourself for the purpose of godliness."
1 Timothy 4:7 NASB

POWER THOUGHT

12

I put God first in my life.

"You·shall have no other gods before or besides Me."
Exodus 20:3

I did not place this power thought last on our list because it is less important, for truly it is the most important. I placed it here because I wanted to leave you with what I consider to be the most vital thing in our lives and that is simply putting God first in everything. We should put Him first in all of our thoughts, words, and decisions. The Bible says that God is a jealous god. That means He is not willing to be second place in any area of our lives. He loves us and wants us to have the very best life possible. He knows for that to happen we must keep Him and His instructions to us as our number one priority at all times. I think the following Scripture says it all:

> For from Him and through Him and to Him are all things. [For all things originate with Him and come from Him; all things live through Him, and all things center in and tend to consummate and to end in Him.] To Him be glory forever! Amen (so be it).
> *(Romans 11:36)*

I love to meditate on that verse because it helps bring me back to the reality that life is all about God. When our lives here end all that remains is God and that is a sobering thought for anyone to ponder. The Earth and the things in it will vanish. They will simply disappear and we will all stand before God and give an account of our lives (see Romans 14:12). I believe each of us should be careful how we live and learn to keep God first in all things.

Everything God asks us to do is for our good. All of His instructions to us are intended to show us the way to righteousness, peace, and joy. Jesus didn't die for us so we can have a religion, but so we might have a deep and intimate personal relationship with God through Him. He wants us to live with, through, and for Him. He created us for fellowship with Him. It is a tragedy for people to live and ignore God unless they have some sort of emergency that they ask Him to help with. In Jeremiah, He said that His people had forgotten Him for days without number and that is sad indeed (see Jeremiah 2:32). Since God is everything how can we forget Him?

Sadly, most people waste a lot of their life, if not all of it, before they realize that having a right relationship with God is the most important thing in all of life. The world struggles to find peace and joy in all the wrong places and the truth is that He (God) is our peace and our joy. He is also everything else that anyone truly needs. God delights in providing for and helping us but He refuses to be treated as a type of spiritual Santa Claus. That is, someone we go to only when we need or want something.

God said that we are to have no other gods before Him. What do you worship? What do you place first in your life? What do you think about, talk about, and spend the most time doing? If we are honest with ourselves, it doesn't take long to locate what or who is number one in our life. We tend to be self-serving, and our number one goal is usually getting what we want. The thing many people fail to realize is that they can never be fulfilled or have the satisfaction they desire apart from God. He created us for His pleasure and delight. He did give us free will so we can choose or reject Him because He has no delight in a heart that does not serve out of choice. He gives us life as a gift and if we will freely offer it back to Him, then and only then we can live it fully and joyfully. However, if we try to keep our life for ourselves, we will lose it. We may live out many years but they will be frustrating, unhappy ones.

I recently realized that it is quite possible to receive Jesus Christ as Lord and yet never give ourselves to Him. We want Him and what He offers, but we are reluctant to give ourselves to Him for His use and will. We are to live dedicated, consecrated lives in which God and His will are our number one priority. Anyone who does not do that will never be truly content and satisfied.

People frequently ask me how I keep my priorities straight. The answer is that I must continually straighten them out. Like most things in life, just because our priorities are straight today doesn't mean they're going to stay that way. In our busy lives we have many things screaming for our time and attention and I realize it is easy to get off track. But we can daily re-establish what our priorities will be. We can daily look at our lives and make sure we are fruitful and not just busy doing things that take time and end up drawing us further and further away from God. We can develop spiritual disciplines in our life that will help us keep God as the center of all that we do. Bible reading and study, prayer, silence and solitude, serving, giving, and many other things should be practiced regularly.

Everything

To become a Christian, all a person has to do is believe that Jesus Christ is the Son of God, that He died for our sins, that He rose from the dead, and that He offers us eternal life. But receiving salvation does not guarantee that anyone will have a close, growing, personal relationship with God—and neither does going to church. Really loving God, having Jesus as the Lord of our lives, and following Him wholeheartedly requires more than praying what is commonly called the "Sinner's Prayer," attending church on Sundays, or even surrounding ourselves with Christian friends.

God loves you. He loves everything about you, and He cares about everything that pertains to you. He wants to be involved in

every aspect of your life. Think about this: A man is highly educated and trained as the CEO of a thriving company. He's a Christian; he prays before meals at home with his family; and he serves
on the finance committee at his church. He rarely misses a service,
plays golf with men from his Sunday school class, and gives generously to the benevolence fund. But in business, this man is known
to lack integrity and total honesty. Somehow in his mind he has
separated the business part of his life from his relationship with
God. When he senses conviction from God about a compromising
business decision, he quickly tells himself, "It is just business."

The problem is, he never prays about business endeavors. He has
never read the Bible to see what it says about work, finances, managing people, making decisions, or anything else relative to business. He respects God's Word in some areas of his life, but doesn't
look to it for guidance in his career. He keeps God in his "God
box" neatly separated from his ordinary everyday life. When we
divide life into sacred and secular, we are embarking on trouble.
God must not be separated from any aspect of life, but instead He
must be at the center of all that we do. When the man we are talking about walks into his office each morning, he puts all his trust in
his training, experience, and instincts rather than in God. After all,
he spent years learning to run a profitable corporation, so why not
make decisions based on proven theories and sound knowledge of
the industry in which he works? As far as the "little lies" he tells to
close a deal, he reasons that everyone does it and it is no big deal.

Now, let's say this man suddenly suffers from a dramatic and
unexpected downturn in the market his company serves. This
economic slump results in layoffs for many of his loyal employees and even affects his own income. Everyone affected has to deal
with difficulties and pressure they have not faced before. It's a terrible situation, and the desperate CEO asks himself every day, *How
on Earth did this happen?* He is nervous, anxious, and worried. He
becomes discouraged and depressed. He asks God to help him with
his problem. He wants God to fix it so he can be happy again and
just live his life.

While there are all sorts of reasons for changes in business climates, we know from this man's story that he is a Christian, but he did not invite God into his work. Maybe, had he understood the wisdom of the Scriptures where business and finances are concerned, he could have made decisions to avert disaster. If God had been first in his entire life, perhaps he would have sensed the market change coming and could have made decisions to avoid it. Maybe, had he prayed and asked for God's help in his business, the people and families affected by layoffs could have remained prosperous. Maybe the man could have avoided the stress of trying to rescue a sinking corporate ship, had he simply allowed God's truth and teachings to guide him, instead of relying on market information and theories. And most certainly, had the man kept Jesus as the center of his life at all times, he could have avoided the negative emotions he experienced when his circumstances changed. His trust in God would have given him assurance of being taken care of no matter what happened in the market or business world.

I am not saying that we should ignore all the information that comes by natural means but we cannot rely on it entirely; I am saying that to ignore God, or limit your time with Him to a quick Sunday morning visit in church is very foolish.

Let me be quick to say that I applaud everyone who works and studies to prepare for careers. I am in favor of gaining all the knowledge, education, and training available. But I am not for *trusting* in these things. I am for trusting God. Theories and textbooks can fail, but God can give a person who seeks His help one creative idea that will cause a business to succeed. While we need to be equipped with natural knowledge, our greater need is to know how to seek and apply God's wisdom. When we put God first, He trumps everything else.

God not only wants to be involved in our businesses and careers, but He also wants to be involved in every other aspect of our lives—our thoughts, our conversations, the way we choose to raise our children, the way we manage our time, the way we spend our money, how we dress, what we eat and drink, how we entertain ourselves, what we watch and listen to, and who our friends are. If we truly put Him first, we will welcome Him into all these areas of our lives. We will study His Word to learn His truth about these things, and we will be diligent to obey the promptings of His Spirit.

Are You Forgetful?

I think Jeremiah 2:32 may be the saddest verse in the Bible: "Can a maid forget and neglect [to wear] her ornaments, or a bride her [marriage] girdle [with its significance like that of a wedding ring]? Yet My people have forgotten Me, days without number." Isn't that sad? God is basically saying in this verse, "My people just forget all about Me." People go for days and don't talk to God, then all of a sudden they have a problem and then they remember Him and come running to Him for help.

I cannot emphasize this point strongly enough: We *must* learn to stop ignoring God when our lives are going well and seeking Him only when we need something. We should seek Him *all the time*. We certainly need Him all the time, but due to pride, self-will, and self-reliance we don't always want Him involved in everything. This is human nature, but as Christians we receive a new nature. The nature of God comes to dwell in our spirit and that is why we must learn to walk by the Spirit and not by the flesh.

When we are not facing crises or having problems, we tend to think we can handle things on our own. But the minute we have a problem that we cannot solve, we suddenly realize we need God after all. Let's honor God by putting Him first in everything—not only when we find ourselves in situations we can't handle on our own.

Too Busy?

I believe that most people would like to have a great relationship with God, but they fail to realize it is dependent on the time they are willing to invest in getting to know Him. Some people don't think it is possible to be intimate with God, many are simply too busy with other things and allow their relationship with God to take a backseat to everything else in life. The truth is, if we believe we are too busy to make spending time with God a priority, then we are simply too busy. It is foolish to never have time for the most important thing in life.

I once read that someone calculated how the average person spends a typical life span of seventy years. Here's the estimate: if you live to be seventy years old, then more than likely you will spend twenty-three years sleeping, sixteen years working, eight years watching television, six years eating, six years traveling, four and a half years on leisure activities, four years being sick, and two years getting dressed. The average person spends six months of his or her life on spiritual activities. If you add the numbers, you will get a total of seventy years—and then life is over. Do you want to spend four times as much of your life getting dressed as you do talking to God, reading His Word, or worshipping Him? I don't!

I even read once that the average minister prays four minutes a day. I realize there are some that pray a lot more than that, but if four minutes is the average, it is no wonder that a lot of people go to church and don't feel they benefit from being there. I discovered years ago that the power that comes from the pulpit when I minister to others is dependent on how I live my private life. I believe anyone's success in business, in ministry, or in everyday life is directly linked to the place of importance they give God in their daily life.

With All Your Heart

When we think about how much time people actually give God, we can understand why the Bible so strongly encourages us to seek Him. The fact is, we are missing the greatest thing in life if we never really get to know God personally. We must seek Him daily. The apostle Paul said that his determined purpose was to know God and the power that flowed out from His resurrection (see Philippians 3:10). The word *seek* is a very strong word. In its original language, it means "to crave; to pursue; to go after with all your might." In Jeremiah 29:13, God Himself promises, "Then you will seek Me, inquire for, and require Me [as a vital necessity] and find Me when you search for Me with all your heart."

Jesus plainly told us what our number one goal and priority should be. When the Pharisees asked Him what was the most important commandment of all, He responded, "You shall love the Lord your God with all your heart and with all your soul and with all your mind (intellect)" (Matthew 22:37). In other words, we can't just love God when we need Him to help us; we can't love Him only when it's convenient for us or popular; we shouldn't just pay attention to Him when we're at church or because we think He might punish us if we don't. No! We are to love Him from our hearts—not out of fear or obligation. And we are to love Him passionately. That's what "with all your heart" means.

He is a wonderful God. He is worth loving! He is worthy of all your passion and devotion. So don't wait until you find yourself in a desperate situation. Determine to seek and love God *with all your heart* from this moment on.

What If You Don't Want To?

More than anything else, I want to help you have the best life you can possibly have. At times, that means answering honest, heartfelt questions, such as, "What if I don't want to seek God with all my heart? What if I don't have any desire to put Him first in my life?"

Most of the time, people who have the courage to ask these questions really *want* to want to seek God. The fact that they don't crave God's presence often makes them feel guilty or embarrassed, but I think it's good that they are honest. If you wish you wanted to seek God, but the thought of praying and reading your Bible doesn't really thrill you, let me help.

Ask

First, ask God to give you the desire you need. If you do not have a genuine desire to know God and seek His ways, you will exhaust yourself trying. You *must* have that desire, because desire is the fuel that enables you to keep going as you grow in God. It makes you want to be in God's presence, and it helps you stay focused as you pray and read God's Word. God is the One who gives us the will and desire to work for His good pleasure (see Philippians 2:13), so ask.

Prayer is the way we ask for what we need from God, and when we pray, He hears and answers. If you don't have a desire to grow in your relationship with God, don't try to convince anyone (including yourself and God) that you do. Admit that you don't really want to do it, then ask Him to help you want to want to. After all, God knows your heart; He knows when you don't really want to seek Him, but He also knows when you wish you could want to. He wants to give you that desire, so ask Him, and He will. If you know that other things are too important to you and that you need to have a change of heart, start praying about it and God will work in you to change your desires. In Psalm 38:9, David told God that all of his desire was before Him. God can give us desires that are good and right and take away ones that are destructive, so ask!

I have had people say, "I wish I felt the way you do about God, but I just don't." They may not realize that I did not always have the passion for God that I have now. I had to do the same things I am encouraging you to do. I prayed to want to pray more, to want to study more, and to want to give and serve more. I pray all the time not to be selfish and self-centered. We have not because we ask not (see James 4:2), so start asking!

Be Disciplined

Second, you'll have to exercise spiritual disciplines. You read extensively about discipline in Power Thought 11, and it applies to your spiritual life as much as it does to other areas of life. Let me give you an example.

You don't want to be physically hungry for very long, do you? Of course not. So you think about what you'd like to eat; you go to the store and buy it; you take it home; you prepare it; you eat it; then you clean up after it. You may spend two hours preparing a meal that takes ten minutes to eat. Nevertheless, you have to make an effort if you don't want to go hungry.

You feed yourself spiritually in a similar manner. The spiritual part of you does want and need to spend quality time with God, but your flesh needs to be disciplined. It needs to form new habits. Prayer is talking to God about all kinds of things. You would never expect to have a good relationship with a human being if you never spoke to that person or took time to listen to him or her, would you? Then why would you think you could enjoy a growing relationship with God if you never spoke or listened to Him?

Spending time in God's Word and in prayer are both spiritual disciplines that help us get to know Him. Worship and praise is another way to connect with God. When you worship God, you focus on who He is; you magnify all the things that are so wonderful about Him and you thank Him for all of His goodness in your life. This causes your faith to grow and it draws you closer to Him. Serving and giving with a right motive also brings us closer to God. All of these spiritual disciplines prevent you from being hungry spiritually. Make the effort to exercise them, and you'll see what I mean.

Educate Yourself

Another way to seek God is to educate yourself concerning the ways and purposes of God. You certainly have to put your heart into seeking God, but you also have to put your mind into it and you have to learn things you may not know yet. Find a good, solid, Bible-based church and get involved in it. Read books; listen to sermons and teachings; take classes or go to Bible studies; attend conferences and seminars; find people who are more mature and experienced in God than you are and ask them questions. If you are truly seeking God, you will need to make an effort. Investing time and money into getting the resources you need to grow is a valuable investment that pays wonderful dividends.

If you went to college, you would expect to purchase textbooks and make an investment of time in order to gain the knowledge you desired. Why should learning about God be any different?

Prove It

In Power Thought 5, I mentioned that love is more than nice feelings; real love includes action. If we say we love God and want to put Him first in our lives, we must act—and we act on our love by obeying Him. Very few of us would say, "I am not going to obey God." Instead we make excuses. I remember many times when I would be easily angered and difficult to get along with and then I would excuse my behavior by saying, "I am tired and don't feel good." It may be more difficult to be kind to others when we are tired, but at all cost we must avoid making excuses because they deceive us and give us permission to continue in disobedience. We are not putting God first if we disobey Him.

If we truly desire to obey God, we steadily grow in learning how to hear His voice and choose the path He is asking us to take. Pray daily that you will receive the grace from God to obey Him. Don't just try...pray!

Prompt Obedience

In Exodus 24, God spoke to Moses and Moses recorded what He said. When he read these words to God's people, they responded, "All that the Lord has said we will do, and we will be obedient" (Exodus 24:7). Obviously, they did not treat God's Word lightly. They understood that they could not simply hear what God said, they also had to obey. When I read this passage, I get the impression the people had come to hear the Word having already decided they wanted to learn what they were supposed to do and how they were supposed to live. Their attitude seemed to be, "No matter what God says, we will do it." Meditating on the power thought, "I put God first in my life," will help you develop a new mind-set. Your attitude will change to one of prompt obedience rather than one of procrastination and excuses.

In James 1:22 we read, "But be doers of the Word [obey the message], and not merely listeners to it." Wonderful things would happen if we made our mind up to do what we hear in God's Word rather than merely listening to it.

In our culture today, we sometimes listen to Bible-based teaching for the sake of gaining knowledge. Though knowledge is important, it won't change our lives unless we act on it. Many people have said to me over the years, "Joyce, I have all your books and tapes, and I watch you on television every day." I appreciate such comments, but I really want to say in response, "That's great, but are you applying what you learn? Are you obeying the Word of God when you hear it?" I have talked in this book about the power of proper mind-sets. If we set our mind in advance to obey God's instructions it will be much easier to do. How much of what you know are you doing? Start confessing, "I put God and His will first at all times." This will renew your mind and soon you will find yourself being more obedient with less struggle. Remember that where the mind goes the man follows. We become what we think (see Proverbs 23:7).

We must not allow ourselves to merely feel good about the fact that we go to church, can quote Scripture, or have a houseful of Christian resources unless we are also making every effort to line our behavior up with what we learn. I realize we are on a lifetime journey and that none of us have arrived, but we do need to make sure that we are daily pressing toward the goal of being like Christ.

Large numbers of Christians live in anger, bitterness, resentment, and unforgiveness yet they know that God strongly instructs us to forgive and to be quick about it. Why would they do that? They do it because obedience requires a decision of the will that goes beyond emotions. We follow our feelings entirely too much. We must own our emotions and not allow them to own us. A person may know that they really need to get out of debt, but they just keep putting it off. They intend to do it but fail to realize that good intentions are not obedience. If we simply listen and don't obey, it really doesn't help us nor does it glorify God.

Putting God first means that we choose what pleases Him rather than what pleases us. Try to learn in your experience what is pleasing to God and set your mind to do it.

Don't Serve Leftovers

I could not write about putting God first without mentioning Matthew 6:33: "But seek (aim at and strive after) first of all His kingdom and His righteousness (His way of doing and being right), and then all these things taken together will be given you besides." In other words, if we put God first, all our needs will be met; everything else will fall into place.

The idea of putting God first appears throughout the Bible. In the Old Testament, God's people gave what was called a "firstfruits offering," which meant they gave to Him the first of everything they had—their produce, firstborn animals, firstborn sons, their gold and silver—everything. So, if a man worked as a farmer, he gave the first crops that appeared in his field to the Lord as an offering.

When we give God our firsts, we are saying, "Lord, I want to give this to You before I do anything else. I trust You to take care of me and meet all of my needs, and I want to honor You with the first evidence of my provision and increase. I don't want to give You my leftovers; I want to give You my 'firsts,' to show that You are first in my life. I'm giving You my firstfruits, and I trust You to bring more." If we give God the first of everything that comes our way, the rest is blessed.

You see, God is a creator, not a consumer. Everything we have comes from Him; He simply asks for the first portion of it back—not because He needs it, but because we need to give it to keep ourselves mindful of the fact that He is preeminent in our lives. Nothing we offer to Him is ever lost; instead it can be multiplied because we put it in His hands.

I urge you to put God first by giving Him your firsts. Give Him the first part of every day by spending time with Him before you do anything else. Begin to schedule your day around God instead of trying to work God into your day. If we give Him the first part, He will make the rest extremely productive. Give God the first portion of your finances by not waiting to see what you have left for Him after you pay your bills. Give God the first of your attention, by turning to Him for guidance before you run to your friends or to the Internet for advice.

God is great and He is our God! He is able and willing to do more for us than we could ever ask or think (see Ephesians 3:20). He desires to enlarge your life and He wants you to enjoy not only your life, but Him. Do you enjoy God? Are you in close fellowship with Him? Is He first in your life? Don't be afraid to answer these questions honestly because God loves honesty. There was certainly a time in my life when God was not first; I went to church but did not enjoy God or have close fellowship with Him. All that has changed in my life and it can change in yours too. Begin practicing the power thought, "I put God first in my life." The more you think it, the more you will do it.

Putting God first is a choice. You have to do it deliberately. But it's a choice that brings greater blessings than you could ever imagine—peace in your heart, joy, fulfillment in life, provision for every need, and every other good thing. Put God first in your life today and every day. And watch to see what He will do!

Think about It

I want you to be totally honest with yourself and ask yourself if you've let anything get ahead of Him. If you have, make an adjustment.

Power Pack

"Then you will seek Me, inquire for, and require
Me [as a vital necessity] and find Me when
you search for Me with all your heart."
Jeremiah 29:13

"You shall love the Lord your God with all your heart and
with all your soul and with all your mind (intellect)."
Matthew 22:37

"But seek (aim at and strive after) first of all His
kingdom and His righteousness (His way of
doing and being right), and then all these things
taken together will be given you besides."
Matthew 6:33

Armed and Ready for Battle

Both the lion and the gazelle have to stay vigilant and active in order to stay alive. The same is true for you and me. I really do believe the quality of your life is at stake and if you want to have the best life you can possibly have, you have to be relentless about thinking right thoughts. You need to think on purpose; you need to discipline your mind; and you need to make sure your thoughts agree with God's Word in every area of your life. I hope this book has built a desire and determination in you to do so.

I had the privilege of writing a book in 2002 that has sold over two million copies and been distributed in many languages. It is called *Battlefield of the Mind.* The book teaches the importance of thoughts and how to control them. This book, *Power Thoughts,* is a step beyond *Battlefield of the Mind.* I think it is a clear study of how to keep our minds renewed daily and enjoy the life God intends for us. Meditating on God's Word, rolling Scriptures over and over in our mind and muttering them verbally, is vital to renewing the mind. I think I can accurately say that it is the key to renewing your mind. The more we think about a portion of Scripture, the more it is changed from information to revelation and that is what we need. When something becomes revelation to us it is alive in us, and has much more impact on us than mere information. This is why Jesus said that the measure of thought and study we give to the truth we hear is the measure of virtue (power) and knowledge that comes back to us (see Mark 4:24).

The mind is definitely the battleground where we do war with Satan and his evil, deceptive thoughts. If we do not war against them, they will turn into actions and our lives will be ruined. The Word of God is our weapon and we must aggressively use it to constantly renew our minds.

Remember, renewing your mind takes time. You may need to finish reading this page and then turn back to the beginning of this book and go through it again in order to get what you need from it. You may need to reread specific chapters or passages over the days and weeks ahead in order to get certain points established in your mind. You may need to find a friend who also understands the power of thoughts and read this book together, talking through it and encouraging each other to do what it suggests. Write down these twelve power thoughts large enough that you can easily read them as you pass by. Put them in several places where you will probably be every day. Write them in the front of your Bible, carry this book with you and reread chapters while you are waiting for appointments. Whatever you need to do to get your mind in the condition God wants it to be in, do it—because your quality of life depends on it.

If you have not read *Battlefield of the Mind,* I strongly encourage that you do so. We even have it available in special formats for children and teens. We want the whole family to think right! *Battlefield of the Mind* is also available in a devotional, on CD and DVD. You can see that I am serious about helping people learn to think right.

Don't forget: Take each power thought and spend a week meditating on it. The entire program will take twelve weeks. You can consider going through the program four times in a year or at the very least go back over the ones that pertain to you the most. Repetition is good! It will help these thoughts get rooted in your heart, then you will begin to say what is in your heart and when your words agree with God's, you will see circumstances change.

I am excited for all of you as you decide to follow through with this program. I know what these principles have produced in my life, and they will do the same in yours. Have a great journey!

NOTES

Chapter 1: The Power of a Positive You

1. "Stripped Gears" (*The Rotarian,* March 1988), 72.

Chapter 2: Teach Your Mind to Work for You

1. Carol Ryff, "Power of a Super Attitude" (*USA Today,* October 12, 2004), http://www.usatoday.com/news/health/2004-10-12 -mind-body x.htm.
2. Robert Roy Britt, LiveScience Web site, "Study: Optimists Live Longer" (November 1, 2004), http://www.livescience.com/ health/041101 optimist heart.html.
3. BBC World News Web site, "Positive Thinking 'extends life'" (July 29, 2002), http://news.bbc.co.uk/2/hi/health/2158336 .stm.
4. Mayo Clinic Web site; "Positive Thinking: Reduce Stress, Enjoy Life More"; http://www.mayoclinic.com/health/ positive-thinking/SR00009.
5. Lauren Neergaard, "Study Verifies Power of Positive Thinking" (Associated Press, November 28, 2005).
6. Chris Tucker, "The Way We're Wired" (*American Way,* March 15, 2008), 26.
7. Steve May, *The Story File* (Massachusetts: Hendrickson Publishers, 2000), 127.
8. Mayo Clinic Web site; "Positive Thinking: Reduce Stress, Enjoy Life More"; http://www.mayoclinic.com/health/ positive-thinking/SR00009.

Chapter 3: More Power to You

1. Steve May, *The Story File* (Massachusetts: Hendrickson Publishers, 2000), 2–3.
2. Robert R. Jackson, "Portia Spider: Mistress of Deception" (*National Geographic,* November 1996), 114.

Power Thought 2: *God loves me unconditionally!*

1. William Bausch, *A World of Stories for Preachers and Teachers* (Connecticut: Twenty-Third Publications, April 1998), 472.

Power Thought 3: *I will not live in fear.*

1. Steve May, *The Story File* (Massachusetts: Hendrickson Publishers, 2000), 127.
2. Caroline Leaf, *Who Switched off My Brain?* (Nashville: Thomas Nelson, Inc.)
3. "Michigan: Fatal Overreaction" (*Time* magazine, August 14, 1989), http://www.time.com/time/magazine/article/0,9171,958326,00.html.

Power Thought 4: *I am difficult to offend.*

1. John Bevere, *The Bait of Satan: Living Free from the Deadly Trap of Offense* (Lake Mary, Florida: Charisma House, 2004), 2.

Power Thought 7: *I am content and emotionally stable.*

1. Deborah Norville, "The New Science of Thank You" (Reader's Digest Web site, October 2007), http://rd.com/content/the-new-science-of-being-thankful.

Power Thought 10: *I live in the present and enjoy each moment.*

1. Steve May, *The Story File* (Massachusetts: Hendrickson Publishers, 2000), 150–151.

ABOUT THE AUTHOR

JOYCE MEYER is one of the world's leading practical Bible teachers. A #1 *New York Times* best-selling author, she has written more than eighty inspirational books, including *The Love Revolution*, *Never Give Up!*, the entire Battlefield of the Mind family of books, and two novels, *The Penny* and *Any Minute*, as well as many others. She has also released thousands of audio teachings, as well as a complete video library. Joyce's *Enjoying Everyday Life*® radio and television programs are broadcast around the world, and she travels extensively conducting conferences. Joyce and her husband, Dave, are the parents of four grown children and make their home in St. Louis, Missouri.

JOYCE MEYER MINISTRIES

U.S. & FOREIGN OFFICE ADDRESSES

Joyce Meyer Ministries
P.O. Box 655
Fenton, MO 63026
USA
(636) 349-0303
www.joycemeyer.org

Joyce Meyer Ministries—Canada
P.O. Box 7700
Vancouver, BC V6B 4E2
Canada
1 (800) 868-1002

Joyce Meyer Ministries—Australia
Locked Bag 77
Mansfield Delivery Centre
Queensland 4122
Australia
(07) 3349-1200

Joyce Meyer Ministries—England
P.O. Box 1549
Windsor SL4 1GT
United Kingdom
+44 (0) 1753-831102

Joyce Meyer Ministries—South Africa
P.O. Box 5
Cape Town 8000
South Africa
(27) 21-701-1056

OTHER BOOKS BY JOYCE MEYER

The Joy of Believing Prayer
Never Lose Heart
Being the Person God Made You to Be
A Leader in the Making
"Good Morning, This Is God!" (gift book)
Jesus—Name Above All Names
Making Marriage Work
(previously published as *Help Me—I'm Married!*)
Reduce Me to Love
Be Healed in Jesus' Name
How to Succeed at Being Yourself
Weary Warriors, Fainting Saints
*Be Anxious for Nothing**
Straight Talk Omnibus
Don't Dread
Managing Your Emotions
Healing the Brokenhearted
*Me and My Big Mouth!**
Prepare to Prosper
Do It Afraid!
Expect a Move of God in Your Life... Suddenly!
Enjoying Where You Are on the
Way to Where You Are Going
A New Way of Living
When, God, When?
Why, God, Why?
The Word, the Name, the Blood
Tell Them I Love Them
Peace
*If Not for the Grace of God**

JOYCE MEYER SPANISH TITLES

Las Siete Cosas Que Te Roban el Gozo
(Seven Things That Steal Your Joy)
Empezando Tu Dia Bien
(Starting Your Day Right)

*Study Guide available for this title.

BOOKS BY DAVE MEYER
Life Lines

I CAN DO WHATEVER I NEED TO DO IN
LIFE THROUGH CHRIST.

GOD LOVES ME UNCONDITIONALLY!

I WILL NOT LIVE IN FEAR.

I AM DIFFICULT TO OFFEND.

I LOVE PEOPLE AND I ENJOY
HELPING THEM.

I TRUST GOD COMPLETELY; THERE IS
NO NEED TO WORRY!

I AM CONTENT AND EMOTIONALLY STABLE.

GOD MEETS ALL MY NEEDS ABUNDANTLY.

I PURSUE PEACE WITH GOD, MYSELF,
AND OTHERS.

I LIVE IN THE PRESENT AND ENJOY
EACH MOMENT.

I AM DISCIPLINED AND SELF-CONTROLLED.

I PUT GOD FIRST IN MY LIFE.